DISCARDED

Beyond Modularity

Beyond Modularity

A Developmental Perspective on Cognitive Science

Annette Karmiloff-Smith

A Bradford Book
The MIT Press
Cambridge, Massachusetts
London, England

Second printing, 1995
© 1992 Massachusetts Institute of Technology

Set in Palatino. Printed and bound in the United States of America.

Library of Congress Cataloging-in-Publication Data

Karmiloff-Smith, Annette.
 Beyond modularity : a developmental perspective on cognitive science / Annette Karmiloff-Smith.
  p.   cm.—(Learning, development, and conceptual change) Includes bibliographical references and index.
 ISBN 0-262-11169-1
 1. Cognition in children. 2. Modularity (Psychology) in children. 3. Constructivism (Psychology) 4. Nativism (Psychology) I. Title.
 II. Series.
 BF723.C5K376 1993
 155.4'13—dc20   92-5006
                                                              CIP

for Marek and Samuel

Contents

Series Foreword

This series in learning, development, and conceptual change will include state-of-the-art reference works, seminal book-length monographs, and texts on the development of concepts and mental structures. It will span learning in all domains of knowledge, from syntax to geometry to the social world, and will be concerned with all phases of development, from infancy through adulthood.

The series intends to engage such fundamental questions as the following.

The nature and limits of learning and maturation: the influence of the environment, of initial structures, and of maturational changes in the nervous system on human development; learnability theory; the problem of induction; domain-specific constraints on development.

The nature of conceptual change: conceptual organization and conceptual change in child development, in the acquisition of expertise, and in the history of science.

Lila Gleitman
Susan Carey
Elissa Newport
Elizabeth Spelke

Preface

This book aims not only to reach developmental psychologists, but also to persuade students and scientists in other areas of cognitive science—philosophy, anthropology, linguistics, ethology, adult cognitive psychology, neuroscience, computer science—to treat cognitive development as a serious theoretical science contributing to the discussion of *how* the human mind is organized internally, and not as merely a cute empirical database about *when* external behavior can be observed. Nowadays much of the literature focuses on what cognitive science can offer the study of development. In this book, I concentrate on what a developmental perspective can offer cognitive science.

As Piaget's conception of the sensorimotor infant is being severely undermined by new paradigms for studying infancy, the battle between nativism and constructivism once again rears its rather unconstructive head. In this book I do not choose between these two epistemological stands, one arguing for predominantly built-in knowledge and the other for a minimum innate underpinning to subsequent domain-general learning. Rather, I submit that nativism and Piaget's constructivism are complementary in fundamental ways, and that the ultimate theory of human cognition will encompass aspects of both. The state of the art in developmental theorizing is currently such that an exploration of the integration of nativism and Piaget's constructivism is timely.

I spent some 13 years immersed in Piagetian theory at Geneva University, first as a student and then as a research collaborator. During that time, the home-grown Piagetians always considered me a heretic, both personally and theoretically. I refused to address Piaget as *Patron*, meaning "Boss," as he expected everyone in his department to do; I dared to put in writing that Piaget had underestimated the role of language in cognitive development; and, worse, I argued that sensorimotor development alone could never explain how language acquisition initially got off the ground—that there had to be some innate component, even if more general processes might operate in subsequent development. Yet each time I went out into the big wide world of psychology conferences, I was considered a prototypical constructivist Piagetian—one who knew about Descartes, Kant, and Hume but who had never even heard of the journal *Child Development*!

Does this strange cocktail of Piagetian and anti-Piagetian theoretical musing mean that epistemological schizophrenia is setting in? No; I think it reflects the state of developmental theorizing in recent years, as dynamical systems theory and connectionism have started to offer some formal modeling of a number of Piagetian ideas while at the same time infancy research has suggested more innate underpinnings to the human mind than had previously been granted. Piagetians attribute the absolute minimum of innate structure to the human infant. Nativists attribute a great deal of built-in, domain-specific knowledge to the neonate, relegating learning to a less important role. Yet these epistemologies are not necessarily mutually exclusive for a theory of development. In this book I argue that a fundamental aspect of human development is the process by which information that is *in* a cognitive system (partly captured within a nativist stance) becomes knowledge *to* that system (partly captured within a constructivist stance). The theoretical discussions are illustrated by empirical findings from both linguistic and nonlinguistic development. This book is intended to excite the reader about the possibilities that a developmental perspective embracing both innate predispositions and constructivism might yield.

Many friends and colleagues have influenced my thinking, not least Jean Piaget, Bärbel Inhelder, Mimi Sinclair, and their numerous collaborators at Geneva University. If at times I seem somewhat anti-Piagetian, this in no way detracts from the enormous influence that my studies and my work at Geneva University still have on my thinking. I should also particularly like to acknowledge thought-provoking debates in recent years with all my present and previous colleagues at the Medical Research Council's Cognitive Development Unit in London—in particular its Director, John Morton. The CDU has been a most stimulating work environment, largely due to John's deep commitment to theoretical as well as experimental advances. Weekly meetings of the University College London's Cognitive Science faculty, organized by David Green, also provided a lively forum for exploring ideas. I should also like to acknowledge stimulating discussions at various times with Liz Bates, Ursula Bellugi, Ellen Bialystok, Susan Carey, Andy Clark, Jeff Elman, Rochel Gelman, Ed Klima, Jay McClelland, Lila Gleitman, Lissa Newport, David Premack, Lolly Tyler, and particularly Jean Mandler. A number of people generously provided comments on different chapters of the book: Simon Baron-

Cohen, Maggie Boden, Mani DasGupta, Jeff Elman, Rochel Gelman, Ron Gold, Francesca Happé, John Morton, Joseph Perner, and Jim Russell. Uta Frith's encouragement was especially helpful in stopping me from throwing in the sponge as I waded through critical comment from others.

Thanks are above all due to Susan Carey, who ploughed through the entire text and provided many pages of constructive suggestions, pointing out inconsistencies and raising deep and difficult questions, and to Julia Grant, who combed every page for linguistic and conceptual inadequacies, acted as a vital go-between when I was in Pittsburgh doing last-minute work on references and figures, and was at all times a wonderful colleague and friend. Rich Lehrer read the manuscript from the stance of an educational psychologist, Marie-Claude Jones from an undergraduate student's viewpoint, and Yuko Munakata from a graduate student's viewpoint. All provided many useful suggestions. Leslie Tucker helped me with proofreading.

It takes a special type of publisher to be generous enough to offer editorial comments despite the book's not being with his house, so special thanks are due to Philip Carpenter for his reactions to chapter 1. Betty and Harry Stanton's midnight calls reminded me in the nicest of ways to get back to the computer when the going was tough. Teri Mendelsohn was of vital help to me as the completion of the manuscript neared—I know that, had it been possible, she would have sent jasmine tea over electronic mail to get me through the final few nights! Paul Bethge of The MIT Press did a splendid editing job. Igor Karmiloff helped with editorial suggestions from a professional outside the field of psychology, and let me use his beautiful home in Provence to do some of the writing.

Finally, particular thanks go to my dear friends Marek Dobraczynski Johnson and Samuel Guttenplan. They read, reread, and ("oh, not again!") re-reread various parts of the text, giving me feedback from the viewpoints of cognitive neuroscience and philosophy, respectively. It is Samuel to whom I shall always be grateful for persuading me to spend all my savings on a good computer, and Marek to whom I owe special appreciation for so many things—not least for enticing me to jazz concerts and art exhibitions as a gentle reminder that there is more to life than writing a book (he had finished his)! Fiona Crampton-Smith and Connie Musicant dragged me out to jog and work out when I least wanted but most needed to. My daughters, Yara and Kyra, read various portions of the manuscript and made rude but helpful comments about its unintelligibility; they also learned to reverse roles and take great care of me.

Beyond Modularity

Chapter 1
Taking Development Seriously

Nature has contrived to have it both ways, to get the best out of fast dumb systems and *slow contemplative ones, by simply refusing to choose between them.* (Fodor 1985, p. 4)

Have you noticed how quite a large number of developmental psychologists are loath to attribute any innate predispositions to the human infant? Yet they would not hesitate to do so with respect to the ant, the spider, the bee, or the chimpanzee. Why would Nature have endowed every species except the human with some domain-specific predispositions? Yet, if it turns out that all species have such predispositions, that most can maintain a goal in the face of changing environmental conditions, and that most have the capacity for learning on the basis of interaction with conspecifics and the physical environment, what is special about human cognition? Is it simply that the *content* of knowledge differs between species? Is it language that makes humans special? Or are there qualitatively different processes at work in the human mind? Does human cognitive change affect all domains of knowledge simultaneously, or does development occur in a domain-specific fashion? Are cross-species differences relevant only to adult cognition, or do humans differ from other species from birth?

This book sets out to address such questions and to demonstrate that one can attribute various innate predispositions to the human neonate without negating the roles of the physical and sociocultural environments and without jeopardizing the deep-seated conviction that we are special—creative, cognitively flexible, and capable of conscious reflection, novel invention, and occasional inordinate stupidity.

Is the Initial Architecture of the Infant Mind Modular?

Fodor's 1983 book *The Modularity of Mind* (which I later criticize) made a significant impact on developmental theorizing by suggesting how the nativist thesis and the domain-specificity of cognition are relevant to constraints on the architecture of the human mind. For Fodor, the notion of "architecture" refers to the organization of relatively fixed and highly constrained innate specifications: the invariant features of the human information-processing system. Unlike Bruner (1974–75) and Piaget (1952b), who argue for domain-general development, Fodor holds that the mind is made up of genetically specified, independently functioning, special-purpose "modules" or input systems.[1] Like Fodor, I shall use the terms "module" and "input system" as synonyms. Each functionally distinct module has its own dedicated processes and proprietary inputs.

According to Fodor, information from the external environment passes first through a system of sensory transducers, which transform the data into formats that each special-purpose input system can process. Each input system, in turn, outputs data in a common format suitable for central, domain-general processing. The modules are deemed to be hard-wired (not assembled from more primitive processes), of fixed neural architecture, domain specific, fast, autonomous, mandatory, automatic, stimulus driven, giving rise to shallow outputs, and insensitive to central cognitive goals.

A further characteristic of modules is that they are informationally encapsulated (or, as Pylyshyn [1980] put it, "cognitively impenetrable"). Other parts of the mind can neither influence nor have access to the internal workings of a module, only to its outputs. Modules have access only to information from stages of processing at lower levels, not to information from top-down processes. In other words, what the mind knows and believes cannot affect the workings of a module.

For Fodor, the essential fact about modules is their informational encapsulation. He is neutral about whether they are resource encapsulated (i.e., whether different modules share, say, inference algorithms[2]). In defense of informational encapsulation, Fodor cites the example of perceptual illusions such as the Muller-Lyer illusion (figure 1.1). In that illusion, even when subjects have measured the

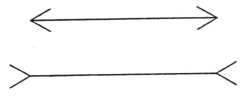

Figure 1.1
The Muller-Lyer illusion.

two lines and thus have explicit knowledge of their equal length, they cannot prevent themselves from seeing one of the lines as longer than the other, depending on the direction of the arrowheads at their extremities. The subject's explicit knowledge about equal line length, available in what Fodor calls the "central system," is not available to the perceptual system's computation of relative lengths. In other words, the module for perceptual processing is self-contained and has no access to the information elsewhere in the mind. Gallistel (1990) gives a similar definition when discussing the cognitive architecture of other species. For instance, although the rat can represent nongeometric data (such as color, smell, and texture) and can use them for various purposes, the rat's system for determining position and heading in space can make use of geometric data only. It is impenetrable to information from nongeometric sources, even when such data are highly relevant to the rat's current goal.

For Fodor, it is the *co-occurrence* of all the properties discussed above that defines a module or an input system. Alone, particular properties do not necessarily entail modularity. For instance, rapid automatic processing can also take place outside input systems. Anderson (1980) provides examples of this from skill learning.[3] He shows that, when learning a new skill, subjects initially focus consciously on component parts, but that once skill learning is complete the parts become compiled into a procedure which is executed rapidly, automatically, and unconsciously. Such task-specific expertise should not be confounded with the Fodorian concept of a module, which includes hard wiring, fixed neural architecture, mandatory stimulus-driven processing, informational encapsulation, and insensitivity to central cognitive goals.

Each module is like a special-purpose computer with a proprietary database. By "proprietary" Fodor means that a module can process only certain types of data and that it automatically ignores other, potentially competing input. A module computes in a bottom-up fashion a constrained class of specific inputs; that is, it focuses on entities that are relevant to its particular processing capacities only. And it does so whenever relevant data present themselves—that is, an input system cannot refrain from processing. This enhances automaticity and speed of computation by ensuring that the organism is insensitive to many potential classes of information from other input systems and to top-down expectations from central processing.

Input systems, then, are the parts of the human mind that are inflexible and unintelligent. They are the stupidity in the machine— but they are just what a young organism might need to get initial cognition off the ground speedily and efficiently.

I argue that development involves a process of going beyond modularity. For Fodor, however, development doesn't really exist.[4] Rather, Fodor posits a built-in dichotomy between what is computed blindly by the input systems and what the organism "believes." It is in "central processing" that the human belief system is built up, by deriving top-down hypotheses about what the world is like from the interface between the outputs of input systems and what is already stored in long-term memory. In contrast with input systems, Fodor considers central processing to be influenced by what the system already knows, and therefore to be relatively unencapsulated, slow, nonmandatory, controlled, often conscious, and influenced by global cognitive goals. Central processing receives outputs from each input system in a common representational format, a language of thought (Fodor 1976). Central processing, then, is general-purpose. It is devoted to the fixation of belief, the building up of encyclopedic knowledge, and the planning of intelligent action, in contrast to the special-purpose, domain-specific computations of modules.

While endorsing the importance of several aspects of Fodor's thesis for understanding the architecture of the human mind, I shall provide a view that differs from the notion that modules are prespecified in detail, and shall question the strictness of the dichotomy that Fodor draws between modules and central processing.[5] I shall also challenge Fodor's contention that the outputs of input systems are automatically encoded into a single common language of thought.

Prespecified Modules versus a Process of Modularization

Fodor's detailed account of the encapsulation of modules focuses predominantly on their role in on-line processing. There is little discussion of ontogenetic change, except to allow for the creation of new modules (such as a reading module). Fodor takes it as demonstrated that modules for spoken language and visual perception are innately specified. By contrast, I wish to draw a distinction between the notion of prespecified modules and that of a process of *modularization* (which, I speculate, occurs repeatedly as the *product* of development). Here I differ from Fodor's strict nativist conception. I hypothesize that if the human mind ends up with any modular structure, then, even in the case of language, the mind becomes modularized *as development proceeds*. My position takes account of the plasticity of early brain development (Neville 1991; Johnson, in press). It is plausible that a fairly limited amount of innately specified, domain-specific predispositions (which are not strictly modular) would be sufficient to constrain the classes of inputs that the infant mind computes. It can thus be hypothesized that, *with time*, brain circuits are progressively selected for different domain-specific computations; in certain cases, relatively encapsulated modules would be formed. Thus, when I use the term "innately specified" in this book, I do not mean to imply anything like a genetic blueprint for prespecified modules, present at birth.[6] Rather, as will be clear, I argue for innately specified predispositions that are more epigenetic than Fodor's nativism. The view that I adopt throughout the book is that Nature specifies initial biases or predispositions that channel attention to relevant environmental inputs, which in turn affect subsequent brain development.[7]

The thesis that development involves a process of gradual modularization rather than prespecified modules remains speculation at this point in time. It will not, therefore, be developed further in the book. However, it does merit mention in this introductory chapter to delineate the extent to which I find Fodor's views useful for thinking about the human mind and the extent to which I call for certain modifications. Together with quite a number of cognitive developmentalists, I think Fodor's thesis has pointed to where a domain-general view of development such as Piaget's is likely to be wrong. However, I shall argue for a more dynamic view of development than Fodor's modularity of mind.

The choice between prespecified modules and modularization is an empirical one. Only future research using on-line brain-activation studies with neonates and young infants can distinguish between the two hypotheses. If Fodor's thesis of prespecified modularity is correct, such studies should show that, from the very outset, specific brain circuits are activated in response to domain-specific inputs. By contrast, if the modularization thesis is correct, activation levels should initially be relatively distributed across the brain, and only with time (and this could be a short or relatively long time during infancy) would specific circuits always be activated in response to domain-specific inputs.[8] The modularization thesis allows us to speculate that, although there are maturationally constrained attention biases and domain-specific predispositions that channel the infant's early development, this endowment interacts richly with, and is in return affected by, the environmental input.

Whatever its shortcomings, Fodor's modularity thesis has offered cognitive science much food for thought. Nonetheless, I aim to challenge Fodor's dismissal of the relevance of a developmental perspective on cognitive science. Development, in my view, is the key to understanding the adult mind. Moreover, I question Fodor's oft-cited claim that "the limits of modularity are also likely to be the limits of what we are going to be able to understand about the mind" (1983,

p. 126). I shall argue that cognitive scientists can go beyond modularity to study the more creative aspects of human cognition. But my contention is that such an endeavor will be greatly enhanced by a developmental perspective on the problem.

What Constitutes a Domain?

Irrespective of whether they agree with Fodor's strict modularity thesis, many psychologists now consider development to be "domain specific." Much depends, of course, on what one understands by "domain," and it is important not to confuse "domain" with "module." From the point of view of the child's mind, a domain is the set of representations sustaining a specific area of knowledge: language, number, physics, and so forth. A module is an information-processing unit that encapsulates that knowledge and the computations on it. Thus, considering development domain specific does not necessarily imply modularity. In other words, the storing and processing of information may be domain specific without being encapsulated, hardwired, or mandatory.

Fodor's discussion of modularity is defined over very broad domains, such as language. He talks, for instance, of the "language module" and the "perceptual module." Others tend to draw finer distinctions within a domain—e.g., the syntactic module, the semantic module, and the phonological module. Still others (Marslen-Wilson and Tyler 1987) reject the notion of on-line modularity of processing altogether. Throughout the book, I shall argue for domain specificity of development rather than modularity in the strict Fodorian sense. I shall retain the term "domain" to cover language, physics, mathematics, and so forth. I will also distinguish "microdomains" such as gravity within the domain of physics and pronoun acquisition within the domain of language. These microdomains can be thought of as subsets within particular domains.

The need for this finer distinction of what constitutes a domain stems from the fact that I will put forward a *phase* model of development, rather than a *stage* model. In a stage model, such as Piaget's, overarching changes occur more or less simultaneously across different domains. One alternative view is that broad changes occur within a domain—for example, that a particular type of change occurs first with respect to language and later with respect to physics. The model discussed in this book differs from both of these conceptions. It invokes *recurrent phase changes* at different times across different microdomains and repeatedly within each domain. Take the case of the domain of language as an example. In the microdomain of pronoun acquisition, a sequence of changes X-Y-Z (e.g., from implicit to explicit to verbal justification) might be complete in a child by age 7, whereas in the microdomain of understanding what a word is the same sequence might already be complete by age 5. I shall thus distinguish the broad domains (language, mathematics, and so forth) from the microdomains (e.g. pronouns and counting) that they subsume. Whenever I refer to domain-general or domain-specific theories, these are situated at the level of broad domains.

Development from a Domain-General Perspective

Fodor's nativist thesis is in sharp contrast with domain-general theories of learning, such as Piaget's constructivist epistemology, which were once popular in the development literature.[9] Piagetian theory argues that neither processing nor storage is domain specific. Of course, implicitly at least, Piagetians must acknowledge that there are different sensory transducers for vision, audition, touch, and so forth. They do not accept, however, that the transducers transform data into innately specified, domain-specific formats for modular processing. For Piagetians, development involves the construction of domain-general changes in representational structures operating over all aspects of the cognitive system in a similar way.

At this juncture I shall risk outraging some of my former colleagues at Geneva University by suggesting that Piaget and behaviorism have much in common. What, link Piaget and Skinner? An aberration, to be sure! Yet I arrive at this *liaison dangereuse* between such unlikely bedfellows by opposing the domain-general view with the domain-specific explanation of development.

Neither the Piagetian nor the behaviorist theory grants the infant any innate structures or domain-specific knowledge. Each grants only some domain-general, biologically specified processes: for the Piagetians, a set of sensory reflexes and three functional processes (assimilation, accommodation, and equilibration); for the behaviorists, inherited physiological sensory systems and a complex set of laws of association. These domain-general learning processes are held to apply across all areas of linguistic and nonlinguistic cognition. Piaget and the behaviorists thus concur on a number of conceptions about the initial state of the infant mind. The behaviorists saw the infant as a *tabula rasa* with no built-in knowledge (Skinner 1953); Piaget's view of the young infant as assailed by "undifferentiated and chaotic" inputs (Piaget 1955a) is substantially the same.

Needless to say, there are fundamental differences between these two schools. Piagetians view the child as an active information constructor, behaviorists as a passive information storer. Piagetians conceive of development as involving fundamental stage-like changes in logical structure, whereas behaviorists invoke a progressive accumulation of knowledge. However, in the light of the present state of the art in developmental theorizing, Piagetians and behaviorists have much in common in their view of the neonate's "knowledge-empty" mind and their claims that domain-general learning explains subsequent development across all aspects of language and cognition.

Development from a Domain-Specific Perspective

The nativist/modularity thesis projects a very different picture of the young infant. Rather than being assailed by incomprehensible, chaotic data from many competing sources, the neonate is seen as preprogrammed to make sense of specific information sources. Contrary to the Piagetian or the behaviorist infant, the nativist infant is off to a very good start. This doesn't, of course, mean that nothing changes during infancy and beyond; the infant has much to learn. But the nativist/modularity stance posits that subsequent learning is guided by innately specified, domain-specific principles, and that these principles determine the entities on which subsequent learning takes place (Gelman 1990b; Spelke 1991).

The domain specificity of cognitive systems is also suggested by developmental neuropsychology and by the existence of children in whom one or more domains are spared or impaired. For example, autism may involve a single deficit in reasoning about mental states (theory of mind), with the rest of cognition relatively unimpaired. Williams Syndrome, by contrast, presents a very uneven cognitive profile in which language, face recognition, and theory of mind seem relatively spared, whereas number and spatial cognition are severely retarded. And there are numerous cases of idiots-savants in whom only one domain (such as drawing or calendrical calculation) functions at a high level, while capacities are very low over the rest of the cognitive system. By contrast, Down Syndrome is suggestive of a more across-the-board, domain-general deficit in cognitive processing.

Adult brain damage points to domain specificity, also. It is remarkably difficult to find convincing examples in the neuropsychological literature of an across-the-board, domain-general disorder (Marshall 1984), although a case might be made for an overall deficit in planning in patients with prefrontal damage (Shallice 1988). But in many instances, disorders of higher cognitive functions consequent upon brain damage are typically domain specific—that is, they affect only face recognition, number, language, or some other facility, leaving the other systems relatively intact.

So if adults manifest domain-specific damage, and if it can be shown that infants come into the world with some domain-specific predispositions, doesn't that mean that the nativists have won the debate over the developmentalists still ensconced on the theoretical shores of Lake Geneva (Piaget's former bastion of anti-nativism and anti-modularity)? Not necessarily, because it is important to bear in mind that the greater the amount of domain-specific properties of the infant mind, the less creative and flexible the subsequent system will be (Chomsky 1988). Whereas the fixed constraints provide an initial adaptive advantage, there is a tradeoff between the efficiency and automaticity of the infant's input systems, on the one hand, and their relative inflexibility, on the other. This leads me to a crucial point: *The more complex the picture we ultimately build of the innate capacities of the infant mind, the more important it becomes for us to explain the flexibility of subsequent cognitive development.* It is toward such an end—exploring the flexibility and creativity of the human mind beyond the initial state—that my work in language acquisition and cognitive development has been concentrated, in an attempt to determine both the domain-specific and the domain-general contributions to development. It is implausible that development will turn out to be entirely domain specific *or* domain general. And although I will need to invoke some built-in constraints, development clearly involves a more dynamic process of interaction between mind and environment than the strict nativist stance presupposes.

Reconciling Nativism and Piaget's Constructivism

What theory of development could encompass the dynamics of a rich process of interaction between mind and environment? At first blush, a theory with a central focus on epigenesis and constructivism, like Piaget's, would seem the most appropriate. The notion of constructivism in Piaget's theory[10] is the equivalent at the cognitive level of the notion of epigenesis at the level of gene expression. For Piaget both gene expression and cognitive development are emergent products of a self-organizing system that is directly affected by its interaction with the environment. This general aspect of Piaget's theory, if more formalized, may well turn out to be appropriate for future explorations of the notion of progressive modularization discussed above. However, much of the rest of Piaget's theory has come under a great deal of criticism. A growing number of cognitive developmentalists[11] have become disenchanted with Piaget's account of the infant as a purely

sensorimotor organism. For Piaget the newborn has no domain-specific knowledge, merely sensory reflexes and the three domain-general
processes of assimilation, accommodation, and equilibration. By contrast, the infancy research that I shall discuss in the following chapters
suggests that there is considerably more to the initial functional architecture of the brain than Piaget's theory posits. Yet the exclusive
focus of nativists like Fodor and Chomsky on biologically specified
modules leaves little room for rich epigenetic-constructivist processes.
Moreover, Fodor's concentration on input systems—he has far less to
say about either output systems or central processing—doesn't help
us to understand the way in which children turn out to be active
participants in the construction of their own knowledge.

Although for Chomsky (1988) and Spelke (1991) a nativist stance
precludes constructivism, I argue that nativism and Piaget's epigenetic
constructivism are not necessarily incompatible—with certain provi-
sos. First, to Piaget's view one must add some innate, knowledge-
impregnated predispositions[12] that would give the epigenetic process
a head start in each domain. This does not imply merely adding a little
more domain-general structure than Piaget supposed. Rather, it
means adding domain-specific biases to the initial endowment. But
the second proviso for the marriage of constructivism and nativism is
that the initial base involve less detailed specifications than some
nativists presuppose and a more progressive process of *modularization*
(as opposed to prespecified modules). Fodor does not, for instance,
discuss the cases in which one of his prespecified modules cannot
receive its proprietary input (e.g., auditory input to a language module
in the case of the congenitally deaf). We know that in such cases the
brain selectively adapts to receive other (e.g., visuomanual) nonau-
ditory inputs, which it processes linguistically (Changeux 1985; Neville
1991; Poizner et al. 1987). Many cases of early brain damage indicate
that there is far more plasticity in the brain than Fodor's strict modularity view would imply. The brain is not prestructured with ready-
made representations; it is channeled to progressively *develop* representations via interaction with both the external environment and its
own internal environment. And, as I stressed above, it is important
not to equate innateness with presence at birth or with the notion of
a static genetic blueprint for maturation. Whatever innate component
we invoke, it becomes part of our biological potential only through
interaction with the environment; it is latent until it receives input
(Johnson 1988; Johnson, in press; Marler 1991; Oyama 1985; Thelen
1989). And that input affects development in return.

The proposed reconciliation of nativism and constructivism will
allow us to adhere to Piaget's epigenetic-constructivist view of the

developmental process, but to drop his insistence on domain generality in favor of a more domain-specific approach. Furthermore, the Piagetian focus on output systems (i.e., on the infant's and the child's *action on* the environment) is an important addition to the nativist's accent on input systems. But Piaget's strong anti-nativism and his arguments for across-the-board stages no longer constitute a viable developmental framework.[13]

The need to invoke domain specificity will be apparent throughout the book. For example, it will become clear in chapter 2 that domain-general sensorimotor development alone cannot explain the acquisition of language. Syntax does not simply derive from exploratory problem solving with toys, as some Piagetians claim. Lining up objects does not form the basis for word order. Trying to fit one toy inside another has nothing to do with embedded clauses. General sensorimotor activity alone cannot account for specifically linguistic constraints; if it could, then it would be difficult to see why chimpanzees, which manifest rich sensorimotor and representational abilities, do not acquire anything remotely resembling human language despite extensive training (Premack 1986).

Despite these criticisms of Piaget's view of early infancy and my rejection of his stage view of development, I hope by the end of the book to have persuaded you that important aspects of Piaget's epistemology should be salvaged and that there is far more to cognitive development than the unfolding of a genetically specified program. If we are to understand the human mind, our focus must stretch well beyond the innate specifications. Infants and young children are active constructors of their own cognition. This involves both domain-specific constraints and domain-general processes.

In sum, there seems to be something right about both Fodor's and Piaget's approaches to human cognition. My own solution to this potential dilemma has been to take an epistemological stance that encompasses aspects of both nativism and constructivism.

The Notion of Constraints on Development

Nowadays, many discussions in developmental psychology concern constraints on development.[14] But domain-general and domain-specific theories treat the notion of constraints differently. For the domain-general theorist, the word "constraints" carries a negative connotation; it is taken as referring to factors which curtail a child's competence. By contrast, for the domain-specific theorist "constraints" takes on a positive connotation: Domain-specific constraints *potentiate* learning by limiting the hypothesis space entertained. They enable the infant to accept as input only those data which it is initially able to compute in specific ways. The domain specificity of processing provides the infant with a limited yet organized (nonchaotic) system from the outset, and not solely at the tail end of the Piagetian sensorimotor period.[15]

New Paradigms for Studying Young Infants

Piaget's pioneering experimental work on development was focused on older children. For his exploration of infancy, Piaget had to rely solely on observation of his own three children. There were no paradigms available then for the experimental study of early infancy. Since the mid 1960s, however, methodological innovations have opened up exciting new experimental possibilities. Experiments now focus on the different input systems through which newborns and young infants compute data relevant to a variety of cognitive domains. And, although I do not share Fodor's pessimism that we shall never understand central systems,[16] he is right that input systems are much more amenable to strict experimental research, particularly in infancy.

Let me digress for a moment to look briefly at the new paradigms for infancy research, since they will crop up throughout the book. These paradigms have been used by researchers interested in the infant's sensitivity to data relevant to language, physics, number, human intention, two-dimensional notation, and so forth. They are thus important for all the chapters in this book.

The new experimental approaches were devised to surmount problems arising from Piagetian-inspired research which required infants to demonstrate their abilities by manual search. Neonates and young infants cannot engage in manual search. What they do well is suck and look (and, alas for parents, cry). These capacities form the basis of the new methodologies. There are three main infancy techniques; two fall under the habituation/dishabituation paradigm, and the third uses preferential looking or listening.

In the habituation/dishabituation paradigm, the infant is presented repeatedly with the same stimulus set until it shows lack of interest by starting to attend for shorter times. Then a different stimulus set is presented. If the infant shows renewed interest by attending for a longer time, it can be concluded that the new stimulus is apprehended (perceived, understood) by the infant as different from the earlier one. The stimulus set can be visual, auditory, or tactile, depending on the experiment. An infant's interest in an event (e.g., seeing a circle after a series of squares of different sizes and colors) typically manifests itself as prolonged attention. By clever manipulation of variables of shape, color, size, and so forth, the researcher can home in on the nature of the difference to which the infant is sensitive. Say the newborn shows decreasing interest in squares despite constant variations in size and color, but suddenly shows renewed interest on the first presentation of a circle; then one can conclude that shape discrimination is present at birth and does not have to be learned. By contrast, if the newborn continues to show lack of interest on presentation of the circle, one can conclude that the circle is apprehended as being equivalent to the set of squares—i.e., that shape discrimination is a later achievement (although in fact, as Slater [1990] has shown, it is present at birth). The same logic is used to test discriminations of other types of stimuli.

"Interest" is measured either by greater amplitude of sucking or by longer length of looking. In the former case, the infant is given a non-nutritive pacifier which is attached to an apparatus that measures sucking amplitude. As the infant habituates to the original stimulus, its sucking amplitude decreases. If the new stimulus is apprehended as different, the infant's sucking amplitude increases; if not, it plateaus or decreases further. As will be discussed in chapter 2, such a technique has been used to explore the infant's preference for listening to its mother tongue over other linguistic input, as well as its capacity for categorical perception of various speech sounds. Thus, if the infant is presented with a set of "va" sounds, and then after habituation with a set of "ba" sounds, increased sucking amplitude demonstrates the infant's sensitivity to the difference between the sounds (i.e., to voice-onset time). Such techniques help us to explore the effects of environmental input on innate predispositions. For a child in a Spanish-speaking environment, for instance, sensitivity to the distinction between "va" and "ba" may be present early in infancy but disappear once the patterns of the input language have been learned, because spoken Spanish does not differentiate between "va" and "ba".

The technique for measuring looking time is based on the same principle as the one measuring sucking amplitude. The infant is repeatedly exposed to a visual stimulus. Each time the stimulus is presented, the infant will look at it for a shorter length of time, until it habituates. After habituation to a given stimulus set, the infant's length of looking at a new stimulus is recorded as a measure of its renewed interest or its boredom. Again, subtle manipulation of variables can determine the features to which the infant is particularly sensitive. The use of this technique will be discussed in chapter 3. For example, infants show surprise (look longer) at a display of a ball that seems to stop in mid-air without support, or at a display of an object that appears to have passed through a solid surface—that is, they are sensitive to violations of certain laws of physics.

Measuring looking time is somewhat more subjective than measuring sucking amplitude. Thus, looking time must be recorded by observers unaware of the particular display being viewed by the infant on any trial. But, as Spelke (1985) has pointed out,[17] the interpretation of test-trial looking and sucking patterns in experiments of this kind depends on the finding, now obtained in hundreds of laboratories throughout the world, that habituation to one stimulus set is followed by longer looking (or longer sucking) for the test display. In other words, the interpretation rests on the fact that infants extract a common feature across the set of stimuli in the habituation display, and differentiate that from a specific feature of the test display.

A third infancy paradigm involves preferential looking or listening. Here habituation and dishabituation are not measured; rather, the infant is presented with two stimulus displays simultaneously and measurement is taken of which display the infant prefers to look at. Again, measurements are determined by observers who cannot see the displays visible to the infant. Chapter 4 illustrates uses of this technique to measure infants' capacity to match the number of auditory stimuli (e.g., three drumbeats) to the number of objects in either of two visual displays, one containing two objects and the other containing three.

Although the infancy data discussed throughout the book are truly impressive, certain questions about the habituation and preferential techniques remain open. Does the violation of a physical principle have to be extreme, or are infants just as sensitive to subtler violations? What conclusions can legitimately be drawn from the demonstration that the infant is sensitive to a novel stimulus: that domain-specific attention biases and principles are built into the infant mind, or merely that we have trained infants to discriminate in the course of the actual experiment? Any particular experiment would remain inconclusive on this issue. However, if results from different experiments demonstrate that newborns or 4-month-olds can make discriminations for one set of stimuli but cannot do so for another, then it cannot be claimed that discrimination is solely the result of task-specific learning. Rather, discrimination is constrained by whether or not the infant can already show sensitivity to the particular characteristics of the stimuli. This allows tentative conclusions regarding innate specifications and those involved in subsequent learning—tentative since many other interpretations are possible.

I discuss the infancy research in some detail in the first part of each of chapters 2 through 6. But every time, I go on to show that development comprises much more than the domain-specific constraints. In particular, it involves "representational redescription," a process that increases the flexibility of the knowledge stored in the mind.

Beyond Domain-Specific Constraints: The Process of Representational Redescription

How does information get stored in the child's mind? I argue that there are several different ways. One is via innate specification as the result of evolutionary processes. Innately specified predispositions can either be specific or nonspecific (Johnson and Bolhuis 1991). In both cases, environmental input is necessary. When the innate component is specified in detail, it is likely that the environment acts simply as a trigger for the organism to select one parameter or circuit over others (Changeux 1985; Chomsky 1981; Piatelli-Palmarini 1989).[18] By contrast, when the innate predisposition is specified merely as a bias or a skeletal outline, then it is likely that the environment acts as much more than a trigger—that it actually influences the subsequent structure of the brain via a rich epigenetic interaction between the mind and the physical/sociocultural environment. The skeletal outline involves attention biases toward particular inputs and a certain number of principled predispositions constraining the computation of those inputs. Note that I am hypothesizing that the human mind has *both* a certain amount of detailed specification and some very skeletal domain-specific predispositions, depending on the domain.

There are several other ways in which new information gets stored in the child's mind. One is when the child fails to reach a goal and has to take into account information from the physical environment. Another is generated by the child's having to represent information provided directly by a linguistic statement from, say, an adult. These are both external sources of change.[19] An internal source of change is illustrated by the above-mentioned process of modularization in such a way that input and output processing becomes less influenced by other processes in the brain. This causes knowledge to become more encapsulated and less accessible to other systems. But another essential facet of cognitive change goes in the opposite direction, with knowledge becoming progressively more accessible.

My claim is that a specifically human way to gain knowledge is for the mind to exploit internally the information that it has already stored (both innate and acquired), by redescribing its representations or, more precisely, by iteratively re-representing in different representational formats what its internal representations represent. I will deal with this in detail in a moment.

Finally, there is a form of knowledge change that is more obviously restricted to the human species: explicit theory change, which involves conscious construction and exploration of analogies, thought experiments and real experiments, typical of older children and adults (Carey 1985; Klahr 1992; Kuhn et al. 1988). But I will argue that this more obvious characteristic of human cognition is possible only on the basis of prior representational redescription, which turns *implicit* information into *explicit* knowledge.

To convey a more tangible feel for the theoretical discussion on which I am about to embark, let me start with a couple of examples— one having to do with learning to play the piano and one having to do with learning to solve Rubik's Cube.[20]

When one is learning to play the piano, initially there is a period during which a sequence of separate notes is laboriously practiced. This is followed by a period during which chunks of several notes are played together as blocks, until finally the whole piece can be played more or less automatically.[21] It is something like this that I shall subsequently call "reaching behavioral mastery." But the automaticity is constrained by the fact that the learner can neither start in the middle of the piece nor play variations on a theme (Hermelin and O'Connor 1989). The performance is generated by procedural representations which are simply run off in their entirety. There is little flexibility. At best the learner starts to be able to play the *whole piece* softer, louder, slower, or faster. It is only later that one can interrupt the piece and start at, say, the third bar without having to go back to the beginning and repeat the entire procedure from the outset. I hypothesize that this cannot be done on the basis of the automatized procedural representations. Rather, I posit, it involves a process of representational redescription such that the knowledge of the different notes and chords (rather than simply their run-off sequence) becomes available as manipulable data. It is only after a period of behavioral mastery that the pianist can generate variations on a theme, change sequential order of bars, introduce insertions from other pieces, and so forth. This differentiates, for instance, jazz improvisation from strict adherence to sheet music. The end result is representational flexibility and control, which allows for creativity. Also important is the fact that the earlier proceduralized capacity is not lost: for certain goals, the pianist can call on the automatic skill; for others, he or she calls on the more explicit representations that allow for flexibility and creativity. (Of course, the playing of some pianists remains at the procedural level.)

In contrast with the beginning pianist's initial conscious attention to particular notes, which gradually becomes proceduralized, I found that I had to "switch off" my consciousness to solve Rubik's Cube. In other words, I had to stop trying to analyze what I was doing until I could actually do it! In the early course of learning to solve the problem, I developed a sort of proprioceptive solution which I could perform very rapidly but which I had much more difficulty repeating at a slower pace. My "knowledge" at that stage was embedded in the procedural representations sustaining the rapid execution. But I did not stop there. After reiterating a solution many times, I found that I started to recognize certain states of the cube and then knew whether or not I was on the path to my solution. But I still could not interrupt my solution and proceed from just any starting state. With more time still, I found that I could predict what the next few moves would be before actually executing them. Finally I came to a point where I could explain the solution to my daughter. She, however, did not use my explicit instructions but went through the same progression from procedural to explicit knowledge that I had experienced (only faster). This movement from implicit information embedded in an efficient problem-solving procedure, to rendering the knowledge progressively more explicit, is a theme that will recur throughout the book. This is precisely what I think development is about: Children are not satisfied with success in learning to talk or to solve problems; they want to understand how they do these things. And in seeking such understanding, they become little theorists.

Development and learning, then, seem to take two complementary directions. On the one hand, they involve the gradual process of proceduralization (that is, rendering behavior more automatic and less accessible). On the other hand, they involve a process of "explicitation" and increasing accessibility (that is, representing explicitly information that is implicit in the procedural representations sustaining the structure of behavior). Both are relevant to cognitive change, but the main focus of this book will be the process of representational explicitation—which, I posit, occurs in a variety of linguistic and cognitive domains throughout development.

The RR Model

For a number of years I have been building a model that incorporates a reiterative process of *representational redescription*. I call this the RR model. I will first make some general points and then provide a summary of the model.

The RR model attempts to account for the way in which children's representations become progressively more manipulable and flexible, for the emergence of conscious access to knowledge, and for children's theory building. It involves a cyclical process by which information already present in the organism's independently functioning, special-purpose representations, is made progressively available, via redescriptive processes, to other parts of the cognitive system. In other words, representational redescription is a process by which implicit information *in* the mind subsequently becomes explicit knowledge *to* the mind, first within a domain and then sometimes across domains.

The process of representational redescription is posited to occur spontaneously as part of an internal drive toward the creation of intra-domain and inter-domain relationships. Although I shall stress the endogenous nature of representational redescription, clearly the process may at times also be triggered by external influences.

The actual *process* of representational redescription is domain general, but it is affected by the form and the level of explicitness of the representations supporting particular domain-specific knowledge at a given time. When I state that representational redescription is domain general, I do not mean to imply that it involves a simultaneous change across domains. Rather, I mean that, within each domain, the process of representational redescription is the same. To reiterate: the RR model is a *phase* model, as opposed to a *stage* model. Stage models such as Piaget's are age-related and involve fundamental changes across the entire cognitive system. Representational redescription, by contrast, is hypothesized to occur recurrently within microdomains throughout development, as well as in adulthood for some kinds of new learning.

I will deal with the RR model and the process of representational redescription again in chapters 7 and 8. But it is essential to outline the model here in order to situate theoretically the empirical research in the following chapters on children as linguists, physicists, mathematicians, psychologists, and notators. At this stage the account may seem rather abstract, but hang in there. I promise that it will become more tangible once I deal with the specific domains in chapters 2 through 6. I also hope that the piano and Rubik's cube analogies will help sustain the discussion.

Let us now look at the RR model in a little detail. Development, I argue, involves three *recurrent* phases. During the first phase the child focuses predominantly on information from the external environment. This initial learning is data driven. During phase 1, for any microdomain, the child focuses on external data to create "representational adjunctions." Representational adjunctions, I hypothesize, neither alter existing stable representations nor are brought into relation with them. Once new representations are stable, they are simply added, domain specifically, to the existing stock, with minimal effect on what is already stored. In other words, independently stored representational adjunctions do not yet entail what I mean by representational change. Phase 1 culminates in consistently successful performance on whatever microdomain has reached that level. This is what I term "behavioral mastery."

Behavioral mastery does not necessarily imply that the underlying representations are like the adult's. Successful performance can be generated by a sequence of independently stored representations that will ultimately have to be linked into a more coherent system. The same performance (say, correctly producing a particular linguistic form, or managing to balance blocks on a narrow support) can be generated at various ages by very different representations. Later (phase-3) behavior may appear identical to phase-1 behavior. We thus need to draw a distinction, as illustrated in figure 1.2, between *behavioral change* (which sometimes gives rise to a U-shaped developmental curve) and *representational change*, because behavioral mastery is not tantamount to the end point of the developmental progression in a given microdomain.

Phase 1 is followed by an internally driven phase during which the child no longer focuses on the external data. Rather, system-internal dynamics take over such that internal representations become the focus of change. In phase 2, the current state of the child's representations of knowledge in a microdomain predominates over information from the incoming data. The temporary disregard for features of the external environment during phase 2 can lead to new errors and

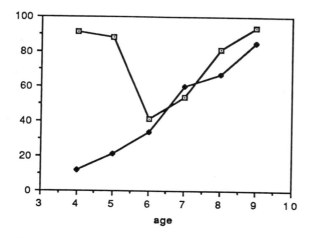

Figure 1.2
Behavioral change (□) versus representational change (◆).

inflexibilities. This can, but does not necessarily, give rise to a decrease in successful behavior—a U-shaped developmental curve. As figure 1.2 shows, however, this is deterioration at the behavioral level, not at the representational level.

Finally, during phase 3, internal representations and external data are reconciled, and a balance is achieved between the quests for internal and external control. In the case of language, for example, a new mapping is made between input and output representations in order to restore correct usage.

But what about the format of the internal representations that sustain these reiterated phases? The RR model argues for at least four levels at which knowledge is represented and re-represented. I have termed them Implicit (I), Explicit-1 (E1), Explicit-2 (E2), and Explicit-3 (E3). These different forms of representation do not constitute age-related stages of developmental change. Rather, they are parts of a reiterative cycle that occurs again and again within different micro-domains and throughout the developmental span.

The RR model postulates different representational formats at different levels. At level I, representations are in the form of procedures for analyzing and responding to stimuli in the external environment. A number of constraints operate on the representational adjunctions that are formed at this level:

> Information is encoded in procedural form.
>
> The procedure-like encodings are sequentially specified.
>
> New representations are independently stored.
>
> Level-I representations are bracketed, and hence no intra-domain or inter-domain representational links can yet be formed.

Information embedded in level-I representations is therefore not available to other operators in the cognitive system. Thus, if two procedures contain identical information, this potential inter-representational commonality is not yet represented in the child's mind. A procedure *as a whole* is available as data to other operators; however, its *component parts* are not. It takes developmental time and representational redescription (see discussion of level E1 below) for component parts to become accessible to potential intra-domain links, a process which ultimately leads (see discussion of levels E2 and E3) to inter-representational flexibility and creative problem-solving capacities. But at this first level, the potential representational links and the information embedded in procedures remain implicit. This gives rise to the ability to compute specific inputs in preferential ways and to respond rapidly and effectively to the environment. But the behavior generated from level-I representations is relatively inflexible.

The RR model posits a subsequent reiterative process of representational redescription.[22] This involves levels E1, E2, and E3. Level-E1 representations are the results of redescription, into a new compressed format, of the procedurally encoded representations at level I. The redescriptions are abstractions in a higher-level language, and unlike level-I representations they are not bracketed (that is, the component parts are open to potential intra-domain and inter-domain representational links).

The E1 representations are reduced descriptions that lose many of the details of the procedurally encoded information. As a nice example of what I have in mind here, consider the details of the grated image delivered to the perceptual system of a person who sees a zebra (Mandler, in press). A redescription of this into "striped animal" (either linguistic or image-like) has lost many of the perceptual details. I would add that the redescription allows the *cognitive* system to understand the analogy between an actual zebra and the road sign for a zebra crossing (a European crosswalk with broad, regular, black and yellow stripes), although the zebra and the road sign deliver very different inputs to the *perceptual* system. A species without representational redescriptions would not make the analogy between the zebra and the "zebra crossing" sign. The redescribed representation is, on the one hand, simpler and less special purpose but, on the other, more cognitively flexible (because it is transportable to other goals). Unlike perceptual representations, conceptual redescriptions are productive; they make possible the invention of new terms (e.g. "zebrin," the antibody which stains certain classes of cells in striped patterns).

Note that the original level-I representations remain intact in the child's mind and can continue to be called for particular cognitive goals which require speed and automaticity. The redescribed representations are used for other goals where explicit knowledge is required.

Although the process of representational redescription can occur on line, I posit that it also takes place without ongoing analysis of incoming data or production of output. Thus, change may occur outside normal input/output relations, i.e. simply as the product of system-internal dynamics, when there are no external pressures of any kind. I will come back to this point in a moment.

As representations are redescribed into the E1 format, we witness the beginnings of a flexible cognitive system upon which the child's nascent theories can subsequently be built. Level E1 involves explicitly defined representations that can be manipulated and related to other redescribed representations. Level-E1 representations thus go beyond the constraints imposed at level I, where procedural-like representations are simply used in response to external stimuli. Once knowledge previously embedded in procedures is explicitly defined, the potential relationships between procedural components can then be marked and represented internally. I examine several examples of this below, particularly in chapters 2 and 3. Moreover, once redescription has taken place and explicit representations become manipulable, the child can then introduce violations to her data-driven, veridical descriptions of the world—violations which allow for pretend play, false belief, and the use of counterfactuals. This I explore in detail in chapter 5.

It is important to stress that although E1 representations are available as data to the system, they are not necessarily available to conscious access and verbal report. Throughout the book we shall examine examples of the formation of explicit representations which are not yet accessible to conscious reflection and verbal report, but which are clearly beyond the procedural level. In general, developmentalists have not distinguished between implicitly stored knowledge and E1 representations in which knowledge *is* explicitly represented but is not yet consciously accessible. Rather, they have drawn a dichotomy between an undefined notion of something implicit in behavior (as if information were not represented in any form) and consciously accessible knowledge that can be stated in verbal form. The RR model postulates that the human representational system is far more complex than a mere dichotomy would suggest. I argue that there are more than two kinds of representation. Levels exist between implicitly stored procedural information and verbally statable declarative knowledge. It is particularly via a developmental perspective that one can pinpoint this multiplicity of levels of representational formats.

The RR model posits that only at levels beyond E1 are conscious access and verbal report possible. At level E2, it is hypothesized, representations are available to conscious access but not to verbal report (which is possible only at level E3). Although for some theorists consciousness is reduced to verbal reportability, the RR model claims that E2 representations are accessible to consciousness but that they are in a similar representational code as the E1 representations of which they are redescriptions. Thus, for example, E1 spatial representations are recoded into consciously accessible E2 *spatial* representations. We often draw diagrams of problems we cannot verbalize. The end result of these various redescriptions is the existence in the mind of multiple representations of similar knowledge at different levels of detail and explicitness.

At level E3, knowledge is recoded into a cross-system code. This common format is hypothesized to be close enough to natural language for easy translation into statable, communicable form. It is possible that some knowledge learned directly in linguistic form is immediately stored at level E3.[23] Children learn a lot from verbal interaction with others. However, knowledge may be stored in linguistic code but not yet be linked to similar knowledge stored in other codes. Often linguistic knowledge (e.g., a mathematical principle governing subtraction) does not constrain nonlinguistic knowledge (e.g., an algorithm used for actually doing subtraction[24]) until both have been redescribed into a similar format so that inter-representational constraints can operate.

In the following chapters, I distinguish three levels of representational format: I, E1, and E2/3. For the present purposes, I do not distinguish between levels E2 and E3, both of which involve conscious access. No research has thus far been directly focused on the E2 level (conscious access without verbal report); most if not all metacognitive studies focus on verbal report (i.e., level E3). However, as mentioned above, I do not wish to foreclose the possibility of consciously accessible spatial, kinesthetic, and other non-linguistically-encoded representations.

There are thus multiple levels at which the same knowledge is re-represented. This notion of multiple encoding is important; development does *not* seem to be a drive for economy. The mind may indeed turn out to be a very redundant store of knowledge and processes.

Before I conclude my account of the RR model, it is important to draw a distinction between the *process* of representational redescription and the ways in which it might be realized in a *model*. The process involves recoding information that is stored in one representational format or code into a different one. Thus, a spatial representation might be recoded into linguistic format, or a proprioceptive representation into spatial format. Each redescription, or re-representation, is a more condensed or compressed version of the previous level. We have just seen that the RR model postulates at least four hierarchically organized levels at which the process of representational redescription occurs. Now, empirical data might refute the existence of this hierarchy (i.e., refute the RR *model*) while leaving the *process* of representational redescription unchallenged. Indeed, as figure 1.3 illustrates, there are several alternative models in which the process of representational redescription might be realized. First, as the RR model presumes, it could involve the passage from implicit representations to a level of explicitly defined representations which are not available to conscious access (level E1), and finally to a format which is available

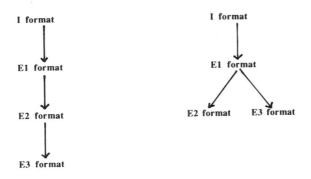

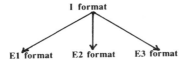

Figure 1.3
Possible models of RR.

to conscious access (level E2) and verbal report (level E3). An alternative view would be that implicit representations are redescribed directly into either the E1, the E2, or the E3 format. Thus, information might be directly recoded into linguistic form, rather than via the E1 level (as the RR model posits).

Models can also differ with respect to constraints on the process of representational redescription. For example, a model might postulate that redescription into one or two different formats occurs automatically every time new input is computed and stored. By contrast, the RR model posits that in most instances a period of behavioral mastery must be reached before redescription occurs. Again, if it were shown that redescription occurs before behavioral mastery, the model would require modification but the general concept of the process of representational redescription would remain. The RR model argues for three recurrent phases leading to behavioral mastery and beyond. Again, were it shown that such phases did not exist, the process of redescription would not necessarily be refuted. On the other hand, if the process of representational redescription were to lose its plausibility (i.e., if all representations in the mind were of equivalent status, or if totally distinct constraints were operative on procedural versus declarative knowledge, rather than each level involving redescription of the previous one), then clearly the model would lose plausibility, too.

Let me again stress the concept of reiterative developmental phases. At any given time the child may have only level-I representations available in one microdomain, but may have E1 representations available in another microdomain and E2/3 representations in yet another. This obviously holds across domains, too. It is hypothesized that there are no overarching domain-general changes in representational format at any given age. There is no such thing as a "phase E2 child". The child's representations are in E2 format with respect to a given microdomain.

The actual *process* of representational redescription is considered domain general, but it operates within each specific domain at different moments and is constrained by the contents and level of explicitness of representations in each microdomain. Again, were each level of representational redescription to turn out to occur across the board at identical ages (e.g., level I up to age 2, level E1 from age 2 to age 4, and E2/3 from age 5 on), which I deem most unlikely, then the model would be refuted and the process would have a different theoretical status.

The model also posits that representational change *within* phases involves adding representational adjunctions. Here negative feedback (failure, incompletion, inadequacy, mismatch between input and output, etc.) plays an important role, leading progressively to behavioral mastery.[25] But in the transition *between* phases, it is hypothesized that *positive* feedback is essential to the onset of representational redescription. In other words, it is representations that have reached a stable state (the child having reached behavioral mastery) that are redescribed.

This success-based view of cognitive change contrasts with Piaget's view. For Piaget, a system in a state of stability would not spontaneously improve itself. Rather, the Piagetian process of equilibration takes place when the system is in a state of disequilibrium. The RR model also runs counter to the behaviorist view that change occurs as the result of failure or external reinforcement. Rather, for the RR model certain types of change take place *after* the child is successful (i.e., already producing the correct linguistic output, or already having consistently reached a problem-solving goal). Representational redescription is a process of "appropriating" stable states to extract the information they contain, which can then be used more flexibly for other purposes.

I do not, of course, deny the role of cognitive conflict in generating other types of change (through, for instance, the mismatch between theory-driven expectations and actual outcomes). What I am stressing here is the additional—and, I hypothesize, crucial—role of internal system stability as the basis for generating representational redescription. And it is from the repeated process of representational redescription, rather than simply from interaction with the external environment, that cognitive flexibility and consciousness ultimately emerge.

The Importance of a Developmental Perspective on Cognitive Science

If our focus is on cognitive flexibility and conscious access to knowledge, why not explore the data from adult psychology? Surely adults are far more cognitively flexible than children, so what justifies a developmental perspective? Not, rest assured, the fact that data from children are cute. One only has to glance at the developmental literature to notice that a sizable number of researchers are absorbed with the ages at which children reach cognitive milestones. But others— and I count myself among them—use the study of development as a theoretical tool for exploring the human mind from a cognitive science perspective. We are not really interested in children per se.[26]

A developmental perspective is essential to the analysis of human cognition, because understanding the built-in architecture of the human mind, the constraints on learning, and *how knowledge changes progressively over time* can provide subtle clues to its final representational format in the adult mind. The work of Spelke (1990), which I discuss in chapter 3, has been particularly influential in pointing to the importance of a developmental perspective on cognitive science.[27] For example, the processes for segmenting visual arrays into objects are overlaid, in adults, by other processes for recognizing object categories. But by focusing on how very young infants segment visual arrays into objects before they are able to categorize certain object kinds, Spelke is able to generate new hypotheses about how the adult visual system may function.[28]

Furthermore, distinctions such as declarative/procedural, conscious/unconscious, and controlled/automatic, which are often used to explain adult processing, turn out to involve far more than a dichotomy when explored within a developmental context. But in assuming a developmental perspective we must take the notion "developmental" seriously. Paradoxically, studies on neonates and infants are often not developmental at all. Like studies on adults, they frequently focus not on change but on real-time processing within steady-state systems. It is of course essential to determine the initial state of the human mind—and for certain abilities the initial state is not necessarily present at birth but is present only after the necessary neurological structures have reached maturation (Mehler and Fox 1985). The notion "developmental" goes beyond the specification of the initial state, however. And a developmental perspective does not apply merely to the details of on-line, steady-state processing in children. Also, it does not simply mean a focus on learning in children of different ages rather than the adult. When making theoretical use of development within a cognitive science perspective, the specific age at which children can successfully perform a task is, to some extent, irrelevant.

The fundamental implication of a developmental perspective involves behavioral and representational change *over time*. I shall often use a later phase in a developmental sequence to understand the status of representations underlying earlier behavior—particularly in the interesting cases where child and adult behaviors are practically identical. This notion of *representational change over time* will be my focus throughout this book. It is for all these reasons that I maintain that a developmental perspective has much to offer cognitive science's efforts to more fully understand the adult mind.

The Importance of a Cognitive Science Perspective on Development

Cognitive science focuses on cognition as a form of computation, and on the mind as a complex system that receives, stores, transforms, retrieves, and transmits information. To do so it uses a variety of disciplines: psychology, philosophy, anthropology, ethology, linguistics, computer science, and neuroscience. I have pointed to the importance of a developmental perspective on cognitive science. But what about the converse? What difference does it make whether or not we study developmental psychology from a cognitive science perspective?

Consider this analogy. Computer scientists use computers in two rather different ways: as a practical tool and as a theoretical tool (Rutkowska 1987). When computers are used to solve practical problems such as designing robots and expert systems, the focus is on successful behavior; how the computer does its job is irrelevant (A. Clark 1987, 1989). Thus, the introduction of a "kludge" (something that remains unexplained but that works for a particular task) poses no problem. But when modelers use computers as theoretical tools for simulating mental processes and testing psychological theories, the focus shifts to questions about appropriate architectures and mechanisms and about the nature of representations. How the computer does its job then becomes a central concern.

Similarly, developmental psychologists fall, *grosso modo*, into two categories: those who see the study of children as an end in itself and those who use it as a theoretical tool to understand the workings of the human mind in general. In the former case, as mentioned above, many developmentalists focus on behavior—e.g., on the particular age at which the child can do X. Decades of developmental research were wasted, in my view, because the focus was entirely on lowering the age at which children could perform a task successfully, without concern for *how* they processed the information. I once began an article (Karmiloff-Smith 1981, p. 151) as follows: "The enticing yet awful fact about child development is that children develop! Awful, because it has provoked a plethora of studies, totally unmotivated theoretically, accepted for publication in certain types of journal because the results are 'significant'—significant *statistically*, since it is indeed easy to obtain differential effects between, say, 5 and 7 year olds, but questionable as to their significance *scientifically*." Fortunately, however, the study of children is used within a cognitive science perspective also—i.e., as a theoretical means of understanding the human mind in general. In such work, the focus is on the initial architecture, the processing mechanisms, and the nature of internal representational change.

Many recent books and articles have focused on what cognitive science and information-processing models might offer the study of development (Bechtel and Abrahamsen 1991; A. Clark 1989; Klahr et al. 1987; Klahr 1992; McTear 1987). In this book, my aim is to highlight why a developmental perspective is essential to cognitive science.

The Plan of the Book

The first part of each of the following five chapters—on the child as a linguist, a physicist, a mathematician, a psychologist, and a notator—concentrates on the initial state of the infant mind and on subsequent domain-specific learning in infancy and early childhood. Each chapter then goes on to explore empirical data on older children's problem solving and theory building, with particular focus on cognitive flexibility and metacognition.

I might have devoted a separate chapter to the child as a concept former, since there has been extensive research on this topic.[29] However, conceptual development is relevant to each of chapters 2–6: how children categorize objects in the physical world, how they mathematize that world, how they conceive of human agents versus physical objects, and how they encode that knowledge linguistically and in external notations such as drawing and maps. Concept formation will thus permeate each chapter rather than be treated separately.

In chapters 7 and 8 I take another look at the reconciliation between nativism and Piaget's constructivism, and discuss the need for more formal developmental models. Here I compare aspects of the RR model with connectionist simulations of development. At all times, I place particular emphasis on the status of representations sustaining different capacities and on the multiple levels at which knowledge is stored and accessible. I end the book by taking a final look at the RR model and speculating on the status of representations in nonhumans, which—however complex their behaviors—never become linguists, physicists, mathematicians, psychologists, or notators.

Chapter 2

The Child as a Linguist

. . . young children know something about language that the spider does not know about web-weaving. (Gleitman et al. 1972, p. 160)

"What's that?"
(Mother: "A typewriter.")
"No, you're the typewriter, that's a typewrite."

(Yara, 4 years)

What makes us specifically human: the complexity of our language? our problem-solving strategies? You may be shocked by my suggestion that, in some very deep sense, language and some aspects of human problem solving are no more or less complex than the behaviors of other species. Complexity as such is not the issue. Spiders weave complex webs, bees transmit complex information about sources and quality of nectar, ants interact in complex colonies, beavers build complex dams, chimpanzees have complex problem-solving strategies, and humans use complex language. And there are humans who acquire fluent language even though they are unable to solve certain problems that the nonlinguistic chimpanzee can solve. So it is not a lack of general problem-solving skills that stops the chimpanzee from acquiring language. Something about the capacity to acquire language must be innately specified in humans. Although language is specific to humans, there is also a domain-general difference between human and nonhuman intelligence. Unlike the spider, which stops at web weaving, the human child—and, I maintain, only the human child—has the potential to take its own representations as objects of cognitive attention. Normally developing children not only become efficient users of language; they also spontaneously become little grammarians. By contrast, the constraints on spiders, ants, beavers, and probably even chimpanzees are such that they do not have the potential to analyze their own knowledge.

This cross-species difference is beautifully captured by the quotation from the 4-year-old at the beginning of this chapter. A "typewrite"! Why doesn't the child simply accept the label provided by the adult and use the correct word, "typewriter"? Why has she bothered to work out that the formal function of the suffix "-er" is agentive—i.e., that one can often take verb stems and add "-er" to form a word for a human agent (baker, dancer, teacher), so why not typewriter? The child's ability cannot be explained away solely on the basis of statistical regularities in the input. The latter might give rise to a sporadic error in output, such as the use of "typewrite" to refer to the object, or to an occasional miscomprehension that "typewriter" refers to a human agent. But statistical regularities cannot explain why the child bothers to go beyond the input/output relations and reflect metalinguistically on the word.

Throughout the book, I shall argue that what is special about humans is the fact that they spontaneously go beyond successful behavior. In the case of language, as in other areas of cognition, normally developing children are not content with using the right words and structures; they go beyond expert usage to exploit the linguistic knowledge that they have already stored. I argue that this is possible via the repeated process of representational redescription discussed in chapter 1. Metalinguistic reflection requires flexible and manipulable linguistic representations.

In every domain that we explore, two major theoretical positions divide developmentalists into rather rigidly opposing camps: either acquisition is domain general or it is domain specific. The modularity/nativist view of language acquisition is that it is domain specific; i.e., that innately specified linguistic structures constrain the child's processing of linguistic input.[1] The strictly domain-general view considers language to be merely a special case of other, domain-general structures and processes.[2]

I shall argue that language acquisition is both domain specific and domain general; i.e., that some initial domain-specific constraints channel the progressive building up of domain-specific linguistic representations but that, once redescribed, these representations become available to domain-general processes. This results in multiple representations of similar linguistic information, but in different representational formats. In other words, I shall agree with aspects of the nativist thesis as far as the very early stages of language acquisition are concerned, but with the proviso that we invoke a less static notion of a fully prespecified linguistic module, in favor of progressive modularization. Overwhelming data now exist to substantiate the hypothesis that, from the outset, infants process linguistic data in linguistically constrained ways. These attention biases serve to build up linguistically relevant representations, not solely domain-general sensorimotor ones. However, unlike dyed-in-the-wool nativists, I maintain that that is not all there is to language acquisition. The innate specification makes infants especially attentive to linguistic input and sets the boundaries within which language acquisition can take place; however, a more constructivist position opens up possibilities for representational flexibility, which ultimately leads to metalinguistic awareness. Let us first look at the rather different ways in which domain-general and domain-specific theorists view early language acquisition.

Language Acquisition as a Domain-General Process: The Piagetian Infant

If you were a disciple of Piaget, how would you explain the onset of language? First, you would not grant the neonate any innately speci-fied linguistic structures or mechanisms which are preferentially attentive to linguistic input. Indeed, Piagetians maintain that both syntax and semantics are solely products of the general structural or-ganization of sensorimotor intelligence. The culmination of the sen-sorimotor period is the first time, according to the theory, that the infant is capable of symbolic representation. In explaining the timing of the onset of language at around 18 months, Piagetians make no appeal to possible maturational constraints. Rather, they maintain that language does not appear earlier because it is an integral part of the onset of the symbolic (or semiotic) function, which includes not only language but also deferred imitation, pretend play, and mental im-agery. For Piagetians, language is not an independently developing capacity. They explain the late onset of language by pointing to the time it takes for sensorimotor action schemes to become progressively coordinated and internalized so as to make symbolic representation possible.

But can one really deny the young infant's capacity for symbolic representation? To do so one would have to ignore the cogent argu-ments of Mandler (1983, 1988, in press), which are based on the now-extensive data suggesting the existence of symbolic representation early in infancy. How, Mandler asks, could a young infant recall an action to be imitated after as long as 24 hours (Meltzoff 1988, 1990) without the benefit of accessible knowledge represented in long-term memory? Likewise, how could an infant of 6–9 months recall the exact size of an object and precisely where it was located behind a screen (Ashmead and Perlmutter 1980; Baillargéon 1986) if it could not rep-resent them in an accessible form? In fact, the data which have accumulated since the early 1980s call into question the very notion of a purely sensorimotor stage of human development prior to language.

But a Piagetian disciple would have to ignore or reinterpret the new infancy data that I am about to discuss, and continue to argue that language is part of the semiotic function, available to the child only with the culmination of sensorimotor intelligence. Indeed, Piagetians seek precursors of all aspects of language in the child's sensorimotor interaction with the environment. Linguistic recursivity, for instance, is not traced to any domain-specific constraint. Rather, the Piagetians' explanation lies in a domain-general recursive process emerging from the infant's earlier embedding of sensorimotor action schemes such as seeing and grasping. This embedding, they argue, is the product of postnatal circular reactions such as reiterated sucking (Sinclair 1971). Piagetians explain the emergence of word order and difficulties therewith purely in terms of prior understanding of the order of sensorimotor actions. Playing with containers—embedding objects one into another—is considered a necessary precursor to the embedding of clauses. Piagetians see the cognitive concepts of agent, action, and patient as the prerequisites of early sentence structures (e.g. subject, verb, and object). Notions such as noun phrase, verb phrase, subject, and clause are labeled adultomorphisms and said not to be available to the young child's linguistic computations before the acquisition of elaborate cognitive structures. Indeed, some Piagetians maintain that "the stages of cognitive development determine the nature and the form of the linguistic structures that children are able to produce and understand" (Ferreiro and Sinclair 1971) and, more recently, that "basic language competence [is] constructed by the child subsequent to and on the model of the child's fundamental achievement during the pre-verbal practical intelligence period" (Sinclair 1987).

But what if, from a Piagetian stance, you favored Chomsky's structuralism while negating the nativist implications of his theory? Indeed, Piagetians tend to hold onto Chomsky's (1965) now-obsolete account in terms of deep and surface linguistic structures and different transformations, only they see these structures and transformations as special cases of prior cognitive structures and operations (Sinclair 1987). Piagetian psycholinguistics remain more compatible with Chomsky's earlier transformational model than with his later model involving innately specified linguistic principles and parameters (Chomsky 1981), which they would have difficulty fitting into their cognitively based thinking about early language development.[3] Yet, paradoxically, Chomsky's more recent theory, which is based not on rules but on principles, could be more readily integrated into an epigenetic view than his earlier rule-based transformational view.

Could the same mechanisms used for parsing visual scenes also account for specifically linguistic principles that determine semantic-syntactic relations? Vision and language seem to adhere to their own domain-specific principles, at least in adults. This does not necessarily imply that the principles have to be innately specified in detail, though they may be. What it does suggest is that the infant would have to start out with innately specified linguistic predispositions and attention biases so as to constrain the class of inputs that it computes in ways relevant to not violating specific linguistic principles, and not simply engage in a data-driven exercise of pattern matching on the basis of the external input and nonlinguistic, domain-general cognitive structures.[4]

Moreover, Piagetians are hard pressed to explain the natural constraints on children's inferential powers. Were domain-general, cognitively based generalizations operative, then, given the input data, the child would make many inappropriate linguistic generalizations. But such generalizations are not made. Inferences that children do and don't make in language acquisition are governed by specifically linguistic principles which constrain the class of inputs open to such generalizations. Domain specificity seems to win out over domain generality in the early stages of language acquisition. Yet Piagetians continue to explain all linguistic notions as deriving from cognitive ones and to see syntax and semantics as generalizations from sensorimotor and conceptual representations.

From the Piagetian stance, then, you might predict that linguistic retardation would necessarily accompany severe cognitive retardation. But such a prediction would turn out to be wrong. Indeed, studies of children with internal hydrocephaly and spina bifida (Anderson and Spain 1977; Cromer 1991; Hadenius et al. 1962; Swisher and Pinsker 1971; Tew 1979) and of those with Williams Syndrome (Bellugi et al. 1988; Udwin et al. 1987) show that complex syntax and lexico-morphology (correct grammar, eloquent vocabulary, etc.) may coexist with very severe general cognitive impairments.

In sum, as a Piagetian you would reduce linguistic universals to general cognitive universals and endorse Sinclair's recent statement (1987) that "language competence and the way it develops in the child [is] an integral part of a general cognitive competence."[5]

Language Acquisition as a Domain-Specific Process: The Nativist Infant

How different your thinking would be if you were a domain-specific theorist! With a growing number of developmental psycholinguists, you would argue that young children focus specifically on language as a problem space in its own right and not as part of domain-general input. Those taking a domain-specific view of language acquisition expect the neonate to possess a number of linguistically relevant attention biases. They attribute the timing of the onset of language to innately specified maturational constraints, rather than viewing it as the final outcome of domain-general sensorimotor development. For many nativists, language is modular (i.e., totally independent of other aspects of cognition).[6] For others, it is domain specific rather than strictly modular. In both cases, children's learning of their native tongue is thought of as an innately guided process.

Thus, if you took a domain-specific stance on language acquisition, you would seek in the neonate and in the early infant specifically linguistic precursors to the onset of language at 18 months. And your efforts would be rewarded.

At least three problems face the language-learning infant[7]: how to segment the speech stream into meaningful linguistic units, how to analyze the world into objects and events relevant to linguistic encoding,[8] and how to handle the mapping between the units and the objects and events at both the lexical and the syntactic level. The nativist argues that these problems could not be surmounted without prior linguistically relevant processes that constrain the way in which the child computes linguistic input compared to other auditory input. There must therefore be some innate component to the acquisition of language—but, to reiterate, this does not mean that there has to be a ready-made module. Attention biases and some innate predispositions could lead the child to focus on linguistically relevant input and, with time, to build up linguistic representations that are domain-specific. Since we process language very rapidly, the system might *with time* close itself off from other influences—i.e., become relatively modularized.

Let us now focus on research aimed at uncovering the linguistic constraints on the neonate's and the young infant's early language, and explore how such very young children build up and store linguistically relevant representations. Recent research suggests that the infant's mind computes a constrained class of specifically linguistic inputs such that, in their interpretation of sound waves, infants make a distinction between linguistically relevant and other, nonlinguistic auditory input. According to Mehler et al. (1986), 4-day-old infants are already sensitive to certain characteristics of their native tongue. Using the non-nutritive sucking habituation technique described above in chapter 1, Mehler tested French babies' sensitivity to the difference between French and Russian input from the same bilingual speaker. Previous studies had already shown that 12-hour-old infants

differentiate between linguistically relevant input and other nonlinguistic acoustic input. But Mehler's new research showed that at birth
infants do not yet react to differences between languages. Thus, the
stimuli received during the 9 months in utero do not provide sufficiently differentiated input for the child to show preferential attention
to its native tongue at birth. But only 4 days after birth—i.e., after
exceedingly little exposure, the infants studied by Mehler et al.
showed sensitivity to the different prosodic patterns of French and
Russian.

It is not merely to overall phonological or prosodic patterns that
young infants are sensitive. They also attend to features which will
ultimately have syntactic value, and they do so extremely early. Jusczyk et al. (1989) studied infants raised in an English-speaking environment and found that at 4 months the infants were sensitive to cues
that correlate with clause boundaries of both English and Polish input.
By 6 months, however, the infants had lost their sensitivity to Polish
clause boundaries, but they continued to demonstrate sensitivity to
clause boundaries in their native tongue. In other words, the architecture of the infant mind is such that it is sensitive at the outset to
the clausal structure of any human language. Thus, some fairly general
features about the prosodic (and perhaps the syntactic) structure of
human languages appear to be built into the system or to be learned
exceedingly early on the basis of some linguistic predispositions.
These early sensitivities channel the infant's computation of all subsequent input and serve to progressively select the appropriate structures for the child's native tongue and stabilize them.

Such data suggest that some specifically linguistic predispositions
and attention biases allow the infant to learn any human language,
and that, in interaction with the particular environmental input from
the child's native tongue(s), particular pathways for representing and
processing language are selected. By puberty the other pathways are
lost, and by then the processing of language in a native-like way has
become relatively modularized.

Further grist for the anti-domain-general mill comes from work
showing that stabilization of phonologically relevant perceptual categories does not require the prior establishment of sensorimotor programs (Mehler and Bertoncini 1988). Experiments have also been
devised to demonstrate that infants are sensitive to the difference
between relative pitch, which is linguistically relevant, and absolute
pitch (e.g., male versus female voice), which is socially relevant; to
rhythmic aspects of linguistic input; to vowel duration; to linguistic
stress; to the contour of rising and falling intonation; and to subtle
phonemic distinctions.[9]

Studies have also suggested that, well before they can talk, young infants are already sensitive to word boundaries (Gleitman et al. 1988) and to clause boundaries within which grammatical rules apply (Hirsh-Pasek et al. 1987). Using a preferential-listening procedure similar to the preferential-looking procedure described above in chapter 1, Hirsh-Pasek et al. had 7–10-month-old babies listen to two types of acoustic input. From a recording of a mother speaking to her child, matched samples were constructed by inserting pauses either at normal clause boundaries or at within-clause locations. Already at 7 months, the babies oriented longer to the samples segmented at the clause boundary than to those in which the pauses violated such natural linguistic boundaries. In other words, the young infant already analyzes auditory input according to phrase-boundary markers—that is, in a linguistically relevant way that will later support the representation of syntactic structure.

Interestingly, there have studies of infants who received no linguistic input at first: congenitally deaf children born of hearing parents who did not know sign language. The exciting finding was that, even though they lacked the benefit of the linguistic model available to hearing children and to deaf children of signing deaf parents, these children nonetheless invented a visuomanual system that displayed several of the constraints of natural language (Goldin-Meadow and Feldman 1979; Feldman et al. 1978). Of course, their visuomanual system did not develop into a full-fledged sign language. Moving from linguistic predispositions to language-specific constraints (French, English, American Sign Language, Spanish, Polish, etc.) requires input. But such case studies once again point to the importance of a domain-specific, innately guided process that can get language acquisition off the ground even in the absence of a model.

And when a linguistic model is available, young children are clearly attentive, not to some domain-general input, but to domain-specific information relevant to language. Many data exist which demonstrate the child's early analysis of language as a formal domain-specific problem space (Bloom 1970; Karmiloff-Smith 1979a; Valian, 1986, 1990). One of the examples I find particularly telling comes from the work of Petitto (1987),[10] who studied children's acquisition of the personal pronouns "you" and "I" in American Sign Language (ASL). Petitto's subjects were congenitally deaf but were growing up in a normal linguistic environment since their parents were native deaf signers. In ASL, personal pronouns are among the few signs that resemble natural gestures. "I" is encoded by pointing to oneself, "you" by pointing toward the addressee. Now, if sensorimotor action schemes were the necessary bases of domain-general acquisition of language, the signs for "I" and "you" should appear very early in ASL acquisition as a natural extension of gestures. Moreover, they should not show the deictic errors typical of spoken language, such as children's temporary mistake of using "you" to refer to themselves (Chiat 1986; Tanz 1980). Neither of these domain-general predictions holds for ASL acquisition. Petitto's data show that nonlinguistic pointing is present well before the syntactic use of pronouns appears in ASL and that the linguistic use of pronouns appears at the same time in ASL as in spoken language. This is not to deny that other signs of a more lexical nature may appear early in ASL (Bonvillian et al. 1983; Meier and Newport 1990).[11] But the point is that pronouns are not an extension of gesture; rather, they are an integral part of the domain-specific development of language as a system.

Important, too, is the fact that deaf children acquiring ASL as their native tongue actually do make subsequent errors in their use of the personal pronouns. They start by using pronouns correctly. However, subsequently in development they temporarily use the ASL sign for "you" (a point to the addressee) to refer to themselves, or they provisionally replace personal pronouns by the use of proper names. And children do this despite their earlier mastery and despite the seeming transparency between the semantic and the syntactic relations. But the deaf child ignores the *indexical* aspect of the signs (the pointing gestures that correspond to semantic information) and focuses on the *formal* aspect of the signs (personal pronouns as a formal linguistic system).

The RR model would explain this development in terms of changing representations. Initially the child focuses on the input data and stores two independent level-I representations for "you" and "I." Subsequently, once the child is producing consistently efficient output, the level-I representations are redescribed such that the linguistic components marking personal pronominal reference are explicitly defined in E1 format. Then links across the two entries' common components can be drawn, such that new representations can form a subsystem of personal pronouns.

Late-occurring errors constitute a striking illustration of how domain-specific mechanisms of data abstraction constrain the child to analyze just those aspects of the input that are relevant to the formal linguistic system. By contrast, different domain-specific mechanisms interpret *identical* input in nonlinguistic ways (e.g., pointing interpreted as a social gesture rather than as an arbitrary linguistic sign).

Another example of the domain specificity of data abstraction and production mechanisms comes from neuropsychological studies of brain damage in deaf adult signers (Poizner et al. 1987). These patients can be shown to be capable of imitating a movement manually and yet be incapable of producing the same form when this is being used in a linguistic context. In other words, the output does not call on domain-general processes; manually realized *linguistic* signs seem to be stored and processed separately from manual *gestures*. It therefore seems that the linguistic system becomes domain specific and relatively modularized over the course of learning. It is these domain-specific processes that are impaired, but such damage may have no effect on the capacity to produce *nonlinguistic* manual gestures of similar form and complexity.

At any time, then, identical input may be open to different interpretations, depending on the particular domain-specific focus of the child (or adult). As far as language is concerned, from the outset and throughout the acquisition process, domain-specific constraints specifying how to abstract and represent linguistically relevant data seem to be operative for both semantics and syntax.

The Infant's and the Young Child's Sensitivity to Semantic Constraints

How do children work out the mapping between concepts and the lexicon of their native tongue? Once again, we shall see that preexisting constraints narrow children's hypotheses about the possible meanings of words (Carey 1982; E. Clark 1987; Dockrell and Campbell 1986; Gleitman 1990; Hall 1991; Markman 1987, 1989; Merriman and Bowman 1989). In this way a virtually insoluble induction problem is avoided. Gleitman (1990) provides a particularly illuminating discussion of the general issue of constraints on word learning. She poses Quine's (1960) problem as follows: Given a linguistic output and a situation to which it refers, how could an intelligent adult, let alone an 18-month-old toddler, settle on the meaning of a new word in the face of the multitude of interpretative options available? For instance, when seeing an adult point toward a cat and say "Look, a cat", how can the child decide whether the speaker uses "cat" to mean the whole animal, the cat's whiskers, the color of the cat's fur, the mat on which it is standing, the bowl of water from which it is drinking, the action of the cat's licking its fur, the noise of its purring, the ribbon around its neck, the fact that the speaker likes animals, or the background details of the scene (and so on, ad infinitum)? We shall see that the same potential induction problems occur not only for nouns but also for verbs. How can one infer from details in the external environment alone the linguistic distinction between, say, "look" and "see", or that between "chase" and "flee"? These induction problems would arise only, Gleitman argues, if the learner's sole ammunition were unaided observation-based interpretations of the scene being described linguistically. But this is not the case. Gleitman proposes that the infant's perceptual and conceptual processing of events and objects in the environment are constrained to specific levels of abstraction and taxonomy. The child does not approach the word-learning task through mere observation. Rather, the child's hypothesis space with respect to the possible meanings of the words in her language is subject to principled constraints. These result from domain-specific biases on mappings between objects/events and words, as well as from sensitivity to distinctions within the linguistic system itself. Let me deal with each of these in turn.

The first involves the interaction between linguistic constraints and those deriving from the child's interpretations of the physical world (via visual or, in the case of the blind, haptic perception). Carey (1982)[12] formulates the problem succinctly by asking: When a child hears a word, to what ontological types does she assume the word refers— whole objects, features of objects, substances, or what? Do children build up word meanings solely on the basis of a composition of semantic features (round, furry, green, sharp, etc.), component by component (E. Clark 1973; Baron 1973), or are there constraints on possible word meanings that bias the way in which the child interprets the linguistic input? There have been several attempts to answer these questions, but the one most relevant to the present discussion comes from a constraints view of early infancy and later word learning.

Mandler (1988 and in press) has provided the most thoroughly worked out speculations about the way in which young infants build representations that are suitable for subsequent linguistic encoding. According to Mandler, young infants engage in a process of perceptual analysis which goes beyond their rapid and automatic computation of perceptual input. Perceptual analysis results in the formation of perceptual primitives such as SELF-MOTION/CAUSED MOTION/PATH/ SUPPORT/AGENT. These primitives guide the way in which infants parse events into separate entities that are supported or contained and which move from sources to goals along specific kinds of paths according to whether the movement is animate or inanimate. Mandler argues that these perceptual primitives are redescribed into an accessible image-schematic format, thereby providing a level of representation intermediate between perception and language. And it is these accessible image schemas that facilitate semantic development (i.e., the mapping between language and conceptual categories). Image schemas are nonpropositional, analog representations of spatial relations and movements; that is, they are conceptual structures mapped from spatial structure.

The redescription of perceptual primitives into image-schematic representations, and of the latter into language, indicates how the RR model outlined in chapter 1 can be applied to very early infancy. I have stressed the fact that representational redescription can occur outside input/output relations. Mandler extends the RR model to on-line processing, suggesting that redescription also takes place as the child is actively engaged in analyzing perceptual input and redescribing it into the more accessible format of image schemas. As with the RR model, Mandler postulates that the formation of image schemas requires an innately specified mechanism of analysis, not necessarily innately specified content.

The redescription into language of image schemas conceptualizing spatial relations suggests a tighter relationship between language and cognition for semantics than in the case of syntax.

How do young children learn the meanings of words in their language? Clearly they attend to the environment in which adults and others use such words and explain their meaning. But is this enough? When the adult points to some object and says "That's an X", such ostensive definitions typically underdetermine a word's meaning severely. To surmount this problem, children must bring to the word-learning situation a limited number of hypotheses about possible types of word meaning. Markman and her colleagues (Horton and Markman 1980; Markman 1980; Markman and Wachtel 1988[13]) have shown that as of 3 years of age (and perhaps as early as 18 months, coinciding with the vocabulary burst [Bloom et al. 1985; Dromi 1987; McShane 1979; Nelson 1973]), children seem to abide by three assumptions about the mapping between words and their referents: the whole-object assumption, the taxonomic assumption, and the assumption of mutual exclusivity. First, 3–5-year-olds assume that a new label refers to an object as a whole, and not to its substance, constituent parts, color, texture, size, shape, etc. Second, children extend a newly acquired label to objects of the same taxonomic kind, rather than to objects that are related thematically to the original one. If a child hears "See the dax" and sees an adult pointing to an object, the child maps "dax" onto the whole object rather than onto one of its parts, although nothing in the adult utterance indicates that. Also, children tend to assume that new words refer to a basic category level (e.g., dog) rather than to a superordinate or subordinate kind (e.g., animal or poodle). The third assumption calls for mutual exclusivity, such that, on hearing a new label (e.g., "viper"), children tend to apply it to an object for which they do not yet have a label, given that other objects present in the array (say dogs, cats, etc.) are ones for which they already have a label. This means that the child can learn a new word without relying on any pointing on the part of the speaker.

Markman points out that these biases are not deterministic but probabilistic.[14] They can be overridden when there is sufficient other information to suggest an alternative interpretation. The mutual-exclusivity assumption, for example, leads children to expect that each object has only one label. Thus, on hearing "Look at its nice *fur*", as an adult points to a cat, a child who already knows the word for cat can use the mutual-exclusivity assumption to override the whole-object assumption and acquire a new word for a feature of the referent (fur). Likewise, on hearing "That's a nice *animal*" the child can override the basic-category-level assumption and learn the superordinate label (animal).

Hall (1991) has recently shown that similar biases constrain the way in which children come to understand what he calls "restricted" versus "unrestricted" meanings of words. For example, whereas the word "person" continues to refer to someone throughout his or her life span and in any situation, words like "youth" or "passenger" refer only at certain times and in certain circumstances; they have restricted meanings. Moreover, someone can be simultaneously both a person and a passenger. These are intricate facts about word meaning with which the child has to come to grips. Hall's research shows that even adults are implicitly aware of these difficulties. They tend to teach young children unrestricted words via pure ostension, whereas restricted meanings are taught via a combination of ostension and direct explanations, providing clues to the learner about how to restrict these special meanings. It is the absence of these extra clues that biases the child to take pure ostension as referring to whole kinds of objects at a middle category level rather than to properties, parts, superordinate, or subordinate levels.

These various default assumptions or biases work to guide children's initial hypotheses about noun meanings, helping them disregard countless possible but incorrect inductions. But they can obviously lead to errors, too. Thus, the biases must be strong, yet flexible enough to be overridden by other, more pertinent information. Clearly we need to draw a distinction between the probabilistic biases operative in the working out of possible semantic mappings for word meanings and the more deterministic constraints of syntax.

The Infant's and the Young Child's Sensitivity to Syntactic Constraints

Those holding the view that the acquisition of language stems from nonlinguistic cognitive constraints would be unlikely to entertain the idea that infants are sensitive to purely syntactic constraints on linguistic input. Yet Katz et al. (1974) showed that 17-month-olds can use syntactic information to distinguish between a noun referring to a class of objects and one functioning as a proper name. And this capacity was apparent well before the infants were using determiners in their own output. Thus, when infants heard "a dax" they chose another doll similar to the one the experimenter already named as "a dax", whereas when they heard "Dax" they chose the individual doll to whom the experimenter had given the proper name "Dax." These data indicate that language is a problem space per se for infants well before they are producing much language themselves. In other words, infants make use of morphosyntactic subtleties within the linguistic system itself to work out meaning.

But what about more complex aspects of syntax? Are infants sensitive to word order in linguistic strings and to differences between transitive and intransitive verb structures? Hirsh-Pasek et al. (1985) used the preferential-looking paradigm described above in chapter 1 to probe infants' sensitivity to word order. Infants with relatively little linguistic output were shown two animated scenes on two screens. While watching the displays, they heard from a hidden speaker a sentence that matched only one of the two scenes. Significantly longer looking at the video that matches the speech output demonstrates infants' sensitivity to the linguistic distinctions being encoded. Hirsh-Pasek et al. showed that 17-month-old infants who were not yet producing anything like sentences could nonetheless distinguish between sentences like "Big Bird is tickling Cookie Monster" and "Cookie Monster is tickling Big Bird". If they were merely relying on the words in the utterances, irrespective of word order, their looking time should have been random between the two displays. But this was not the case. They looked significantly longer at the display that matched the linguistic output, demonstrating that at this young age word order was already *linguistically relevant* to them.

Although infants are sensitive to word order, one should not confound this with sensitivity to serial order. The order to which they are sensitive in language is dependent on structure (i.e., the relative order of noun phrases and verb phrases) (Chomsky 1987; Crain and Fodor, in press), not on the order of single words. Domain-neutral theories argue that infants work out how their language functions on the basis of rules that order conceptual categories or real-world events. But this is not so. There is no *conceptual* reason why, for instance, pronouns and proper names cannot be modified by prenominal adjectives. What, conceptually, would preclude children from pointing to two individuals and, using deictic pronouns, saying "Big he, little she"? But according to studies by Bloom (1990), children never violate this specifically linguistic constraint of English. Rather, both production and comprehension experiments show that, in computing language, children order abstract *linguistic* categories, not *conceptual* categories. Children analyze pronouns as noun phrases, not as single words. Noun phrases cannot be modified by prenominal adjectives. That violates a constraint on English. Now, if children generated general cognitive hypotheses (i.e., not specifically linguistic ones) in order to understand adult language, surely they would opt for the simplest hypothesis (order of elements) instead of the cognitively more complex hypothesis (order of structure-dependent phrases). But it is the linguistically relevant, domain-specific hypothesis that young children use.

Hirsh-Pasek et al. (1988) explored children's understanding of an even more complex linguistic distinction. They were interested in children's processing of constraints on causative verbs. Children heard outputs such as "Big Bird is turning Cookie Monster" (or "Big Bird is turning with Cookie Monster") and saw two scenes on the video screens: one depicting Big Bird making Cookie Monster physically turn around, the other with the animals both turning next to one another. The preferential-looking procedure was again used to assess whether children looked longer at the scene matching the verbal output. Other trials used verbs which these young children were unlikely to have ever heard before, such as "flexing", in both transitive and intransitive sentences. Although stable effects were not established consistently at 24 months, by 27 months (long before such distinctions figure in their output) children looked significantly longer at the display matching the linguistic output. These results allow us to conclude that shortly after the second birthday a child knows that only a transitive verb expresses the presence of a causal agent and that causal agency cannot be in an oblique argument position (the *with* clause). Further, the child understands that the *with* clause excludes a transitive reading. It is difficult to see how children so young could have learned such subtle linguistic distinctions solely on the basis of domain-general sensorimotor actions.

The Need for Both Semantic and Syntactic Bootstrapping

Gleitman (1990) draws a distinction between semantic bootstrapping (the use of semantics to work out syntax) and syntactic bootstrapping (the use of syntax to predict semantics). While most developmental psycholinguists have focused on one or the other of these processes,

Gleitman argues that language development involves both. Both make critical use of canonical relations between syntax and semantics.

The semantic bootstrapping hypothesis involves word-to-world mappings by which the child searches the observable environment for possible referential candidates (see Pinker 1984, 1987 for detailed accounts). Gleitman calls this the "observational learning hypothesis" and agrees that part of the child's acquisition of verb meanings takes place via this route. The distinctions between some closely related verbs (e.g. break/tear, shatter/crumble) must be worked out by observational learning, because these verbs do not differ in their syntactic frames (Filmore 1968).

However, semantic bootstrapping, although necessary, is not sufficient to explain the normal child's acquisition of many verb meanings.[15] In support of this claim, Landau and Gleitman (1985) analyze the problems besetting the congenitally blind child's distinction between the verbs "see" and "look". How, they ask, could blind children use observational learning to guide their hypotheses about the meanings of these two verbs? In fact, the problem obtains for sighted children, too. Evidence for word meaning does not simply lie in the external environment of physical objects and actions. Rather, the evidence resides in the design of language itself, in the different subcategorization frames in which these verbs can be used.[16] Some verbs take three argument structures, some two. Some verbs encode paths and goals expressed in prepositional phrases, others do not. The use of particular verbs with particular subcategorization frames depends on the perspective taken by the speaker. Do you interpret an action between two people as one of "giving to" or "taking from", as one of "fleeing from" or "chasing after", and so forth? The same event can be described in very different ways. To work out the linguistic meanings, the young child must be sensitive to these *intralinguistic* differences. The structure of subcategorization frames helps children figure out speakers' intentions as well as the differences in verb meanings used to describe potentially equivalent extralinguistic contexts.

The major thrust of Gleitman's argument is that, blind or sighted, children cannot rely on observational learning alone. Rather, the child must also bring to the language learning situation relatively sophisticated presuppositions about the structure of language itself. Caretakers do not provide a running commentary on events and scenes in the world. And even if they did, ostensive definitions are underdetermined. In any case, adult output also refers to things not happening in the here and now. For example, a father might say to his infant: "When you're done with eating your dinner, we'll look at Sesame Street. Then Daddy'll get you undressed, and take you up to the bath before Mummy gets back from work. Oh, dear, look what you've done now. You've dropped it all over the floor. I'll get the broom. And, we're late, listen, I can already hear Mummy's car." Simple word-to-world mappings would lead to umpteen erroneous hypotheses about word meanings in general, and verb meanings in particular.

Gleitman takes a different stance. She maintains that children must be using *sentence*-to-world mappings in trying to work out the semantic distinctions between such closely related verbs as look/see, listen/hear, fall/drop, hide/disappear, and chase/flee. The differences are rarely observable from the extralinguistic contexts in which they are used, but they can be inferred from the intralinguistic contexts in which they are used because of their different subcategorization frames. One says "I hid the ball" but not "I disappeared the ball"; "I fled from the man" but not "The man chased from me"; "I looked at the ball" but not "I saw at the ball". It is the fact that similar meanings can be expressed via verbs with different subcategorization frames that narrows the interpretative options. In this way, the syntax functions, to use Gleitman's words, "like a kind of mental zoom lens" for fixing on just the interpretation among many possible ones that the speaker is expressing. Again, it is difficult to see how domain-general data-abstraction mechanisms could alone give rise to an understanding of such subtle linguistic distinctions.

Beyond Infancy and Early Childhood

The extraordinary feat of language acquisition takes place effortlessly in a short span of time. By the time a child is 3 or 4 years old, she is speaking and understanding rather fluently. So is that all there is to language—a set of constraints for attending to, processing, and representing linguistically relevant input; biases that constrain the way in which the child represents objects and events in the world; and the subsequent processes of semantic and syntactic bootstrapping? Does acquisition involve nothing more than reaching behavioral mastery of each aspect of the linguistic system? Let us explore these questions by jumping a couple of years and imagining our infant as having become a fluent speaker of her native tongue.

The RR Model and Becoming a Little Linguist

The RR model, outlined in chapter 1, argues that normal development involves considerably more than reaching behavioral mastery. Mandler has posited the formation of image-schematic representations that mediate between perception and language, and has used the process of representational redescription to account for the passage from one representational format to another. The RR model further postulates that the linguistic representations themselves also undergo subsequent redescription, such that they become linguistic objects of attention outside their on-line use in comprehension and production. In other words, young children go beyond behavioral mastery, beyond fluent output and successful communication, to exploit the linguistic knowledge they have already stored. It is this that ultimately allows them to become little linguists.

The linguistic representations built up during infancy and early childhood serve young children for comprehending and producing their native tongue. But these initial linguistic representations are not, I argue, available as data for metalinguistic reflection. They are stored and run as procedures for effective comprehension and production. They are, to use the metaphor from chapter 1, information *in* the mind and not yet knowledge *to* the mind.

To become flexible and manipulable as data (level-E1 representations) and thus ultimately accessible to metalinguistic reflection as well as to cross-domain relationships with other aspects of cognition (level-E2/3 representations), the knowledge embedded implicitly in linguistic procedures (level-I representations) has to be re-represented.

It is, of course, easy to determine when a child has verbally statable metalinguistic knowledge. But the RR model postulates a first level of redescription which is not available for verbal report and for which more subtle empirical clues must be sought. The fact that such redescription does take place can be gleaned from late-occurring errors and self-repairs. Let us briefly consider three examples.

The first is from the acquisition of French. In French, the word "mes" is a plural possessive adjective (my + plural marker). "Ma voiture" means "my car"; "mes voitures" means "my cars". But, in contrast with English, in spoken French the plural marker is heard on the possessive adjective ("mes"), not on the noun ("voitures"). So the little word "mes" conveys a lot of information in spoken French. My experiments showed that 4-year-olds use this term easily in situations where possession and plurality have to be expressed ("mes voitures" implying "all my cars"). They have efficiently functioning level-I representations. By contrast, 6-year-olds spell out redundantly the meaning components of the word "mes". They use explicit markers for each of the implicit features in "mes", producing outputs such as "toutes les miennes de voitures", where totality is expressed by "toutes", plurality by "les", and possession by "miennes". Metalinguistic questioning at this age shows that the reasons for this explicit overmarking of features (level-E1 representations) are not available to conscious access. That requires yet another level (E2/3) of redescription. The overmarking subsequently disappears; older children again use "mes", but they can also explain the various meaning components of the possessive determiner system (Karmiloff-Smith 1979a, 1986).

A similar example comes from Newport's (1981) studies of the acquisition of American Sign Language. In ASL signs have morphological structure, but initially children use holistic signs (level-I representations). Deaf parents who are non-native signers (i.e., who acquired sign language late in life) cannot analyze the signs into their morphological component parts. By contrast, children acquiring ASL as a native language analyze its morphological structure. They express that knowledge via late-occurring errors in their output after they have been using the sign correctly for some time. The errors involve separate staccato movements isolating two separate morphological markers, instead of the normally flowing holistic sign. It is something like the equivalent in spoken language of pronouncing the word "typewriter" correctly at first, and then subsequently pronouncing it as "type - write - er". This extraction of component parts from the initial holistic signs is again suggestive of representational redescription (level-E1 representations). Nothing in Newport's data suggests that children are consciously aware of the segmented form of their new productions. In other words, the representations are not yet in E2/3 format. The overmarking subsequently disappears; older children again use signs that look like the ones they used when younger. However, the RR model posits that the later identical output stems from representations more explicit than the procedural ones that underlie the initial productions.

Note that in neither the ASL nor the French examples can the children get the component morphological information directly from environmental input, because parents do not spell out the separate morphological marking in their productions. The "errors" in the French and ASL examples suggest that the child analyzes the level-I representations and extracts the implicit information that they contain. Since the original procedures remain intact and are produced concurrently with the explicit overmarking, I argue that this analysis is carried out on redescriptions (E1 format) of the procedures. And it is these redescribed representations that are the basis for normal children's subsequent building of theories about language and for their responses to metalinguistic tasks[17] (level-E2/3 representations). In other words, the external environment serves as input to linguistic attention biases to form and store linguistically relevant representations, but redescriptions of internal representations serve as the basis for further development and for children's spontaneous folk theories about how language functions as a system.

The third example is from spontaneous self-repairs and their relation to subsequent metalinguistic awareness. Here is a metalinguistic explanation from a 10-year-old. The context was two pens, one eraser, one earring, and the child's own watch. The experimenter hid the child's watch and then asked "What did I do?". The exchange was as follows:

Child: You hid the watch.

Exp: Why did you say *"the* watch"?

Child: Well . . . *"my* watch" because it belongs to me, but I said, "you hid *the* watch" because there are no other watches there. If you'd put yours out, I would have had to say "you hid *my* watch", because it could have been confusing, but this way it's better for me to say "you hid the watch" so someone doesn't think yours was there too.

This is an eloquent example of how children can produce elaborate verbal statements once they have access to that part of their linguistic knowledge. (Note that correct *usage* of "the", "my", etc. occurs much earlier, around 4–5 years of age.)

Now, if one were to consider only the difference between young children's correct usage and older children's metalinguistic statements, one would merely postulate two levels of representation: the implicit level-I representations sustaining correct usage and the level-E2/3 representations sustaining the verbal explanations. To posit the existence of E1 representations between the two, one needs to find other kinds of data. Spontaneous self-repairs turned out to be the clue I was seeking. Take the hiding game outlined above. During testing, children often make self-repairs. They sometimes make lexical repairs: "You hid the pe . . . no, the watch." At other times they make referential repairs: "You hid the blue pe . . . the red pen." But they also make what I call "systemic repairs": "You hid my wat . . . the watch." (Note that this is precisely equivalent, at the repair level, to the metalinguistic statement above.) Such repairs are not corrections of errors; "my watch" identifies the referent unambiguously. Rather, they denote children's sensitivity to the force of different determiners, which are no longer independently stored but are part of a linguistic subsystem. Such subsystems, I argue, are built up from the extraction of common features after representational redescription. Younger children do not make these self-repairs, but this is precisely what children of around 6 display in such circumstances. In other words, although they are unable to provide verbal explanations of their linguistic

knowledge about the relationship between "the" and "my" in referential communication, their self-repairs bear witness to the fact that
something has changed in their internal representations since the
period of correct usage.

I would now like to take you through a little more detail of some of
my psycholinguistic experiments aimed at testing aspects of the RR
model. The data demonstrate the progression from behavioral mastery, to subsequent representational change, and finally to children's
consciously accessible theories about how language functions as a
system. We will start with children's use and thoughts about what
counts as a "word", then look at how they build theories about the
functioning of little words like "a" and "the" in sentences, and finally
go beyond the sentence to extended discourse.

From Behavioral Mastery to Metalinguistic Knowledge about Words

How do young children segment the continuous speech stream into
appropriate formal word boundaries? There is no simple physical basis
in the input to cue children about how to isolate words (Tunmer et al.
1983). Of course, if children were pure behaviorists, this would pose
a serious problem, and segmentation errors would pervade their output. Yet, although segmentation errors occur at the very earliest stages
of language acquisition (Peters 1983), they are rare once morphology
and functors appear in the child's output. Moreover, when segmentation errors do occur (e.g., "a nadult" or "un léléphant"), they do not
persist. Children do not learn language by passively soaking up the
input with all its inherent problems. Children actively construct representations at formal word boundaries on the basis of linguistically
relevant constraints and of abstractions—not copies—of the linguistic
input. Indeed, once young children are beyond the very initial stage
of language acquisition and are consistently producing both open-
class and closed-class words in new, nonformulaic contexts, there can
be no question that at some level these are represented internally as
words. That is, whereas 3-year-olds represent and process formal word
boundaries as such, they seem to know little if anything explicit about
what counts as a word.

Numerous studies[18] have shown that it is not until about age 6, and
for some tasks even later, that children know explicitly that both open-
class words (e.g. "boy", "chair", "silence", "run", "think") and closed-
class words ("the", "any", "to", "in", "when", "of") are *words*. When
asked to count words in a sentence, young children frequently neglect
to count the closed-class items. When asked directly if "table" is a

word, they agree; but when asked if "the" is a word, they answer in the negative. Yet 3-year-olds can correctly perceive and produce words like *the*.

The RR model posits that 3-year-olds' representations of formal word boundaries are in level-I format. By age 6 a child's statable knowledge that *the* counts as a word is, according to the model, in the E2/3 format. But what happens between these two ages?

The RR model predicts that there must exist a level of representation between that underlying the correct segmentation of the speech stream into words like *the*, in which formal word boundaries are represented as part of on-line input/output procedures, and the level of representation that allows for direct off-line metalinguistic reflection about the fact that *the* is a word. This middle level is the E1 representational format. It involves a redescription of information into a format that is accessible to certain tasks outside normal input/output relations but not yet to metalinguistic explanation.

I set out to test this prediction (Karmiloff-Smith, Grant, Jones, and Cuckle 1991). Previous studies in which children were asked whether X is a word, or to count the number of words in a sentence, did not engage normal language processing and required a totally off-line stance. Such tasks therefore demand a high level of explictness (E2/3 representations). If we are to capture something between the totally on-line use of word representations and the full metalinguistically accessible knowledge in off-line tasks, we need to devise a way of engaging children's normal language processing while getting them to access that knowledge for partially off-line reflection. The following technique did just that: Children of ages 3–7 were given a series of partially on-line tasks of a similar design. They listened to a story in which the narrator paused repeatedly on open-class or closed-class words. Depending on the task, the child was asked to repeat "the last word" "the last sentence," or "the last thing" that the storyteller had said each time she stopped. No explanation was given as to what counted as a word, a sentence, or a thing. The design of our task did not preclude the types of errors found in previous research, including responding with more than one word (e.g. "on the floor" instead of "floor" or "knock over" instead of "over"), responding with single syllables ("lence" instead of "silence", "kind" instead of "kindness", "thing" instead of "nothing"), or making segmentation errors ("isa" instead of "a"; "kover" from "knock over").

This partially on-line technique engages normal language processing and causes an interruption of the construction of a representation of the speech input. Note, however, that the task also has an off-line metalinguistic component.[19] The child must know what the term *word* means and differentiate this from instructions to repeat the last *sentence* or the last *thing*. To access and reproduce the last word, the child must focus on her representation of the acoustic input, make a decision as to which segment of it constitutes the last *word*, and repeat that segment.

In another experiment, we compared a group of subjects' data from the on-line word task with their responses to off-line direct questioning about whether closed-class and open-class items are *words*.[20] For the latter, we simply asked children to help a teddy bear find out what counts as a word and read out one by one a list of words, asking "What do you think about X? Tell Teddy if X is a word."

We hypothesized that the off-line task would require level-E2/3 representations, whereas the partially on-line task would require the level-E1 format. We thus predicted that 3- and 4-year-olds would fail both types of task because their representations of words are still in procedurally encoded level-I format, that children around 5 would succeed on the partially on-line task but be less successful on the fully off-line metalinguistic task, and that children of age 6 or 7 would succeed on both tasks, because by then they have multiple levels of representation with respect to the concept *word*.

These predictions were borne out. A number of the youngest subjects could do neither task well, suggesting that their representations of formal word boundaries were still implicit in the level-I format. But our results show that some children as young as 4½, and the majority from age 5 on, treat both open-class and closed-class words as *words*, and that they differentiate *word* and *sentence* when the task has an on-line component engaging normal language processing. These children were significantly worse, however, on the off-line task that involved E2/3 representations. On that task, although young children accepted exemplars from the open-class category as *words*, they rejected several exemplars from the closed-class category. Only the older subjects were very successful at both tasks.

In general, then, the older child's level-E2/3 theory is one that has changed from rejecting words like "the" but accepting words like "chair" (because they denote something in the extralinguistic context) to considering "chair", "the", etc. as all equivalent in their status as *words*, by virtue of the fact that they are part of a system whose elements combine in principled ways. The latter—an intralinguistic account—was found to be available only at around age 6 and beyond.

The developmental progression highlighted by this study is important. First, as of age 3, when their output is more or less devoid of segmentation errors, we must grant that children represent formal word boundaries for both open-class and closed-class words. However, these representations are inaccessible for purposes outside input/ output relations. They are, according to the RR model, in the level-I format. Second, something occurs internally between ages 3 and 5 such that by around age 4½ children can access the represented knowledge and succeed on our partially on-line task. The RR model posits that this is possible because the level-I representations have been redescribed into an accessible E1 format. And, third, something must again occur internally beyond age 5 or 6 to explain why, by then, children can engage in more consciously accessible theory construction about what *words* are and can access such knowledge in off-line tasks. This, I maintain, requires a further redescription into the E2/3 format.

The RR model posits that this developmental progression can be explained only by invoking, not one representation of linguistic knowledge, to which one either has or does not have access, but several *re*-representations of the same knowledge, allowing for increasing accessibility.

From Behavioral Mastery to Metalinguistic Knowledge of the Article System

Nominal determiners such as articles exist in one form or another in all languages, but their obligatory contexts differ markedly from one language to the next. English marks the indefinite/definite contrast ("a"/"the") and uses two different surface forms to express the indefinite article ("a") and the numeral "one". Although French also marks the indefinite/definite contrast by different articles, in that language the numeral and the indefinite are realized by a single form ("un" or the feminine counterpart "une"). Russian marks the indefinite ("adna"), but the definite has no surface realization; for definite reference the noun is used without a determiner. Swedish places the indefinite before a noun as a separate word ("et hus"—a house), but the definite marker is suffixed to the noun ("huset"—the house). And so on. Children have to be sensitive to nominal marking in general and must also learn about the particular syntactic realization of the nominal system in their own language.

Recall how infants show sensitivity to distinctions conveyed by articles, well before they are part of their own output? One reason concerns the phonological and prosodic patterns of language. As we saw earlier in this chapter, 4-day-old infants are already sensitive to the phonological patterns of their native tongue. And well before they are producing articles, they can use the presence or absence of articles to decide whether a noun is a proper name (no article; e.g., "Dax") or a common noun (e.g., "a dax"). Gerken (1987) has also demonstrated this early sensitivity to syntactic cues.[21] She asked very young children who were not yet producing articles to imitate short sentences in which either articles or nonce filler syllables of equivalent length and stress were also placed before nouns. If children were simply constrained by length, phonological or prosodic cues, their imitations should be equivalent for both types of sentence. It turned out, however, that they selectively omitted articles, whereas they imitated the nonce syllables. This suggests that, in their comprehension of the sentences to be imitated, these young children were processing articles *syntactically*—i.e., differently from the fillers, which they probably processed phonologically.

It turns out, too, that articles appear early in production (Brown 1973; Karmiloff-Smith 1979a; Maratsos 1976; Tanz 1980; Warden 1976), despite the fact that early on they seem to carry far less meaning than nouns and verbs. So what is the status of these early representations of articles? Let us look at this question via an experiment that specifically explored children's understanding of the contrast between definite and indefinite articles.

Imagine a very simple experimental setup that I used some years ago, in which two dolls—a boy and a girl—have playrooms where various objects are displayed. In one situation, the girl doll has three cars, one book, and one ball, and the boy doll has one car, one pencil, and three balls. The crucial difference between the two dolls' possessions is that for some trials the girl doll has several Y's and the boy doll one Y, whereas for others the boy doll has several X's and the girl doll one X. Take the context illustrated in figure 2.1 as an example. Now, if you were to hear me say "Lend me the car" you could infer that I must be talking to the boy because he's the only one with one car. Likewise, were I to say "Lend me a car" you could infer that I am more likely to be talking to the girl because she has several cars. This was the child's task: to guess which addressee I was speaking to in a series of trials with varying contexts.[22]

Now, this is a task at which children of ages 3 and 4 succeed easily. Much developmental research stops at the point when children's performance is at ceiling. But my research strategy has always been to explore development beyond behavioral mastery in an attempt to uncover subsequent changes in internal representations. As of age 3, children are almost 100% successful at the mapping between each of the indefinite and definite articles and one of their deictic functions. This is a healthy start as far as behavioral mastery of one of the article's functions is concerned. But what can we say about what children "know" about the definite and indefinite articles? More precisely, what can we say about young children's internal representations of these

Girl doll's playroom   Boy doll's playroom

Child seated here

Figure 2.1
Definite-indefinite discrimination. (After Karmiloff-Smith 1979a; used with permission of Cambridge University Press.)

linguistic forms? Nothing very substantial beyond a guess. It is not until we take a truly developmental perspective—until we know something about children's *subsequent* development—that we can infer the status of the early representations sustaining such efficient understanding.

It turns out that later, around the age of 5 or 6, French speakers—although they continue to be successful at interpreting the definite article—start to make mistakes with respect to the indefinite article. They temporarily interpret "prête-moi une voiture" (with no stress on "une") to mean "lend me one car" rather than the indefinite "lend me a car". They pick the doll with a single car instead of the one with several.[23] This late-occurring failure is an important clue to representational change. It points to the fact that the 5-year-old has become sensitive to the dual function of the indefinite article in French, and not just to the distinction between the definite and the indefinite article. The phonological form "une" (or its masculine counterpart, "un") is a homophone which, as mentioned above, conveys both indefinite reference (English "a") and the numeral function (English "one").

The RR model accounts for this developmental progression as follows. Although 3-year-olds reach behavioral mastery for each of these functions in separate contexts and make no errors, they do so because they have two independently stored procedures for producing the same phonological form for indefinite reference and for the numeral. Subsequent representational redescription of each of these procedures into the more explicit E1 format makes it possible to link the common phonological form across the two representations of form-function pairs. But, since there is a fairly strong one-form/one-function constraint during language acquisition (Slobin 1985), 5-year-olds temporarily mark the two meanings by two different forms in production. They produce "une voiture" for "a car" and "une de voiture" for "one car".[24] In comprehension, as pointed out above, they start to make mistakes as to which of the two functions (numeral or indefinite reference) is intended.

With these new facts in mind, are we getting any closer to being able to say anything about the child's internal representations of the indefinite and definite articles? Since the errors and repairs with respect to the dual function of the indefinite article occur later than behavioral mastery, something must have happened internally between ages 3 and 5 to explain this. The RR argument is that when 3-year-olds can first correctly understand or produce simple functions of the definite and indefinite articles (such as deictic functions, which point to the current extralinguistic context), they do so by calling on two independently stored level-I representations which map a phonological form onto a specific functional context. In other words, these young children know how to interpret the definite article "the" to refer deictically to a context where a singleton (e.g., one car) is focused upon. And they also know how to interpret the indefinite article "a" to refer to a context where the speaker is referring to any one of several examples of a group of similar items, or to use an identical form in French to refer to the numeral. What the 3-year-old does not "know" is that there is a functional relationship between these efficiently functioning procedures—that the articles together form part of a linguistic subsystem. In other words, the RR model posits that nowhere in the very young child's internal representations is there any explicit indication of the common functional links between the articles. If such relationships were explicitly represented, then these specific errors and repairs should occur at any time, not solely after behavioral mastery. This suggests that the knowledge embedded in the efficiently functioning but independently stored representations of very young children is not yet encoded in the E1 format, and that links across the procedural representations for the different functions are as yet only implicit in level-I representations.

What happens, then, after behavioral mastery? The RR model postulates that once behavioral mastery has been achieved (i.e., once part of the system functions efficiently and a pattern of internal stability has been reached), the level-I representations undergo a process of redescription. The original level-I representations remain intact and can still be called for certain purposes, but the redescribed knowledge embedded in them is now also available as explicit internal data in the E1 format. Thus, the French-speaking child's internal representations now explicitly mark the relationship between identical forms—i.e., the fact that, say, the phonological form "un" paired to the nonspecific reference function is the same as the phonological form "un" paired to the numeral function. Thus, children begin to represent determiners internally as part of a linguistic subsystem rather than as independently stored form-function pairs. It is this newly formed representational link that explains the sudden occurrence of errors of interpretation of the indefinite article in 5-year-olds—errors that are not apparent in the successful performance of 3- and 4-year-olds because their independently stored representations do not explicitly represent the link between the different functions of the articles. For the 3-year-old (and, I hypothesize, for certain fluent-speaking yet otherwise severely retarded children), the representational link is potential, or implicit, in the fact that, from the observer's external viewpoint only, each independently stored procedural representation contains analogous information. However, it is only as of age 5, after behavioral mastery in this part of the linguistic system, that the relationship between the representations is explicitly stored.

Storing representations in the E1 format does not mean that the knowledge is available to conscious access and verbal report. The child still has a way to go before he or she can consciously access that linguistic knowledge for verbal reporting. For the articles, this tends to occur around age 7 or 8. To gain a sense of young children's passage from explicitly represented knowledge to consciously accessible and verbally statable metalinguistic knowledge, let us take a peek at some more data. To simplify, let us take the same linguistic category of nominal determiners ("a", "the", "my", "some", etc.).

What if a child is asked to actually give a verbal explanation, rather than merely interpret and use the constraints on articles? Let us return to the simple experimental context of the boy doll and the girl doll, and their respective playrooms, illustrated in figure 2.1. The child has correctly guessed which doll the experimenter is addressing, depending on whether the output contained the definite or the indefinite article. How do children explain their correct guesses when your questions involve accessing knowledge represented at level E2/3?

Well, the youngest subjects, although they must have *used* the contrast between the articles to make their correct guess, explain this on the basis of real-world knowledge, saying something along the lines of "You must have been talking to the boy, because boys like cars" (irrespective of the fact that the girl doll has more cars than the boy doll). Later in development, children explain their correct guesses by referring to contextual features—for example, "You were speaking to the boy, because he's got one car". It is really rather late in development, around age 8 or 9, that children make explicit reference to the *linguistic* clue that all children must have in fact used when making their correct guess: "You must be talking to the boy, because you said 'lend me *the* (stressed) car'." Around age 10, children even provide information about the linguistic subsystem from which the referential clue was taken, as in the following explanation: "It's got to be the boy, because you said 'the'; if you'd been talking to the girl, you'd have had to say 'lend me a car' or, maybe, 'one of your cars'."

Let me reiterate that all children making successful guesses *used* the linguistic clues. These must therefore be represented internally, but only in the I or the E1 format. It takes several years before children can consciously access their representations of such linguistic knowledge and report on them verbally. By then, I argue, their representations of this linguistic category are also in the E2/3 format.

In the developmental literature, when children cannot report on some aspect of their cognition it is often implied that the knowledge is somehow absent (i.e., not represented at all). The RR model postulates something different: that the knowledge *is* represented internally, but still in the I or the E1 format, neither of which is accessible to verbal report. The end state is such that the same information is re-represented at several different levels of explicitness. This allows for different levels to be accessed for different goals: from level I (for rapid input/output computations) to level E2/3 (for explicit metalinguistic tasks).

I should also mention that children do not reach behavioral mastery for all the functions of the articles by age 3. For many other functions (including the anaphoric function of the definite article, such as the use of the expression "the man" after one has introduced "a man" into the discourse), behavioral mastery is reached considerably later in development.[25] And those functions also later undergo the same three steps at various ages—behavioral mastery, representational redescription, verbally statable theory about how that part of the linguistic system functions.

It is clear that development involves far more than the infant's initial sensitivity to the presence or absence of articles or the toddler's fluent usage. In order for a child to become a potential linguist, the child's representations have to undergo multiple levels of redescription.

Beyond the Word and the Sentence

So is that it? Is the developmental picture of language acquisition one in which the child starts with innately specified attention biases and data-abstraction mechanisms, reaches behavioral mastery, proceeds from there through several levels of representational redescription, and finally becomes able to formulate verbally communicable theories about how the system functions? Does all linguistic knowledge take this route? Clearly not.

Among the many developments to occur in children's later language is the passage from the sentential functions of various linguistic markers to their discourse functions. An earlier study of children's production of spans of discourse in narrative had shown that initially children merely juxtapose a sequence of correct sentences, making only minimal use of discourse constraints (Karmiloff-Smith 1980, 1985). However, with development, children structure their narratives as a single unit rather than as a mere juxtaposition of sentences, and they then adhere to what I called the "thematic subject constraint" (see examples below).

Spontaneous repairs turned out to be very informative about children's developing capacity for discourse organization and about their adherence to the thematic subject constraint. The following are typical examples of such repairs taken from the data of a task in which children generated stories from a sequence of pictures. (It is important to note in these examples that the pronoun repaired to a noun phrase is not ambiguous with respect to the intended referent, because the story has only one female protagonist.)

> There's a boy and a girl. He's trying to fish. And to get her bucket, he hits the girl and she star . . . he hits the girl who starts crying.

> This boy and girl are out playing. He's gonna catch some fish but she . . . but the girl won't lend him her bucket. So he just takes it and the girl gets real sad.

These and many other examples suggest that as of age 6 or 7 children operate under the "thematic subject constraint," a discourse constraint which stipulates that pronominalization in subject position be reserved for the thematic subject of the total discourse (in this case, the boy). By contrast, subsidiary characters tend to be referred to with full noun phrases (or proper names, or stressed pronouns), despite the fact that the different sexes of the protagonists would obviate any potential ambiguity with pronominal reference. As can be seen above, the pronoun is repaired even though it is perfectly clear that "she" refers to the girl; the girl is the only female referent in the sequence of pictures. Other research has shown similar constraints to obtain in the discourse production of both adults and children (Reichmann 1978; Tyler 1981, 1983; Tyler and Marslen-Wilson 1978, 1981).

We have seen in this chapter that older children often have level-E2/3 representations which allow them to explain metalinguistically a number of aspects of the way language functions at the sentential level. Do children (or adults, for that matter) have metalinguistic knowledge of the discourse constraints on the very same markers? In other words, are we again to witness behavioral mastery followed by representational redescription and finally by conscious access?

Some recent research indicates that neither children nor adults can provide metalinguistic explanations of discourse constraints (Karmiloff-Smith et al., in press). They cannot explain why speakers use pronouns or full noun phrases in particular discourse contexts. Even as adults, we clearly do not have access to all aspects of the linguistic system that we use. Certain aspects of spoken language are inaccessible to metalinguistic reflection whereas others, as we saw earlier in this chapter, are available for spontaneous theory-construction and conscious access. The rules governing discourse constraints do not seem to reach the E2/3 format, and it remains an open question whether they are redescribed into the E1 format. Two related linguistic facts seem to be operative. First, there is a difference between the local, sentential function of linguistic markers and their more global discourse function. Take as an example the pronoun "she". At the local, sentential level, "she" provides information about features such as feminine, singular, and pro-form—i.e., the referent is female, is alone, and either is in the present deictic space, has just been referred to linguistically, or can be taken for granted through shared knowledge between the interlocutors. Children and adults have metalinguistic access to these features. According to the RR model, they must be represented in the E2/3 format. But in an extended span of discourse involving more than one referent, use of the pronoun "she" also provides information beyond these features. It encodes the role of one referent (e.g., the main protagonist) relative to others in the overall story structure. In other words, it reflects the speaker's mental model of the span of discourse as a whole. When in subject position, the pronoun can usually be taken to refer by default to the main protagonist. Reference to a subsidiary protagonist is usually marked linguistically by use of a full noun phrase, a proper name, or a stressed pronoun in subject position. There is a complex interplay between nouns, and zero anaphora, marked differentially as discourse unfolds rapidly in real time. It is this discourse function of the pronouns and noun phrases to which neither child nor adult subjects have metalinguistic access. The only way the linguist can have access to constraints on the dynamics of discourse functions is by freezing the fast-fading message of on-line spoken text into a static written form that leaves a trace in a different representational format (Karmiloff-Smith 1985).

The RR model focuses on knowledge growth outside normal input/output relations. But discourse constraints operate *only* on line. The discourse function or meaning of a particular use of a pronoun to mark the thematic subject is relevant only while that discourse is being uttered. In other words, discourse constraints are relevant only to rapid on-line computations of the output system. Decisions as to whether to use a pronoun or a full noun phrase at *this* particular point in *this* stretch of discourse are not stored in long-term memory. Thus, such on-line computations are probably rarely if ever redescribed and so cannot be available to metalinguistic reflection.

From the Nativist Infant to the Constructivist Linguist

This chapter began by exploring domain-general versus domain-specific perspectives on language acquisition. The bulk of work on neonates and very young infants suggests that the domain-specific solution is likely to be correct. Human babies attend preferentially to language over other auditory input, require only a few days of input to differentiate certain characteristics of their native tongue from other languages, and are sensitive very early on to many abstract structure-dependent features of language. Certain children with otherwise severe cognitive retardation acquire language late but easily, whereas, despite rich representational capacities, the most intelligent of chimpanzees can at best be taught—through incredibly extensive training—strings of manually encoded lexical items (Gardner and Gardner 1969) or a simple form of language-like logic (Premack 1986). This involves a one-to-one mapping between concepts and arbitrary symbols, probably through the use of domain-general mechanisms. But this is not language (Premack 1986; Seidenberg 1985). The symbols are not signs within a structured system. A list of lexical items, however long, does not constitute naming and bears little or no relationship to the linguistic competence of even a 2- or 3-year-old.

Much of the recent infancy work seems to move in the direction of Chomsky's claim that the abstract structure of language is innately specified in humans in some detail. Clearly, we must invoke *some* innately specified attention biases and linguistic predispositions. It may turn out that the innate principles sustaining language are more detailed than those sustaining other domains, such as number. Nonetheless, let's not foreclose the possibility of an epigenetic process that gradually creates the domain specificity of language. Whatever the level of detail of the innate linguistic specification, there must be *some* predispositions for language; that is why other species can never learn a structured linguistic system. But the innate specification does not alone explain language acquisition. We saw that the mapping between innate predispositions and the input of the child's native tongue requires complex semantic and syntactic bootstrapping. For normal development, this is still only part of the picture. To understand how our linguistic representations become flexible and manipulable (i.e., open to metalinguistic reflection), we need to invoke several levels of representational redescription beyond the semantic and syntactic bootstrapping that leads to behavioral mastery. This, in my view, also differentiates human capacities from those of other species. Thus, even if the chimpanzee were to have an innately specified linguistic base, I speculate that it would still not go as far as the normal human child. It would never wonder why "typewriter" isn't used to refer to people. It would simply repeat the linguistic labels that it was given. But children do not simply reach efficient usage; they subsequently develop explicit representations which allow them to reflect on the component parts of words and to progressively build linguistic theories. Although this holds for some aspects of language, it does not hold across the board. There are facets of syntax and discourse cohesion that are never available to metalinguistic report, even in adults.

Chapter 3
The Child as a Physicist

All theories tend to shape the facts they attempt to explain. Wassily Leontief, upon receiving the Nobel Prize for economics

How I wish Piaget were alive today. What, I wonder, would he have made of the exciting new findings on infant knowledge about the physical world? Well before it is a year old, the infant "knows" a surprising amount about various properties of objects and the principles governing their behavior in the physical world. As I did in chapter 2 with regard to language, I shall argue here that to account for development in general, and for children's spontaneous theory building about the physical world in particular, it is necessary to invoke an integration of aspects of nativism and constructivism, along with a cognitive architecture that enables representational redescription.

Understanding the Physical World: The Piagetian Infant

How would a Piagetian conceive of the infant's developing knowledge of the physical world? He or she would start by evoking an unprepared mind faced with a chaotic perceptual input, with no innately tuned attention biases to channel its computations of input from the physical world.

Piaget argued that during the first 12 months the infant lacks object permanence and knowledge about the physical laws that constrain the behavior of objects. Where did Piaget's conclusions stem from? Try a little experiment yourself. Hold out a coveted toy to a young infant. As she reaches for it, cover it with a cloth. You'll see that she withdraws her hand and seems to make no attempt to find the toy under the cover. A slightly older infant may seek the toy under the cover, but if you move it to a second location in front of her eyes she will continue to look in the first hiding place. This observation has come to be known as the "A not B error." Piaget concluded from such behavior that once an object disappears from sight it ceases to exist for the infant. Piagetians consider the attainment of object permanence to be one of the fundamental outcomes of sensorimotor intelligence. They argue that the progressive construction of object permanence underlies all subsequent developments, such as conservation of matter, weight, and volume. (Had you taken coffee with Piaget, as I did in my Genevan days, you might have worried about *his* conservation of volume as you watched him add ten sugar cubes to a tiny espresso!)

As with language, Piagetians claim that the young infant's acquisition of knowledge about object behavior develops slowly, and initially only via sensorimotor action on the physical world. The young infant is considered to be unable to develop symbolic representations of object properties until it has internalized sensorimotor action schemes, after the first year of life. Domain-neutral sensorimotor developments are used to explain progressive achievements in the young child's understanding of the physical world.

Later reasoning about physical properties (substance, weight, gravity, compressibility, animacy/inanimacy, and so forth) depends, according to Piagetian theory, on the progressive development of the logic of concrete operations. Piaget (1952b) and his collaborators postulated developmental stages extending through the preoperational period (ages 2–7) the concrete operational stage (ages 7–11) to the formal operational stage (ages 11–16). Each stage is sustained by a particular logico-mathematical structure. The same structure underlies development in language, mathematics, spatial cognition, and physics. Domain-neutral changes are used to postulate across-the-board changes in structural organization at specific developmental milestones from infancy through adolescence.

Understanding the Physical World: The Nativist Infant

In sharp contrast, a domain-specific nativist would assert that from the first few months of life the young infant is constrained by a number of domain-specific basic principles about the persistence of objects and several of their distinctive properties. Let us now examine some studies carried out within the nativist framework.

Research has progressed vastly in recent years because of methodological innovations in studying babies, such as the habituation/dishabituation and preferential-looking/sucking paradigms described in chapter 1. By contrast, many of Piaget's conclusions about infancy were drawn from experiments involving manual search. The object-permanence task mentioned above is a typical example. But at birth and in the early months of life infants cannot engage in manual search.

Thus, to a nativist who hypothesizes the existence of principles of physics guiding young infants' perceptual and inferential processes, tasks involving manual search are obviously unsuitable. To surmount such difficulties, Liz Spelke—one of the pioneers in exploring young infants' perception and knowledge of the properties of objects in the physical world—devised an ingenious program of habituation and preferential-looking experiments to assess the extent to which physical principles are already present during early infancy.

Spelke's work is based on the general hypothesis that infants come into the world equipped with a number of domain-specific principles which guide their segmentation of complex visual arrays into objects. She negates the Piagetian notion of an initially chaotic perceptual input. She also claims that the same principles underlie both infants' perception of objects and their subsequent reasoning about the behavior of objects.

Constraints on Object Perception in Early Infancy

As adults we take so much for granted about the physical world that it is impossible, by introspection, to know how we perceive objects. Even for the researcher, it is difficult to separate the processes by which adults simply perceive from the processes by which they recognize and categorize familiar objects. Here again a developmental perspective can help us to delineate the processes operating in the adult mind. According to Spelke (1988, 1990), in both adults and children the general processes for perceiving objects operate *before* those for recognizing and categorizing objects.[1] Spelke's studies suggest that infants perceive objects by analyzing three-dimensional surface arrangements and by following the continuous motion of the display. They do not seem to perceive objects by maximizing simplicity of form, uniformity of substance or other Gestalt properties of the visual array. Spelke claims that infants must be endowed with mechanisms capable of segmenting objects partially occluded by, or adjacent to, others, as well as being able to perform computations on representations of objects that have moved out of view. In other words, in sharp contrast to the Piagetian position, Spelke asserts that some form of object persistence must be operative from the outset.

Four principles—boundedness, cohesion, rigidity, and no action at a distance (i.e., no action without some form of contact)—underlie the basic constraints on the motions of objects and guide the infant's perceptual analysis of the array. Such principles make it possible for the infant (and the adult) to distinguish between the presence of a single object and more than one object when they are adjacent or partially occlude each other. In normal visual arrays, partial occlusion is the rule rather than the exception; objects rarely present themselves in isolation against a neutral background. Hence, principles for segmenting the complex array into separate objects must be called upon. Spelke's boundedness principle stipulates that two surface points lie on distinct objects only if no path of connected surface points links them. The cohesion principle specifies that two surface points lie on the same object only if the points are linked by a continuous path of surface points. The principles of rigidity and no action at a distance determine additional connections and separations that obtain among surfaces. These principles, which hold for both object perception and subsequent reasoning about object behavior, stipulate that objects move as connected wholes on continuous paths, that they do not pass through one another or change shape as they move, and that they cannot act on one another unless they come into contact. The principles operate automatically each time the infant perceives a visual array.

If you were to see a display like the one depicted at the top of figure 3.1, you could infer that the occluded array was either two short objects or a single long one. But you would be much more likely to infer that it was a single unified object. And infants as young as 4 months make the same inference when the two parts of the object are moving together to and fro behind an occluder. Recall that, after habituation to a stimulus, infants look longer at a display that they consider novel. Thus, after habituating to the display shown at the top of figure 3.1,

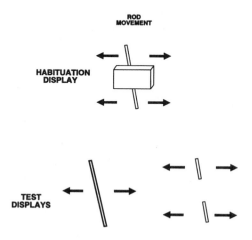

Figure 3.1
Perception of partially occluded objects. (From Kellman and Spelke 1983. Reprinted with permission of Academic Press.)

infants shown the display of a single object (bottom left) continue to be bored (their looking time decreases). By contrast, infants shown the display of two objects (bottom right) show renewed interest (their looking time increases suddenly). They must have inferred from the unitary movement and connected path of the habituation display that a single long object was occluded. The posthabituation display of two short objects is thus considered novel. At 7 months infants can make similar inferences even when the objects are stationary. Movement seems, therefore, to be essential to the 4-month-old's perceptual inferences, whereas by 7 months a developmental change in object perception has occurred such that inferences can be made on the basis of properties of a stationary array. But, according to Spelke, what has been learned by 7 months about Gestalt principles such as good figural form enriches the earlier capacity for object perception without changing it developmentally. Indeed, as we shall see from the following experiment, Gestalt principles are *always* overridden by the principles underlying the perception of objects *in motion*.

An experiment by Kellman and Spelke (1983), also designed to test the perception of object unity, made use of objects with irregular shapes and different coloring (see figure 3.2). Now, contrary to the previous experiment, if the non-occluded parts differ in color, shape, texture, etc., then adults are likely to infer that there are two occluded objects. Such features are not relevant to infants between 3 and 4 months, however. They perform at chance when the objects are stationary. However, if the two parts move together as a unit, then the infant does consider them as parts of a single unitary object[2]—an

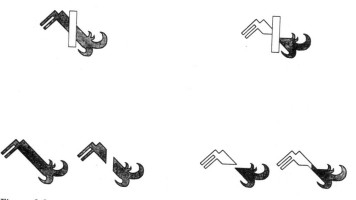

Figure 3.2
Perception of Gestalt properties. Top: habituation displays. Bottom: test displays. (From Spelke 1990. Reprinted with permission of Ablex Publishing Corporation.)

excellent survival mechanism, for if a tiger is running behind some trees, you had better realize that the simultaneously moving, perceptually different parts are the unitary body of one hungry tiger!

As mentioned, adults infer that two objects are occluded in the stationary display in figure 3.2, because of the different colors and shapes of the parts. Once the parts move together, adults first experience a paradox (because of their earlier inference) but then immediately infer that the object must be a single unitary one. This feeling of necessity demonstrates that movement is a more basic constraint on object perception than Gestalt properties of figural goodness of shape, continuance of color, substance, and texture. Young infants learn the Gestalt properties later than the principles that enable them to sort the perceptual array into objects. It is true that young infants have been shown to be sensitive to Gestalt relations such as shape, texture, and symmetry in some circumstances (Bornstein et al. 1981; Slater et al. 1983), but Spelke's work reveals that they do not make use of these relations in organizing surfaces into objects. The Gestalt principles do help the slightly older infant to discover properties of objects in stationary arrays, but movement always overrides Gestalt properties for both infants and adults.

Are the constraints of cohesion, boundedness, and rigidity in apprehending objects modality specific? Or are the outputs from different sensory transducers redescribed into image schematic format, as Mandler (1988) has proposed, so that comparisons across modalities can be made? To explore this issue, Streri and Spelke (1988) presented 4-month-old infants with the setup illustrated in figure 3.3. The infants first explored haptically (by touch only) a stimulus that they could not see. For one group of infants, this consisted of two independently movable rings connected by a flexible string. For another group, the rings were attached to a rigid rod, thus forming a single object. The infants were then presented with a visual display. Did they show renewed interest when the visual display depicted one rigidly connected object or when it depicted two separate objects? Recall that in the haptic condition all that the baby can feel in her hands is the existence of two rings. She must infer from the rigid or flexible linkage between them the presence of one or two objects.

The results were clear cut. Habituation to the independently movable rings was followed by longer looking at the connected display. Similarly, habituation to the rigidly connected rings was followed by longer looking at the two separate rings. It is important to note that in both cases the posthabituation displays were in a new (visual) modality, so the infants could have found either display novel. But they did not focus on the change in modality. Rather, what they found

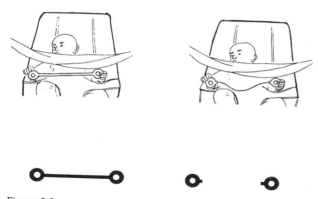

Figure 3.3
Cross-modal perception of objects. Top: (left) rigid motion. (right) independent motion. Bottom: visual text displays. (From Spelke 1990. Reprinted with permission of Ablex Publishing Corporation.)

salient were the physical principles that allowed them to infer object-hood. Thus, only the connected object was considered new by infants habituated to the independently movable rings (and vice versa). They must therefore have inferred from the haptic exploration that the independently movable rings were two distinct objects and translated that knowledge to their analysis of the visual arrays. Hence, the privileged role of movement for the cohesion and boundedness constraints on object perception obtains not only for vision but also for the haptic modality. Indeed, if constraints on object perception obtained only for vision, how could the blind infant develop relatively normal cognition?

The results of this study indicate that Spelke's constraints on object perception are not modality specific. The outputs of haptic perception can be represented in a format that is available for comparison with the outputs of visual perception. These representations may be in the image-schematic format suggested by Mandler, so that they will be available for subsequent redescription into more explicit formats such as language.

Spelke and her collaborators' demonstrations of the sensitivity of very young infants to the principles governing objects and their properties seems irreconcilable with the Piagetian view. This body of research suggests that infants store knowledge about the object world in far greater sophistication and far earlier than Piagetian theory asserts. Whether or not such computations are domain specific from the very outset or progressively become domain specific awaits more sophisticated experimentation involving brain activation. My guess is that this is precisely what developmental cognitive science research will see much more of in the 1990s.

Spelke's experiments reveal that 3–4-month-old infants can make inferences on the basis of perceptual input. This inferential capacity does not seem to be operative in neonates, however. Slater et al. (1990) have recently demonstrated that although visual perception (orientation, discrimination, form perception, size constancy, etc.) is highly organized at birth, newborns are not good at making inferences from perceptual input in tasks similar to Spelke's. So is the capacity of the infant of 3–4 months learned? Spelke argues that, whereas other physical principles such as gravity and inertia are learned, the four principles underlying object perception are innately specified and not learned. Slater's results do not rule out innate specification, however. They can be reconciled with Spelke's theory by invoking a maturational account, in that the principles are innately specified but await cortical maturation at around 4 months (Johnson 1990a, b). But the difference between Slater's and Spelke's results can also be used to suggest that the processes guiding object perception do not start out as a fully specified perceptual module, but become modularized as a product of development. None of this detracts from the fact that Spelke's data and arguments yield a picture of infancy very different from Piaget's.

We have seen that some of the principles of object perception may be innately specified (present at birth or after maturation), whereas others are learned. Such learning takes place very early—within the first 6–7 months of life—and is constrained by the domain-specific principles relevant to object perception. Spelke compares the acquisition of knowledge of physics to that of knowledge of language, in particular Chomsky's model in which innately specified parameters are set with respect to the environmental input. She suggests that a set of innately specified principles about the physical world serves as the basis for infants' subsequent learning and to direct their attention to relevant aspects of the input.

Understanding Object Behavior: Innate Principles and Subsequent Learning

Beyond the question of children's perception of objects, Spelke has explored infants' understanding of the behavior of objects. Are infants sensitive, for instance, to principles of object substance, such as the fact that objects cannot pass through a solid surface? To test this, Spelke and her collaborators (Spelke et al. 1992) habituated 4-month-old infants to a falling ball which came to rest on a supporting surface (see figure 3.4). The infants were then shown either a possible or an

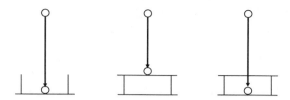

Figure 3.4
Principle of object substance. Left: habituation. Center: possible test event. Right: impossible test event. (From Spelke et al. 1992. Reprinted with permission of the authors. Copyright American Psychological Association.)

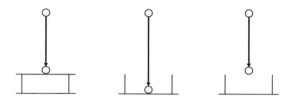

Figure 3.5
Principle of gravity and supporting surface. Left: habituation. Center: possible test event. Right: impossible test event. (From Spelke et al. 1992. Reprinted with permission of the authors. Copyright American Psychological Association.)

impossible event. The possible event was visibly different from the habituation display; the ball came to rest at a different location. In the impossible event, the ball came to rest in the same location as in the habituation display, but in order to do so it would have had to pass through a solid surface. Now, if the infants were interested only in the visual characteristics of the display, they should have found the possible test event new and more interesting, because the ball was in a different location. However, they showed longer looking times at the impossible but visually similar event; they focused on the properties of the displays relevant to laws of physics. They seemed to be sensitive to the violation of a principle of object substance and found it surprising that one solid object appeared to have passed through another.

One other study by Spelke suggests that not all principles are innately specified but that, although infants have to learn about certain types of object behavior, they do so much earlier than Piagetian-inspired theories would have predicted.

A falling object cannot stop in mid-air if there is no supporting surface. Do young infants know about this? Figure 3.5 is self-explanatory with respect to the habituation setup. It turns out that 4-month-olds know nothing about the principles governing gravity, for they do not show surprise when the object stops in mid-air. But 6-month-old infants show significantly longer looking times if a falling object does not continue its trajectory until it encounters a supporting surface. By 6 months, infants' perceptual experience of the physical world has been sufficient to generate new sensitivities to how object behavior is constrained by gravity; they show surprise when viewing the display in which an object stops in mid-air without support.

Other examples showing the effects of either maturation or learning about principles of physics in early infancy are now pouring into the developmental literature, painting a very different picture of the growing infant than the one Piagetians depict.

Rethinking Object Permanence

Spelke has argued that if object perception obeys her four principles even when objects move out of sight, then one must infer that object persistence is implicit in the inferences that young infants make. Recall Piaget's position that object permanence is based on the culmination of sensorimotor achievements relatively late in infancy. Choosing between these very different perspectives requires a more direct focus on the question of object permanence in early infancy.

In a series of ingenious experiments, Baillargéon and her collaborators (Baillargéon 1986, 1987a, 1987b, 1991; Baillargéon et al. 1986) habituated 3–4-month-old infants to the sight of a screen rotating 180° until they showed boredom. Then, in full view of the infant, she placed a solid object behind the screen. Next, babies either saw the screen rotate to 112° (a normal event now that an object prevented the full rotation) or saw the screen continue to rotate 180° (an impossible event, because the babies did not see that the object had been surreptitiously removed) (see figure 3.6). As far as the visual input was concerned, the infants who saw the normal event were receiving new visual input (a 112° rotation), whereas the infants who saw the impossible event were receiving the same visual input as before (a 180° rotation). If Piagetians are correct and young babies do not have object permanence, then infants should not infer that an object that has disappeared from sight ought to block a screen from rotating the full 180°. However, if infants' inferences are based on the representation of the persistence of objects out of sight, and if they comply with the physical principle that two objects (the screen and the object behind it) cannot occupy the same space simultaneously, then they should show increased attention with respect to the impossible event yet identical visual input. And this is exactly what happened. In other words, 3–4-month-

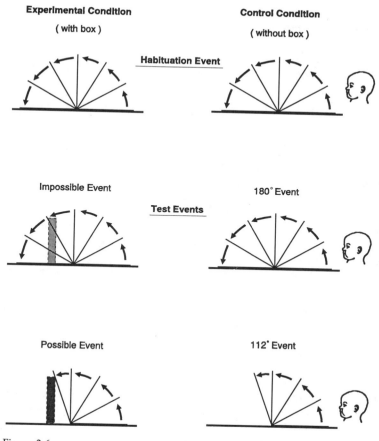

Figure 3.6
Principle of object persistence. (From Baillargéon 1986. Reprinted with permission of the author. Copyright American Psychological Association.)

old infants are sensitive to the fact that, even when an object is occluded by a screen, it persists and should therefore block the screen's rotation.[3]

Now, it is an open question whether this is merely some form of perceptual persistence constrained by the visual system or whether it calls on the beginnings of conceptual knowledge and inferences about objects.[4] My guess is that it is the latter, and that the conceptual representations on which such inferences take place are redescriptions of the perceptual input (i.e., the image-schematic formats that Mandler has invoked and that I discussed in chapter 2). But whichever turns out to be the correct interpretation, the data suggest that young infants can represent the continued existence of objects out of view and can make inferences on the basis of those representations—not what one would expect from a strictly Piagetian infant. Other research generated from various theoretical stances (Butterworth 1981; Slater and Bremner 1989; Harris 1989; Slater et al. 1983, 1985) also challenges the Piagetian view of early infancy.

Baillargéon (1987b) went on to use a similar rotating-screen paradigm to demonstrate that 3–4-month-old infants can compute the relation between the height of objects and the angle of rotation that they allow. Only later, but still during infancy, did they show knowledge about the rigidity or compressibility of objects, lending support to Spelke's view that knowledge of physical principles is partly innately specified and partly learned during early infancy by the same mechanisms that constrain early object perception.

So, if by 3–4 months infants display considerable knowledge about the continued existence of objects, their precise locations, and principles that govern their behavior, and if by 7 months they have learned new facts about physics, why do 9-month-olds fail to seek an object that they have just seen hidden under a screen—the Piagetians' demonstration of the absence of object permanence? The data on 3–4-month-olds suggest that knowledge of the object's persistence is represented in the infant's mind. So what precludes the somewhat older infant, who is by then capable of manual search, from looking under a cover? One explanation (Baillargéon et al. 1990) is based on the limitations of infants' problem-solving abilities, in particular the planning of means-end sequences and the chaining of subgoals. Recent work by Willats (1989) tends to confirm this. Willats put infants in situations where they had to plan how to reach an object by removing a series of obstacles in a certain sequence. He showed that although infants are better at planning than Piaget maintained, their capacities are very limited.

A further fact is that in the Spelke and Baillargéon tasks infants only have to respond by computing a visual array and looking longer at it (still a visual activity). In the Piagetian task, infants have to make computations in the visual system and then translate that information into a motor output system for manual search. According to Diamond (1985), the 9-month-old infant's difficulties with manual search tasks require a maturational explanation: that the correct motor behavior must await the development of the prefrontal cortex.

The pioneering work on infants' knowledge of principles of physics has made it abundantly clear that the Piagetian picture of the knowledge-free sensorimotor infant is likely to be wrong. So have the nativists won the battle? Many developmentalists would reply in the affirmative. Clearly, once again, we must invoke *some* innate component to the infant mind as it processes and interprets the physical world. But perhaps you have by now acquired (as, indeed, I hope you will by the end of this book) some of my epistemological schizophrenia—accepting the need for some innate predispositions for the initial architecture of the infant mind while maintaining a constructivist view of subsequent development. Clearly the nativist perspective does not rule out the need for learning. But, more important for our present purposes, the static nativist view cannot explain why children go beyond successful learning and beyond effective interaction with their physical environment.

The Representational Status of Early Knowledge: Do Infants Have Theories?

In referring to young infants' knowledge, Spelke (and, more recently, Baillargéon and Hanko-Summers [1990]) uses the term "theory". The RR model postulates, by contrast, that for knowledge to have theoretical status for the cognizer (the young infant, in this case), it must be represented explicitly at level E1 or higher. Indeed, an issue that has not been raised in any of the work on infant physics is the format of the representations that sustain the behavior reported by Spelke, Baillargéon, and others. Are these level-I representations and the principles embedded in them simply implicit, or are they the holistic image-schematic format postulated by Mandler (1988 and in press), or are they E1 representations? They obviously do not reach level E2/3, because the infants are far too young to express such knowledge verbally.

The four principles of boundedness, cohesion, rigidity, and no action at a distance operating in very early object perception are likely to be in the form of procedures for responding to environmental stimuli. These could be supported by level-I representations. However, the inferential processes in which infants engage to determine the precise location and height of an object blocking the rotation of a screen, for instance, would seem to require at least Mandler's holistic image-schematic format. It would not, however, seem to require representations at level E1 that extract component parts of representations. These are questions which clearly need further exploration. My own work on representational redescription has focused on children past infancy. However, the issue of the theoretical status of the infant's knowledge is important, since I have consistently argued that older children's knowledge has theoretical status. In other words, older children are theorists, not simply inductivists.

Within the framework of the RR model, my argument is that very young infants do *not* have theories. That their knowledge is rich, coherent, and stable has been amply demonstrated. My intention is certainly not to invoke the more traditional picture of development in which shaky knowledge is progressively replaced by richer, more coherently organized, stable knowledge. On the contrary, the principles and attention mechanisms of infancy are rich and coherently organized. My point is that coherently organized information about objects is first *used* by the infant to respond appropriately to external stimuli. Despite its coherence, it does not have the status of a "theory." To have theoretical status, knowledge must be encoded in a format usable outside normal input/output relations. It is these redescriptions that can be used for building explicit theories.

Becoming a Little Theorist

Clearly, young children do not automatically have explicitly statable knowledge of the principles they adhere to during infancy. Now, one could argue that children's theory building is based solely on linguistic encoding, with little or no relationship to the earlier knowledge. Some of children's theories may indeed be built up in this way from knowledge that they acquire directly in linguistic form from adults' responses to their questions. But the RR model posits that not all theory building during childhood is derived directly from linguistic encoding. Another way young children spontaneously come to theorize about the physical world is by the internal process of representational redescription which abstracts knowledge the child has already gained from interacting with the environment. There are three reasons to infer that the repeated process of representational redescription should be considered part of theory building. First, it takes time for children to be able to access explicit knowledge. For example, whereas 4-month-olds show surprise when one object passes through another, 2-year-olds display no such knowledge when an explicit response rather than a habituation response is required (Susan Carey, personal communication). Second, the knowledge that is initially mentioned in children's explicit theories often bears a strong resemblance to the constraints operative in earlier behavior. Third, there are clear-cut examples of theory-like knowledge (what I call "theories-in-action") which the child cannot yet encode linguistically. Thus, there are many different levels of representations of physical knowledge.

From Behavioral Mastery to Metacognitive Knowledge about the Animate/ Inanimate Distinction

A nice illustration of children's progressive theory building comes from work on the animate/inanimate distinction. We saw earlier that motion plays a crucial role in making it possible for young infants to segment the perceptual array into bounded objects. They also use movement to differentiate between animates and inanimates (Golinkoff et al. 1984). And, as we shall see later, this sensitivity to movement also forms the basis of their subsequent theories about animacy. But first let us look at work on how the distinction between biological and mechanical movement underlies infants' categorization of objects.

Mandler and Bauer (1988) gave 12-month-old infants a series of toys to play with. Since these were preverbal infants, the experimenters could not ask them to sort the toys into animals (animate) and vehicles (inanimate). They simply left the toys in front of the infants and took note of their sequences of touching the various toys. The results were clear. Left to their own devices, with no explicit instructions from the experimenters, the infants showed very distinctive and statistically significant touching patterns. They did not pick up the toys randomly. Rather, they first touched a series of, say, vehicles one after another, and then touched a series of animals (or vice versa). In another experiment, infants' manipulation times were recorded. The experimenter handed infants a series of different toys from the same category (e.g., animals such as birds, dogs, and giraffes). After a certain number of different exemplars, the infant was then given a toy from the other category (e.g., inanimates such as airplanes, trucks, and spoons). Assessment was made of whether the manipulation time suddenly increased when a category change took place (e.g., bird to airplane), versus a within-category change (e.g., bird to dog). The design was similar to that of the visual/sucking habituation techniques used with younger infants.

It is crucial to note that, perceptually, some of the animates looked and felt more like the inanimates than other toys within the animate class. The plastic bird and the plastic airplane were more perceptually similar than the bird and the dog. But infants did not base their groupings on perceptual similarity. When the dog, the horse, the rabbit, the bird, etc. were presented sequentially they were explored similarly, but when the airplane followed it was treated as a new category (i.e., a longer manipulation time was recorded). Infants' groupings were not based on *perceptual* similarity, then, but on *conceptual* similarity between potential animate versus inanimate movement—the only feature that would make the infants categorize the similar plastic toys into two distinct sets.

Experiments using the visual habituation paradigm came to similar conclusions. Smith (1989) cut up three-dimensional replicas of mammals and vehicles, removed obvious pieces that had eyes, faces, and wheels, and then randomly assembled the within-animal and the within-vehicle pieces to make novel "animal" and "vehicle" categories. The habituation technique referred to in chapter 1 was used. Twelve-month-old infants rapidly habituated to within-class displays despite the potential visual novelty of every assemblage. They dishabituated only when an assemblage from outside the habituation class was presented. Once again, the clear-cut distinction between animate and inanimate could not have been made solely on the basis of the perceptual properties of the visual arrays. The conceptual distinction does not lie in the visual input; it is made on the basis of fundamental differences in potential movement between the two classes. For the RR model, it is essential to determine whether this same knowledge is used in the somewhat older child's theory building.

If you were shown a picture of a statue, you would know immediately that it could not move alone. Likewise, if you saw a picture of an unfamiliar animal (without being told it was an animal) you would immediately recognize its capacity for self-propelled movement. And so do 3–4-year-old children. Gelman (1990a, 1990b; see also Massey and Gelman 1988) asked young children a series of questions about entities depicted in static displays in photographs: were they alive, could they move alone up and down hills, and so forth. Some of the photographs of inanimate objects were more perceptually similar to animates (statues that had familiar animal-like forms and parts) than to complex, wheeled, machine-like objects. Yet others were photographs of mammals and nonmammalian animals which were totally unfamiliar to the children (e.g., an echidna). When 3- and 4-year-olds were asked for explicit judgments (i.e., to call on E2/3 representations), it turned out that their judgments were not based on perceptual similarity between the photographs (e.g., two very similar photographs depicting spikey bodies, one animate and one inanimate). Rather, the children's judgments were solely a function of whether they considered the depicted object to be capable of self-propelled movement or to require an external agent. In other words, even though a photograph of an animal and a small statue might both have spikes, children considered them to be different in that one could move alone and one had to be moved by a human agent. And to maintain their theories about such distinctive movement, these 3–4-year-old children went as far as inventing observable attributes (e.g., "I can see its feet" when justifying that a photograph was of an animate although no feet were depicted, versus "It can't move alone, it's got no feet" when referring to a photograph of a statue clearly depicting feet)! Children either invent or ignore observables to maintain consistency in their explicit theoretical commitments.

A very similar phenomenon occurred in a study of much older children's explicit judgments about action and reaction as compensating forces (Piaget et al. 1978).[5] Children were asked to explain what happens when a number of items were placed on top of others. For instance, when a piece of wood is placed on a sponge, the sponge becomes slightly indented. What is happening? When the same piece of wood is placed on a table, no visible effect occurs. Why is this? What is happening? Children of ages 4–10 were asked such questions with a series of items and surfaces made of iron, sponge, wood, polyethylene, etc. By about age 8, the children had developed a theory that everything exerts force on whatever it is placed upon and that all causes must have *observable* effects. Holding onto such a theory is easy in any case where something heavy is placed on, say, a sponge, which becomes visibly indented. One might expect the placing of an iron bar on a solid wood surface, with no observable effects, to have threatened the child's theory of action and reaction. Not so! To explain the force exerted by the bar on the surface, children claimed that they saw the surface "flinch a little and quickly re-flatten"! As in the Massey-Gelman study, to maintain their theory children went as far as inventing "observable" data. And, obviously children aren't alone in this!

When children invent observables, they are not simply responding to perceptual information. They are working with explicit internal representations. In the animate/inanimate task, the knowledge about self-propelled versus caused motion is represented explicitly by age 3. The motion principles and the understanding of the role of an external agent are similar to those operating early in infancy, but on the basis of level-I representations. The close resemblance between the constraints operating in infancy and those invoked explicitly in subsequent development (which might not have been the same) suggests that the later knowledge stems from a redescription into more explicit format of the earlier level-I representations.

Beyond the principles allowing for the basic animate/inanimate distinction, children still have much to learn. They need to assimilate information about the insides of animates and objects, the role of levers, wheels, blood, brains, bones, and so on. But further learning is always constrained by earlier principles. As Gelman points out, the innards principle and the external-agent principle allow children to differentiate between relevant and irrelevant data for the animate versus inanimate categories and to make generalizations such that new information can be stored in a coherent way. The new information has to be learned in further interaction with the physical and sociocultural environments. As of age 3–4, although children continue to actively explore the physical environment, they also start to plague adults with questions and thereby obtain linguistically encoded information directly.

In one of the major studies of how children build theories about animates, Carey (1985, 1988) focused on the child as a biologist.[6] She explored the extent to which children understand that all animate things are alive, grow, reproduce, and die and the way in which their concepts of "alive" and "dead" change. Carey showed that knowledge about biological kinds, although relevant to the animate/inanimate distinction, involves a different set of principles than those governing physical motion. Thus, domain specificity of knowledge reorganization operates even in what seem to be closely related domains.

From Behavioral Mastery to Metacognitive Knowledge about Gravity and the Law of Torque

Earlier in this chapter, it was noted that very young infants are not yet sensitive to violations of the law of gravity, but that by 6 months an infant shows surprise if an object stops in mid-air without resting on a supporting surface. Another study on support relations and the principle of gravity explored whether young infants realize that when objects are placed one on top of another the center of gravity of the top object must lie on the surface of the supporting object. Using the habituation paradigm, Baillargéon and Hanko-Summers (1990) showed 7–9-month-old infants objects in possible and impossible support relations.

In figure 3.7, which objects will fall? You know immediately, to be sure. You probably first call on your level-I representations (you can literally see which will fall), but when asked to justify your decision you can call on your level-E2/3 representations. Infants can call on

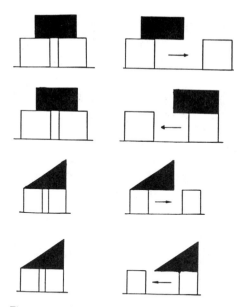

Figure 3.7
Principle of support relations. (After Baillargéon and Hanko-Summers 1990. Used with permission of Ablex Publishing Corporation.)

level-I representations too. Baillargéon found that 7–9-month-old infants looked significantly longer at the display shown at upper right in figure 3.7, which suggests that they were surprised that it did not fall. However, they failed to show discrimination in the case of the asymmetrical objects. Their looking times were equal for the two lower displays; they demonstrated no surprise when asymmetrical objects were displayed in impossible support relations, as in the bottom right diagram. Thus, the sensitivity that young infants already demonstrate to some aspects of the laws of gravity is constrained by symmetry. They still have to engage in further learning as far as asymmetrical objects are concerned. But what about older children? Are they also constrained by symmetry in progressively building a theory about gravity and the law of torque?

When still at Geneva University, I entitled an article "If you want to get ahead, get a theory" (Karmiloff-Smith and Inhelder 1974–75). In part it was meant to be an in-house joke about the Piagetian enterprise, in which big theories were sometimes built on small but important anecdotal data. But my title was also meant to be an apt depiction of the child as a spontaneous theoretician rather than a mere inductivist.

Although the innate predispositions and early-learned principles set the boundaries within which development takes place, I have repeatedly stressed that they do not rule out the need for subsequent representational change, even after successful interaction with the physical environment.

Here again, taking a developmental perspective on cognitive science can enhance our understanding of human discovery processes because the *relation* between theory and data shows subtle changes repeatedly throughout development as children build theories in different microdomains (Karmiloff-Smith 1984, 1988).[7]

A nice illustration of children's passage from behavioral mastery to verbally statable theories about gravity and the law of torque can be found in a study of children's block balancing (Karmiloff-Smith and Inhelder 1974–75; Karmiloff-Smith 1984). Most attempts to understand children's developing knowledge in this microdomain have used the conventional balance scale (Inhelder and Piaget 1958; Siegler 1978). However, many children tested on the balance scale have never encountered one before and must therefore bring to the experiment knowledge that they have acquired elsewhere. I therefore decided to capitalize on an activity that children engage in spontaneously: trying to balance objects on various supports. In the experiment, 4–9-year-olds were asked to balance a series of different blocks on a narrow metal support. Some of the blocks had their weight evenly distributed and balanced at their geometric center. Others had been filled with lead at one end; although they looked identical to the first type, they actually balanced way off-center. A third type of block had a weight glued visibly on the surface at one end; it also balanced off-center. The various block types are shown in figure 3.8.

Now, if one were merely to record successful versus unsuccessful balancing attempts, then 4- and 8-year-olds score far better than 6-year-olds. But such results tell us little. An analysis of microdevelopmental details of children's behavior reveals much more. In a nutshell, 4- and 5-year-olds do this task very easily. They simply pick up each block, move it along the support until they feel the direction of imbalance, and correct the positioning of the block by using proprioceptive feedback about the direction of fall until the block balances. By contrast, 6–7-year-olds place every block at its geometric center and seem incapable of balancing anything but blocks with evenly distributed weight. The 8–9-year olds succeed in balancing all the types of block, as do the youngest group.

How do we explain this developmental progression? The 4-year-olds are only sensitive to information emanating from observable data. They treat each block as a new task. Negative and positive propriocep-

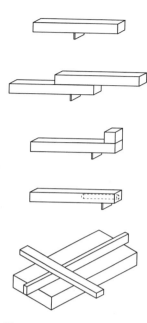

Figure 3.8
Stimuli for block-balancing task. (From Karmiloff-Smith 1984. Reprinted with permission of Laurence Erlbaum Associates, Inc.)

tive feedback about its direction of fall is used to find the point of balance. Information obtained from balancing each block is stored independently, without being linked to what happened in previous attempts or to what follows. This data-driven phase is sustained by level-I representations. It is noteworthy that these youngest subjects made no selection among the blocks; for example, even if two blocks were identical and the child had just succeeded in balancing one of them, she did not subsequently pick up an identical block to make use of the information just obtained from the previous balancing success. These children simply treated the balancing of the blocks as a series of isolated problems. Their actions were mediated by striving for behavioral mastery.

By contrast, the behavior of 6-year-olds is mediated by a theory-in-action that is in the E1 format but is not yet explicable verbally in the E2/3 format. This theory-in-action makes them ignore the proprioceptive feedback of the direction of fall, which is so useful to 4-year-olds. Recall that for infants using the visual input system, symmetry played a crucial role in the principles determining balance. For 6-year-olds using motor output, the first E1 representation is also constrained by symmetry: the geometric-center theory stipulates that all objects balance symmetrically along their length. From redescriptions of their stored level-I representations of objects that balance, children extract a common feature that holds for many (but not all) objects in the world: they are symmetrical and balance at their geometric center. This is the core of the reduced, redescribed representation; other proprioceptive details are not included.

The redescription is an internal process, not due to more experience with the environment. Indeed, it is not always by seeking further information from the *external* environment that children move from level I to higher representational formats to elaborate a theory. Rather, as argued above, they analyze their *internal* representations of previously independently stored entries and generate a theory from relevant patterns across stored entries (e.g., many objects in the world do balance at their geometric center). The 6-year-old treats negative feedback as if she (the *child*) were in difficulty, not as if the theory might be at fault. Indeed, the theory remains unquestioned for a surprisingly long time. These children do exactly what Kuhn (1962) has argued scientists do: They do not abandon or amend their theory despite glaring counterexamples! Instead, they look for an error in their behavior. When a weighted block placed at the geometric center falls, they put it right back at the geometric center—but very much more gently! Finally, when these children can no longer treat the failure as an error in their behavior, they simply push aside any unevenly weighted block as impossible to balance—as an anomaly to be ignored. The observable data are brushed aside as irrelevant!

Why do children finally give up their simple geometric-center theory? First, because of an accumulation of anomalies which call for explanation and cannot be reconciled with the original theory. Yet the reevaluation of anomalies as counterexamples depends crucially on a prior and very firm commitment to a theory. Potentially, all the information (that weighted blocks fall when placed at their center, that evenly distributed blocks fall when placed off-center, etc.) was available for all ages. Like behavioral mastery at level I, the consolidation of a theory at level E1 takes time developmentally. The theory itself must be consolidated before counterexamples are explained via a different theory. Interestingly, though, the accumulation of anomalies does not immediately induce the child to elaborate a comprehensive theory to encompass *all* the data. Rather, children tend to stick to the geometric-center theory, with length as the sole criterion, for one set of blocks. And they create a new theory, based solely on weight, for the set of visibly weighted blocks. It is as if they believe for one set of blocks that there is length but no weight, and for the other set there is weight but no length! And they continue to view the invisibly weighted blocks as anomalies fitting neither theory.

At first, then, children temporarily create two microdomains rather than try to explain all the data within a single microdomain. But in so doing, they lose both the unity of a potentially broader view and the simplicity of their earlier geometric-center theory. The problem is reconciled finally when the child develops her correct, albeit naive, version of the law of torque.

At different moments in development, then, children alternate between focusing on data and on theory. In the present microdomain, when a weighted block balances off-center, this represents *positive* feedback for the younger children because it meets their goal. However, the very same stimulus represents *negative* feedback (a balanced block) for older children holding the geometric-center theory. Similarly, when a block placed off-center falls, this represents negative feedback for the younger children, whereas the same stimulus represents positive feedback for the somewhat older children because a failed off-center attempt confirms their geometric-center theory. This developmental progression demonstrates how the same stimuli can represent different data for children at different ages.

As was pointed out already, by 8 or 9 years of age children do succeed in balancing unevenly weighted blocks, replicating the *behavior* of the youngest group. Note that the RR model posits that the *representations* underlying the behavior are very different. In fact, although both age groups use proprioceptive feedback, the 8-year-old has explicit knowledge about the geometric center and also has a naive theory of the law of torque. This is based on representations in the E2/3 format.

Of course there is still a lot to learn. The qualitative understanding of the law of torque has to be quantified as the precise product of length and weight (Siegler 1978). Moreover, children (and adults) have to come to grips with the subtle effects of torque with decentered fulcrums (Karmiloff-Smith 1975, 1984).

Representational Redescription and Theory Building

At a certain point in development there is no doubt that children's knowledge in this microdomain has a theoretical status in contrast to that of the infant. The coherence in the infant's responses to the environment is a combination of the input and the principles sustaining the processing of that input. The environmental stimuli are always taken into account, and infants show surprise if certain principles are violated. But there is an important phase later in development during which the older child ignores environmental feedback totally or invents observables in the environment to meet her theoretical commitment. Some may not want to call the geometric-center theory a "theory" in the strong sense of the term,[8] and may prefer to think of it as a belief the child entertains. But I argue that these examples in children have all the beginnings of theory building. Rather than simply responding to the proprioceptive data, children use an explanatory structure to shape the data, even if their explanation needs to be broadened and enriched before it can become the conceptual equivalent of the adult's. It is also important to note that 6-year-olds retain the level-I representations. Ask them to close their eyes and they can balance all the blocks easily. Ask them to build a house with the blocks, so that their new explicit goal is the building of a house, and they access level-I representations for balancing the blocks (since this is the means to the main goal). It is when their explicit goal is to balance each block that they call on explicit representations. These are in the form of a not-yet-verbalizable E1 theory-in-action. And while language may be important in scientific reasoning (Gelman, Massey, and McManus, in press), the beginnings of theory building seem to take place without linguistic encoding. Theories-in-action cannot be based on level-I representations. Theory building starts with explicitly defined E1 representations and does not immediately require linguistic encoding.

To summarize: Children are not just problem-solvers. They rapidly become problem generators, and move from successful data-driven actions to theory-mediated actions that are often not influenced by environmental feedback. If ever children are empiricists, it is only very briefly as they first approach a new microdomain. Then, data are all-important. But subsequently children exploit the information that they have already stored in their internal representations. Children constantly develop theories, and they simplify and unify incoming data to make them conform to their theories. As I argued in the introductory chapter, this both potentiates and curtails learning. The theories give the child predictive control, because they refer coherently and stably to several events in a microdomain. But in order to maintain their theories, children treat what should be counterexamples as mere anomalies, and they invent or ignore data in order to maintain their theoretical commitments.

In earlier work not reported on here (Karmiloff-Smith 1975, 1984), I looked at the way much older children enrich their theories about the physical world by expressing their more qualitative explanations in mathematical form. To take the intuitive knowledge of physics further, the child must translate it into quantitative form. This creates new cognitive problems. Moreover, the RR model postulates that representations across different codes can be linked only if the representations are all explicitly defined in at least E1 format. Thus, for knowledge of physics to be related to mathematical knowledge, the latter must also undergo representational redescription.

Chapter 4

The Child as a Mathematician

The failure of children younger than 5 to conserve number . . . is one of the most reliable experimental findings in the entire literature on cognitive development." (Gelman and Gallistel 1978)

"There are 35 horses and 10 ducks on a ship. What is the age of the captain? . . . When given to young children in school, many will immediately begin to manipulate the numbers in the question in order to come up with an answer: 35 + 10 = 45 for example! This situation captures beautifully the meaninglessness of so much of what is perceived by children as 'school' maths." (Hoyles 1985) Yet these schoolchildren started life with some number-relevant predispositions.

Just as for the domains of language and physics, Piaget's view of the number-free infant and his interpretation of the older child's acquisition of number has been seriously called into question. Yet, the original data are very robust. I will begin this chapter with a brief account of Piaget's well-known number-conservation task and the challenges thereto, and then go on to explore the recent infancy and toddler research. Again, I shall end up inviting you to opt for an integration of aspects of both nativism and constructivism.

Number Acquisition as a Domain-General Process

For a Piagetian, it would be inconceivable to attribute number-relevant principles to the neonate or the young infant, or to consider number as domain specific. Piaget postulated that all aspects of number are part of domain-general cognitive development and constructed as a result of general sensorimotor intelligence and the subsequent coordination of seriation and classification. He argued that representation of linear order and seriation (the capacity to represent objects of varying length in correctly ordered sequences) are necessary for number conservation, but not sufficient. Also required is a hierarchical classification system of inclusive relations, in which the class containing only one element is included in the class containing two elements, which in turn is included in the class containing three, and so on (Piaget and Szeminska 1952a).[1] In this way, according to Piaget, the child ultimately achieves conservation of number. What does it mean to conserve number?

Take ten objects and spread them equidistant in a row. Then place exactly the same number of objects in a one-to-one correspondence in a row beneath. Children of age 4 readily accept that there are equal numbers of objects in each row. Now spread out the objects in one of the rows so that they form a longer line, as in figure 4.1, and ask the child whether there is still the same number of objects in each row, or whether one line has more. Children under 5 years old will invariably maintain that one of the two lines (usually the longer, but for some layouts the denser [Piaget 1968]) now has more objects than the other line.

In 1971 I worked in Beirut in the Palestinian refugee camps of Bourj-el-Barajneh and Shattila. My task was to set up guidelines for the introduction of cognitive development into the camps' teacher-training correspondence courses (Karmiloff-Smith 1971a, 1971b). The most convincing demonstration to the camps' teaching staff about children's problems with number was to use real money as the stimulus material for the conservation-of-number task mentioned above. The teachers were initially convinced that for these refugee children the use of real coins would induce even very young subjects to give correct responses. But they were wrong. In fact, the choice of stimulus materials

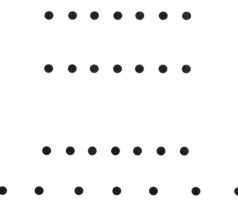

Figure 4.1
Number-conservation task.

(flowers, chocolates, money, geometric shapes) makes little difference.[2] Whatever the stimulus materials, in this now-classic task young children often seem to believe that altering the spatial layout of a line of objects changes its numerosity; hence, they choose the longer line. Though younger subjects sometimes succeed with small numbers, it is not until age 6 or 7 that children consistently pass this seemingly simple test irrespective of the number of objects involved. And these older children justify their responses by invoking the fact that nothing has been added or subtracted, that although one line is shorter it is denser, and that the transformation is merely spatial and does not alter number (since, at all times during the transformation, one-to-one correspondence can be reinstated). Important, too, is the fact that those who successfully conserve number do not feel the need to count the objects after the transformation. Given the type of transformation, they know that the initial one-to-one correspondence suffices to maintain the equivalence of nonspecified quantities throughout.

Challenges to Piaget's View

Challenges to Piaget's account come from two very different approaches to cognitive development. Some researchers have focused solely on lowering the age at which Piagetian number conservation is attained. Others have shifted attention away from number conservation per se and have concentrated on early counting principles in infants and toddlers.

A plethora of variations on an experimental theme have been used in attempts to show that young children are far more competent mathematically than Piaget had concluded. Donaldson (1978) took the number-conservation task to hand. She claimed that the pragmatics of the experimenter-child interaction were misinterpreted by young children who thought that their answers must focus on some salient act performed by the experimenter, such as lengthening one of the lines. She and her colleagues then changed the experimental paradigm such that the spatial transformation of one of the equal rows turned into an accident (involving a naughty teddy bear) rather than a purposeful act of the experimenter (McGarrigle and Donaldson 1975). With such a paradigm, children were successful at a younger age than in the classical Piagetian version of the task. Donaldson claims that development consists in a shift from knowledge embedded in pragmatically relevant contexts to disembedded knowledge.

Markman (1979) took a different line in critically evaluating Piagetian theory, drawing a distinction between classes (soldiers, trees) and collections (army, forest) and the linguistic terms that encode them. Her experiments demonstrate that younger children find it easier to conserve number when the objects in two lines are referred to by a term denoting a collection ("Does your army have as many as my army?") than when they are referred to by a term denoting a class ("Do you have as many soldiers as I?").

Other studies, particularly a series of seminal experiments by Bryant (1974), indicated that the child's problem might reside in learning to distinguish between relevant and irrelevant perceptual cues to number. Thus, if an experiment is designed so as to camouflage irrelevant perceptual aspects of the situation, the age of successful performance can be lowered. But as several authors have stressed,[3] Piaget's conception of number conservation is not the same as learning to ignore spatial layout or to recognize that the configuration of two static arrays is irrelevant to number. Conservation involves specifically focusing on, and reasoning about, *transformations.*

However, Bryant is right that spatial layout is one of the problems besetting young children. To demonstrate this, Gelman (1982) devised a task in which the arrays of objects were not placed one under the other, as in figure 4.1, but side by side. In this way, changes in spatial layout do not directly affect perception of one-to-one correspondence between sets. The children in this study had to keep track of additions and subtractions of objects in each of the two sets, which changed in spatial layout, but they were not faced with the conflicting perceptual data typical of conservation tasks in which objects are placed one under the other. Gelman showed that as long as the sizes of the sets are small, preschoolers know that the operations of addition and subtraction alter set size and that a change in the spatial layout of the array does not.

Another line of research was directly aimed at demonstrating that, although young children do not conserve "large" numbers, they are capable of "small-number conservation" (Bever et al. 1968; Lawson et al. 1974; Siegler 1981). Children under 5 years can pass the conservation task if only three or four objects are used. Bever and his colleagues argued that young children possess the logical operators for number conservation but cannot yet apply them to numbers larger than 5. However, subsequent work suggested that success with small numbers is not necessarily based on the principle of number invariance across spatial transformations. Rather, the precocious success was attributed to number identity via rapid subitizing (a fast enumeration process for numbers up to 4 or 5) (Chi and Klahr 1975), or to one-to-one correspondence checks *after* the transformation had taken place

(Tollefsrud-Anderson et al., in press). In other words, the success of young children can be explained via counting solutions to small-number conservation tasks. By contrast, what Piaget deemed to be true conservation reasoning does not require post transformation checks on cardinality. It is for logical-cum-algebraic reasons that older children know the number is conserved (nothing has been added or subtracted, one-to-one correspondence can be reinstated, etc.), and not because they have specifically counted the objects in each set and compared the resulting cardinal numbers.

In fact, successful conservation does not require knowledge of the precise cardinality of the set; provided you have established one-to-one correspondence at the outset, you can work with unspecified quantities. The focus must be on what happens *during the transformation*, not simply on the post-transformational product. Indeed, true conservers perform better on conservation tasks involving spatial transformations of very large numbers than on static tasks in which they merely have to count such numbers. The reaction times of young children in small-number conservation tasks are significantly longer than those of older children in large-number tasks (Gold 1987). This is because young children are counting or performing one-to-one matching after the transformation, whereas older children use logical reasoning in which the actual number of objects involved is always irrelevant because nothing has been added to or subtracted from the original quantities. It is worth noting that a young child who uses quantification procedures to solve a conservation task is more advanced than one who relies solely on the spatial layout of the lines. The quantifying child constrains her interpretation of the conservation task to number-relevant procedures, although the knowledge embedded in counting procedures (such as sequence and one-to-one correspondence) is not yet explicitly represented.

Some of the efforts at lowering the age of number conservation to refute Piagetian theory boiled down to a form of narrow experimentation for experimentation's sake. As Gold (1987) has shown, much of this research was insensitive to central Piagetian themes, and thus the experiments were irrelevant to the Piagetian theory of number. No consequential theoretical alternatives of Piagetian breadth were offered to account for the lower age of success. The most serious and theoretically profound challenge to the Piagetian view of preschool number acquisition (Gelman and Gallistel 1978; see Resnick 1986 with respect to older children) was not aimed at lowering the age of performance on number-conservation tasks; the epistemological starting point for Gelman and Gallistel's argument was a nativist stance.

Number Acquisition as a Domain-Specific, Innately Guided Process

Is number conservation the appropriate focus for understanding children's acquisition of number? Gelman maintains that it is not. For Gelman and her collaborators,[4] some knowledge about number, such as one-to-one correspondence, is present from early infancy.

The nativist stance posits that the child's learning about number is highly constrained by innately specified number-relevant principles. These principles enable the infant to focus attention on number-relevant inputs and to build up in memory number-relevant representations. Such principles also subsequently stipulate for the toddler what are and are not valid instances of counting. Gelman's arguments about number are similar to those developed in earlier chapters with respect to other domains—i.e., that innate biases channel the infant to focus attention selectively on those inputs that are relevant to each particular domain (in this case, number). This does not necessarily imply that the infant starts life with a number module. Rather, as I argue throughout the book, the innate predispositions provide constraints through which to compute number-relevant inputs. In this way, it is possible that the set of number constraints becomes progressively modularized as development proceeds.

How does one discover these number-relevant predispositions? A series of experiments with infants and preverbal toddlers shows how they respond in numerically relevant ways to displays that they could successfully process in, say, color-relevant or shape-relevant ways.

Via the habituation and dishabituation paradigms described in chapter 1, Antell and Keating (1983) exposed neonates to stimulus cards containing the same number of dots but varying in length of line and density between dots.[5] After reaching habituation criterion, the infants were exposed to a second card containing a novel number of dots but maintaining either the line length or the dot density of the habituation arrays. Figure 4.2 shows examples of the displays used in the Antell-Keating study; other similar studies used objects of different shapes and colors instead of dots, but with the same results. The experiments indicate that neonates can detect numerical differences in arrays consisting of small numbers. Infants showed renewed attention to changes in number, but not to changes in line length or dot density. However, this ability breaks down when sets are too large.

Overall, the results indicate that dishabituation is due to the infant's making the numerosity distinction by abstracting the numerical invariance of earlier displays and recognizing different numerosity in the new display. A further interesting fact pointed out by Antell and Keating is that, to succeed on such tasks, neonates must recall the

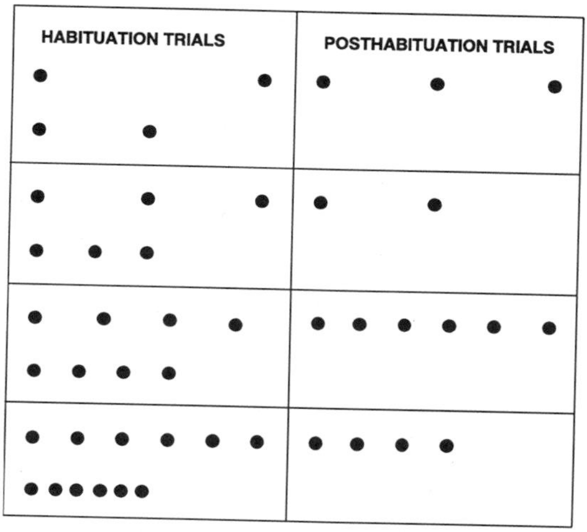

Figure 4.2
Number-discrimination task. (After Antell and Keating 1983. Reprinted with permission of The Society for Research in Child Development.)

numerosity of displays previously perceived but no longer visible and then relate the number-relevant information to a display currently being viewed. This would seem to require some form of image-schematic representations, and to be a far cry from the traditional Piagetian view of infants' capacities.

Perhaps such data can be explained away by suggesting that the infants are merely reacting to different light intensities between the two-item and three-item displays and that their discriminatory responses have nothing to do with the numerosity of the displays. Starkey et al. (1985) argue that such explanations cannot hold because, although Antell and Keating used uniform dots, many other experiments involve changes in color, size, or shape every time a new numerical display is presented. There are thus light-intensity changes *within* the set of two-item stimuli, just as there are *between* the two-item and three-item stimuli. The discriminatory responses of the young infants must therefore be due to their attending to number-relevant changes in the displays while ignoring other perceptually interesting features. Indeed, it is important to stress that color and shape discrimination are already part of the infants' capacities, and that if an experiment focuses on either of these features infants perform exceedingly well. However, if the habituation and dishabituation displays single out numerical changes, then infants ignore color and shape changes and attend to the numerically relevant aspect of the stimuli.

We saw in the previous chapter that infants' early sensitivity to physics principles is cross-modal. Recall the experiment using haptically and visually presented displays of rings connected to rigid or flexible rods. Does cross-modal matching exist in the number domain too? It turns out that 6–8-month-old infants can detect numerical correspondence between a set of visible items and a set of audible items; that is, they can perform cross-modal matching relevant to the numerosity of displays. Thus, when presented with two visual displays each with a specific number of objects, infants will focus consistently on the one with the same number of objects as an auditory input of drumbeats (Starkey et al. 1985) or consistently on the visual display with a different number (Moore et al. 1987). Irrespective of whether the infant opts for focusing on matching number across the two modalities or finds a new number more interesting,[6] their increased attention to one or the other is consistent, showing that they are attending to the number-relevant properties of the displays rather than to other potentially attractive features. Further, infants as young as 12 months can order different-size sets (Cooper 1984) and can take into account surreptitious changes in number of an expected set (Sophian and Adams 1987). This too seems a far cry from Piaget's view of the lack of number sensitivity in infancy.

As with cross-modal matching in physics, the above results show that sensitivity to different numerosities is not modality specific. This raises important questions about whether a number module simply receives inputs from different transducers in a single, number-relevant format, or whether the outputs of all the modality-specific computations are fed to central processing. In the latter case, we would have to grant the 6–8-month-old infants in this experiment the capacity to recall numerical information when making the cross-modality comparison and to be able to redescribe number-relevant data from different modalities into a common format. The question awaits further research. Again, whichever explanation turns out to be correct, there is no doubt that this body of research has shown that infants process and store number-relevant data in far greater sophistication and far earlier than Piagetian theory asserts.

The Role of Subitizing: Perceptual or Conceptual?

The sensitivity of infants to numerosity has not been explained away in terms of light-intensity changes on the retina. But what about "subitizing," a fast enumeration process that works for adults for numbers up to about 5? Mandler and Shebo (1982) and Gallistel and Gelman (1991) argue that subitizing is the result of enumeration processes, whereas von Glaserfeld (1982) sees subitizing as a purely perceptual operation not involving number-relevant procedures. The latter position explains subitizing as the capacity to recite a number word in association with a given visual pattern, much as one might associate common nouns with common objects. This may indeed be the way we recognize the numbers on dice, which always appear in the same spatial configuration. One can, in some sense, "perceive" 5 on a die. But in general, one cannot "perceive" number, as one perceives "red". Number is something the mind imposes on reality. And once privileged spatial layouts such as those on dice are not used, subitizing involves rapid enumeration and not purely perceptual processes (Mandler and Shebo 1982; Gelman and Meck 1986). Infants' use of subitizing, then, is number-relevant. Whatever the subitizing mechanism turns out to be, it is important to recall that there seem to be no restrictions on the degree to which one can vary the inputs in terms of size, color, shape, orientation, and texture and still capture the infant's attention by number-relevant changes. By contrast, if quantity changes for every display in the stimulus set and color or shape remains constant during the habituation phase, then of course the infant dishabituates to these features.

The conclusion to be drawn from these various studies is that infants show sensitivity to numerical relations that are defined by one-to-one correspondence and can disregard a variety of interesting non-numerical features in the visual displays. It does not seem to matter what the actual entities are, or what size, color, or shape they are; nor does the mode of presentation (visual, auditory, tactile, etc.) matter, or whether they project different light intensities on the retina individually or as a collection against a given background, or the visual angle at which they are viewed. Young infants' attention seems to be captured by changes in the numerosity of displays. As Gelman has repeatedly argued, this indicates that number is an important feature to which the young infant is sensitive in the environment to which she is exposed.

It is crucial to note that in neonates and infants up to 6–8 months, this capacity is limited to numbers up to 3 and breaks down for larger quantities. Nonetheless, we can conclude that a predisposition to numerically relevant data is built into the architecture of the human mind. It directs the infant's attention and makes it possible for number-relevant representations to be stored for subsequent representational redescription. It would thus seem that children do not first learn some undifferentiated "many" versus "few", nor do they use purely perceptual processes to compute numerosities. From the outset, they use number-relevant principles, and these constrain their subsequent learning also.

That the infant's sensitivity to numerical relations is defined by one-to-one correspondence does not, of course, imply that the infant knows all there is to know about number. First, the principle operates only for small numbers. Second, the capacity to recall the numerosity of a two-item display or to match a two-set visual display to a two-set audible one is clearly not the same as knowing what "2" means or understanding the notion of "+1". The implicit knowledge embedded in procedures has to be subsequently redescribed to be used outside numerosity-detection procedures. But the early capacity is likely to be the foundation of toddlers' subsequent capacity to judge numerosity and to make numerically relevant searches (Starkey 1983). Whatever innate predispositions one ascribes to the child, there is still a great deal to acquire. Gelman's principles-first model is a model of learning—i.e., of the role of innate, number-relevant principles that the infant and the toddler bring to subsequent learning. What are these principles?

Constraints on Learning How to Count

The innately specified principles posited by Gelman and Gallistel are principles that constrain learning how to count. Surely, you object, learning the list of count words can easily be explained within an associationist framework and hardly requires innately specified number-relevant knowledge. Is it not simply rote learning, via numerous opportunities for practice? How many times have you seen parents take children up and down stairs, counting aloud "1, 2, 3, 4, 5, 6, 7, 8, 9, 10!" When toddlers learn to repeat such sequences, is this ability initially very different from chanting "Baa baa black sheep"?

In an impressively vast study of how preschool children learn to count, Gelman and Gallistel demonstrated that early counting is much more than rote learning and that, although children make errors as they learn to count, their efforts are constrained by a set of counting-relevant principles.

We have just seen that the first principle—one-to-one correspondence—may already be operative in the neonate's and the young infant's discriminations of arrays with different numerosities. The one-to-one correspondence principle captures the fact that one must match each and every item in one collection with one and only one item in another collection to decide whether or not the collections are equal. Infants can do this for small numbers. This does not, of course, mean that infants know everything about one-to-one correspondence; they don't (Cowan 1987). But what it does mean is that when toddlers subsequently learn to count, their efforts are also constrained by one-to-one correspondence. They may make numerous errors in their counting attempts, but they rarely violate one-to-one correspondence. Each and every item in the collection to be counted is tagged once and only once with a unique, symbolic tag. The early knowledge thus directs the way in which young children attend to examples of counting in their environment.

The second principle involves stable ordering. The tags need not initially come from a conventional counting list, as long as they obey counting constraints. Say a child counts "one, three, seven, ten" when counting a group of four objects. As long as each tag is unique and as long as the ordinal sequence is the same for each counted set, then, despite the oddity of the list, Gelman considers the child to be counting according to number-relevant constraints. And it is these constraints that dictate the way in which the child eventually learns the conventional sequence of number words.

Gelman and Gallistel identified three other counting principles that constrain the way in which children learn to count: item indifference, order indifference, and cardinality. The principles of item indifference and order indifference stipulate that any type of item can be counted, and that the order in which different items in a set are counted is irrelevant to its cardinal value: one can start counting a line of objects at either end, or from the center, as long as each and every item is counted and once only.

The cardinality principle stipulates that only the final count term of any particular trial represents the cardinal value of the set. This principle has come under a lot of attack from developmentalists. First, Gelman and Gallistel's criterion for cardinality is weaker than that used by other researchers. For Gelman and Gallistel the child possesses the principle of cardinality if she consistently produces the last tag in a set as the total number in that set. However (like Piaget), Frydman and Bryant (1988) and Fuson (1988) use a more stringent criterion: that cardinality involves using counting, not for one set, but to make a numerical comparison between two or more sets. This is a later achievement, but the point of Gelman and Gallistel's model is to identify the foundational principles guiding initial number-relevant learning. This is why they, unlike Piaget, believe that counting is relevant to number conservation.

A more serious challenge to the principle of cardinality comes from the work of Wynn (1990), who showed that for an entire year after children have been counting (i.e., honoring one-to-one correspondence and stable ordering principles) they do not seem to know that counting yields a particular cardinality on each count. Asked "How many?", 2-year-olds promptly perform adequately: "1, 2, 3, 4, 5." But they do not say the last tag a second time after counting. By contrast, 3-year-olds repeat the cardinal value after ending the count sequence (e.g., "1, 2, 3, 4, 5 . . . 5"). Moreover, when 2-year-olds who can count to five when asked "How many?" are instructed to get "five objects" from a pile, they just pick up a handful and never use the counting procedure to solve the task. Again, 3-year-olds spontaneously use counting to determine the cardinality of the set.

Wynn interprets her results as demonstrating that although the counting behavior of 2-year-olds obeys some of Gelman's principles, they do not yet have the cardinality principle. This takes another full year of development. So if 2-year-olds lack the crucial principle of cardinality, their counting procedures may actually have less to do with number than Gelman supposes. Another possible explanation, however, comes from the extensive work on strategy choice by Siegler and Robinson (1982) and Siegler (1989a).[7] Siegler has shown that children do not automatically realize that a strategy thoroughly practiced in one situation is also relevant to another. Flexible strategy choice also takes time to develop. But the fact that the younger children not only fail to use a counting strategy for all relevant goals but also fail to repeat the last tag suggests that their knowledge of cardinality may be weak. Moreover, as we shall see in a moment, the representational status of early counting behavior is also an important part of an adequate explanation.

Gelman, too, reports data which could be used to challenge the stability of the principle of cardinality, even in somewhat older children (Gelman and Meck 1986). When asked to give the cardinal value of a set, 2-year-olds correctly count the set on the first trial and repeat the last tag. However, even when every trial involves exactly the same set of objects, they recount on every new trial. By contrast, 3-year-old children also count aloud on the first trial, but on subsequent trials with the same set they simply state the last tag of an earlier count. They do not repeat the procedure in its entirety each time, but they are able to focus specifically on the part of the procedure that is relevant to the cardinality question. So do the younger children really understand cardinality?

According to Frydman and Bryant (1988), they may not. They designed some elegant experiments to probe this question further. To avoid the problems with spatial mappings, they used temporal one-to-one correspondence in the form of a sharing game children love to play: one for you, one for me. When 4- and 5-year-olds were asked to distribute a pile of sweets equally to a group of dolls so that each ended up with the same number, they had no difficulty. Afterward, when asked how many sweets one of the dolls had, the children counted. They were then asked how many sweets each of the other dolls had. Only the 5-year-olds inferred spontaneously that the cardinal value after the distribution was the same for each of the dolls. As in the Gelman data, the younger children wanted to recount for each doll. This was true irrespective of set size.

In another experiment, children were asked to distribute chocolate bars to dolls. The bars came in one-, two-, and three-segment lengths (each segment was of equal size). In this experiment, then, to ensure an equal amount of chocolate at the end, children had to adapt their distribution strategies to the different number of segments per bar. Again only 5-year-olds performed correctly. The 4-year-olds tended to use the distribution procedures (one bar for X, one bar for Y), irrespective of the number of chocolate segments in a bar. However, a training experiment showed that 4-year-olds were not totally unaware of the relationship between one-to-one correspondence and cardinal values. They benefited from a training schedule in which the different sizes of the chocolate bars were color coded. In a post-test with no colors, they performed like 5-year-olds and were no longer blind to the fact that an equal number of actions to each recipient will not automatically ensure that each recipient gets the same amount as the other.

Frydman and Bryant's study shows that 5-year-olds have a good grasp of the quantitative significance of temporal one-to-one correspondence at an age before they can manage traditional tests of spatial one-to-one correspondence. The capacity seems to develop spontaneously between the ages of 4 and 5. The 4-year-old, however, requires some explicit external marking, such as color coding, as a reminder to take into account the quantitative implications of the one-to-one correspondence.

This work shows that, although the infant may start with some innately specified number-relevant attention biases and principles, much has to be learned during the first few years of life so that the early principles take on richer meanings and more flexible usage. This requires, as I argue below, the process of representational redescription. Moreover, it is possible that the principle of cardinality is not innately specified, as Gelman and Gallistel presuppose, but grows out of the coordination of simpler principles (such as stable order and one-to-one mapping) once these have become explicitly represented.

The Representational Status of Early Number Knowledge

What is the representational status of the principles with which young children come to counting-relevant tasks? According to Gelman, one reason why children who abide by counting principles fail on number-conservation tasks is that they lack an *explicit* understanding of the principle of one-to-one correspondence by which conservation of non-specified values is achieved. It is not clear from Gelman's description what mechanisms allow for the passage from implicit to explicit knowledge, or exactly what is meant by "explicit."

How can the RR model help us to think about development in the number domain, and in particular about some of the data reported above? Recall that in chapter 1, when I discussed the RR model, I pointed out that an important step in development was first to reach behavioral mastery and then to redescribe efficient procedures so that their component parts could be focused upon individually. I took as an analogy learning to execute a tune on the piano. The RR account of the development of counting is similar. First the toddler has to routinize the counting procedure so that it becomes automatic. Asked "How many?", she can rapidly run off the first few numbers of the count list in accordance with the Gelman-Gallistel principles. She has reached behavioral mastery on the basis of level-I representations. Implicit in these representations are principles like one-to-one correspondence and ordinality. The toddler who can readily count to 5 but needs to count the same display again and again is unable to focus on the individual component of the counting procedure that yields the array's cardinality. This is precisely what the RR model would predict. The toddler is running a procedure in its entirety and can use it adequately in certain circumstances, such as when asked how many objects are in a set. In other words, she knows that using the count list is relevant. However, the knowledge embedded in the procedure is not yet manipulable as separate components. That is why it is run afresh each time, even when the trial involves the same set just counted.

Other research testing the RR model, which I discuss in detail in chapter 6, has shown that ends of procedures are the first to become manipulable after representations have been redescribed into non-bracketed E1 format. The final tag with respect to the cardinal value of the whole count once redescribed is the first to become accessible explicitly, because it is at the end of each counting procedure. Ultimately all the component parts of the counting sequence, and its semantics (e.g. an abstract notion of +1), become accessible to cognitive manipulation.

Focusing on the representational status of children's number knowledge helps us to understand the limitations on early counting knowledge. But why do children who do have the cardinality principle fail the number-conservation task? Before we try to answer this, let us briefly look at the potential problems besetting the child in learning the language of counting.

Learning the Language of Counting and Mathematics

In the mass of linguistic input to the child, how does she know that certain words refer specifically to counting? The young child hears "one, two, three, four . . ." or "un, deux, trois, quatre . . .", as the case may be. How does she know that these are not the names of the items being pointed at? Gelman and Meck (1986) and Gelman (1990a, 1990b) show that very young children keep the set of count words ("one", "two", "three") separate from the set of object labels ("cat", "dog", "spoon"), and use each in their appropriate contexts. Gelman and Meck maintain that the learner's task is facilitated by the very fact that different innate principles and attention biases underlie the domains of language and number.

Let me briefly return to the case of language with which I dealt at some length in chapter 2. For naming objects, a specific set of principles obtain (Markman 1987; Spelke 1988; Au and Markman 1987; Hall 1991; Waxman 1985). The first specifies that if objects are from the same category they will share the same unique label (e.g. "spoon"). A second principle stipulates that once an item has a label it cannot be given a different label at the same category level. All items from the same category must have the same basic-level name—a spoon can be called by a superordinate name (e.g. "utensil"), but it cannot be called a "car" (except, of course, in pretend play, which violates these very constraints).

Take the case of four spoons in an array. For labeling, they must all have the same unique basic-level name: "spoon", "spoon", "spoon", "spoon". For counting, a very different set of principles obtains (Gelman, Cohen, and Hartnett 1989). Each spoon must have a different label: "one", "two", "three", "four" (or "blonch", "conch", "minch", "binch", if you do not yet know the conventional list). On repeated counting trials, any particular spoon may receive a different label, i.e. be the "one" on one trial and the "three" on another trial, depending on the order in which the items are counted. Domain-specific knowledge of counting principles serves to identify the class of behaviors that are potentially counting behaviors, as opposed to those that are potentially labeling behaviors.

These various considerations led Gelman and her colleagues to conclude that it is on the basis of principles of item-irrelevance and stable order—very different from the principles governing labeling—that children induce that the number words they hear are not names for objects but tags for counting. In other words, the domain-specific principles make certain aspects of the linguistic input particularly salient for number, such as the count list, and others germane to naming. The two are not confused.[8] Faced with the overwhelming volume of verbal input in their environment, toddlers use the domain-specific principles to attend to and demarcate these different functions, to treat some inputs as relevant to counting and others as relevant to naming, and to store counting-relevant representations in one case and naming-relevant representations in the other. This would be impossible if innately specified principles were not there to guide the infant and toddler learning the language of counting by defining which linguistic entities are part of a given domain and which are not (Gelman and Cohen 1988). But development involves more than these domain-specific principles.

Beyond the early capacities that guide them in learning the language of counting, children will later have to learn to apply mathematical language to the principles governing arithmetic operations. This turns out to be crucial to subsequent number development and leads to a richer understanding of the number domain (Kitcher 1982, 1988; Resnick 1986). The language of mathematics has a specific syntax and lexicon of its own which children must master. For example, in everyday language the term "multiply" always implies an increment (e.g., cells multiply). Its technical meaning in mathematical language does not; multiplication of fractions, for example, produces a decrement. Interestingly, in mathematically gifted children, level of mathematical understanding and use of mathematical language are positively correlated (Gelman 1990a, 1990b; Resnick 1986). Less gifted children tend to understand mathematical language in terms of everyday language. Nonetheless, the role of language remains unclear. In some cases, language seems essential to rendering implicit principles explicit. Yet we cannot lose sight of the fact that there are idiots-savants with very little language who can perform extraordinary mathematical feats, such as recognizing whether or not a number is prime at very great speed (O'Connor and Hermelin 1984). Research shows that such idiots-savants do not rely on rote-memory, but the precise status of the representations that sustain their mathematical calculations remains a mystery.

Is Mathematical Notation Essential to Number Development?

Mathematical notation embodies constraints that differ from those of writing and drawing. Number notation is often an integral part of number development. Tolchinsky-Landsman and Karmiloff-Smith (in press), Bialystok (1991 and in press), Hughes (1986), and Sinclair et al. (1983) have made extensive studies of children's invented writing, number notation, and drawing. Bialystok argues that external notation helps the child understand the symbolic nature of number. She showed children boxes, each filled with a quantity of toys, had them count how many were in each box, closed the boxes, and asked them to write down on the box cover how many were in it so as to be able to remember later. Children produced either numbers, analogical representations (five lines or squares to represent five objects), or drawings. When brought back to the experiment room some time later, mainly those who had used number notation, even if wrong, were able to recall the previous quantities. Analogical notations were of less help for recall of number even when children had made the right number of marks. So understanding the symbolic nature of number notation and the relationship between encoding and decoding takes time developmentally.

Cross-cultural studies have demonstrated that number notation is not a necessary condition for the development of arithmetic principles. Cultures without systems of number notation nonetheless use number computations that obey formal arithmetic principles. This is true, for example, of the cloth merchants and tailors of the Dioula culture of the Ivory Coast (Petitto 1978). Sophisticated practical base-6 mathematics, via iterated groupings of six cowry shells, has also been identified within other African cultures despite an apparent absence of written symbols (Zaslavsky 1973).[9] More recently, Carraher et al. (1985) have shown that mental arithmetic (partition and iterative addition, but not multiplication) is performed by Brazilian street-vendor children who also do not make use of externalized notations. So an external number notation system is not universal, but counting, additive arithmetic operations, and conservation seem to be.

Reconciling Domain-Specific Counting Principles with the Failure to Conserve: Cultural Universals

We are still left with the issue of why children whose successful counting embodies number-relevant principles fail on the conservation-of-number task. As was noted above, some aspects of counting principles and a rudimentary numerosity invariance are available to the neonate and the young infant, and toddlers learn to count and progressively come to understand cardinality under the constraint of five number-relevant principles. Yet they fail on the number-conservation task. Why?

Piaget has argued that counting is irrelevant to number conservation, and Bovet et al. (1972), Dasen et al. (1978), and Cole and Scribner (1974) point to the fact that conservation seems to be universal to all cultures. But if number conservation is a universal human capacity and has nothing to do with counting, why is it that almost all human societies also invent enumeration procedures (Carraher et al. 1985; Petitto 1978; Saxe 1981; Zaslavsky 1973)? Even when these are not composed of a list of linguistically encoded count terms, they obey the counting principles identified by Gelman and Gallistel. Cross-cultural research has identified the numeration system of the remote Oksapmin village populations in Papua New Guinea as a stably ordered list of body parts—wrist, forearm, elbow, and so on (Saxe 1981). This bodily encoded system is constrained by number principles and is the formal equivalent of linguistically encoded counting systems. So, despite surface differences, counting systems share abstract counting principles and, like number conservation, seem to be acquired almost universally.

So far I have said little about the role of the sociocultural environment. Taking a constructivist stance means that we consider the innately specified number-relevant attention biases and principles only as a potential for number acquisition. Without a relevant environment, number competence cannot develop. Gordon (1991) reports preliminary studies suggesting that the Piraha tribe of Amazonia in Brazil have only a 1/2/many system and that adults are unsuccessful on simple number-conservation tasks. They also fail to learn to perform accurate one-to-one numerical correspondences. Young Piraha children, however, do seem to be able to benefit from training. The research is still in progress, but the preliminary adult data seem to indicate that innately specified number-relevant principles may decay if not put to use early in development in a sufficiently relevant environment.[10]

Another seemingly universal fact about number has been highlighted by Resnick (1986), who reports that almost every society invents or uses additive composition operations. According to Resnick, the only numerical concepts that are easy to acquire and that will be acquired early and universally are those based on additive composition. Groen and Resnick (1977) have provided eloquent demonstrations of children's spontaneous inventions of addition algorithms prior to schooling. And cross-cultural work by Carraher et al. (1985) demonstrates that unschooled children and adults obey the abstract additive composition principles identified by Resnick and her group.

What, then, is the relationship between the counting and additive composition principles, on the one hand, and conservation of number, on the other, since all seem to be universal across most cultures, whether schooled or not? Is it simply that children can conserve if the numbers are small enough (Bever et al. 1968)? We have already seen that there is an initial constraint for infants on discriminating numerosities up to 3. A similar constraint obtains initially for toddlers' counting up to 3. Could it be, then, that conservation of number simply involves the capacity to operate on larger numerosities? Gelman and Gallistel disagree. Rather, they place particular emphasis on the difference between operations on counted numerosities and operations on *unspecified quantities*. The latter, they argue, involve a more abstract understanding of number. The true conserver has developed the ability to reason about numerical relations in the absence of representations of instantiated numerosities. In some sense, then, the conserving child has started to operate on algebraic inputs, rather than merely on numerical ones.

The Gelman-Gallistel position with respect to the implications of failure to conserve differs substantially from Piaget's. For Piagetians, the failure to conserve is interpreted as a lack of a coherent set of number-relevant principles. For Gelman and Gallistel, by contrast, the preschooler has a coherent set of principles for operating on number-relevant inputs; what the young child lacks, and has to learn, is the more abstract algebraic representation of these concepts.

How could this learning take place? Innately specified principles are never directly available, but become embedded in procedures for interacting with the environment. Clearly nothing in the external environment will directly inform the child. The RR model postulates that the movement to algebraic concepts involves a focus on the child's *internal* representations. What elements of the successful counting procedures must be rendered explicit to enable the child to work on unspecified quantities and conserve number? First, the one-to-one correspondence operation implicit in counting must be explicitly defined. One-to-one correspondence is an implicit feature of successful counting procedures. The principle embedded in the procedure must then be abstracted, redescribed, and represented in a different format independent of the procedural encoding. This level-E1 representation, once it is lifted from its embedding in the level-I counting procedure, can then be used for unspecified quantities.

Important, too, is the fact that the level-E1 knowledge is not yet available to verbal report. Indeed, Tollefsrud-Anderson et al. (in press) provide data from a reaction-time study that they carried out on the conservation task. Their results turn out to be directly relevant to the RR model. At first blush, all their subjects seemed to conserve: they answered that both lines were equal in number despite the difference in length and density. But a subtle analysis of reaction times showed that there were three very different levels of performance. The most advanced were the so-called "true-conservers," who passed the conservation task *and* could provide verbal justifications about one-to-one correspondence. Next was an interesting group for the RR model in that they could *not* provide verbal justifications but their reaction times for the conservation responses were as fast as those of the true conservers. Finally there was a group whose reaction times for correct responses were considerably slower. It turned out that they were making post-transformation one-to-one matching checks.

Since the middle group's reaction times were as fast as those of the verbally explicit group, they were clearly conserving and not doing one-to-one post-transformation checks. But they could not provide verbal justifications. We can thus use the RR model to suggest that these children seem to be at a level at which they have explicitly represented one-to-one correspondence in the E1 format and can use that knowledge on unspecified quantities. However, further redescription into the E2/3 format had not yet occurred and thus the knowledge was not yet accessible to verbal report. The existence of this middle level is particularly revealing with respect to the many different levels of representational explicitness that exist.

Becoming a Little Mathematician

Redescription of knowledge into increasingly explicit formats which ultimately enable the child to provide verbal explanation is at the heart of the RR model's account of how children subsequently develop their intuitive theories about different domains. Theories are built on explicitly defined representations. How do children's theories change with respect to what a "number" is? Do children ultimately come to understand number as part of a structured *system*, much as they ultimately come to understand the concept of "word" as part of a structured linguistic system?

Metamathematical Knowledge: The Child's Changing Theory about Number

According to Gelman, Cohen, and Hartnett (1989), children's initial theory about number is that numbers are what you get when you count. Both zero and fractions are therefore rejected as numbers because they are not part of the counting sequence. Assigning the concept of numberhood to fractions and zero is the first step in a fundamental theory change about what a number is. It involves a change in the core concepts of what constitutes a number (Carey 1985). The child's theory moves from a core constraint that number is a property of countable entities to a different core constraint: that number is something with which, and on which, one performs mathematical operations. This issue in mathematics has been eloquently discussed by Resnick (1986) with respect to the difficulties children have recognizing the dual function of mathematical notations. Resnick points out a paradox central to mathematical thinking. On the one hand, the algebraic expression $a + b$ takes its meaning from the situations to which it refers. On the other hand, it derives its mathematical power from divorcing itself from those situations. The movement from conserving number identity via counting real-world objects to conserving equivalence of nonspecified quantities is of a similar type of abstraction.

Such a theory change also embodies changing ideas about the number zero. This is a particularly abstract concept mathematically. Counting plays little role here because counting real-world objects cannot yield the empty set zero. Does the child understand that zero is a number among others, with its own unique value, namely nothing? Zero is the smallest (non-negative) whole number, and as a "small number" it might be part of other small-number acquisitions. In fact, it is not. As part of the number system (and not simply representing "nothing"), it is a particularly difficult notion. This causes children initially to reject zero as a number.

Wellman and Miller (1986) showed that children's understanding of zero passes through three steps: First they acquire familiarity with the name and the written notation of zero. This precocious notational knowledge is independent of the young child's conceptual understanding that zero refers to a unique numerical quantity—none or nothing. It is this latter that constitutes the second step in acquisition. Lastly, children understand that zero is the smallest number in the series of non-negative integers, whereas earlier they believed 1 to be the smallest number. And they still do not conceive of the operator "+1" as relating zero to one. This more abstract representation "+1" is likely to be a late acquisition, rather like the generic use of the definite article (Karmiloff-Smith 1979a). To understand abstract notions like "+1" or the generic statement that "the lion is a dangerous animal", the child must know that such expressions do not involve a concrete instantiation. After such a statement, you cannot then ask, e.g., "Which lion is a dangerous animal?" The generic relates to the intension of a concept and not to its extension. Likewise, the concept "+1" is not the same as understanding instantiations: $5 + 1 = 6$, $7 + 1 = 8$, etc.

A similar theory change takes place with respect to fractions. Initially the role of fractions in mathematical operations is taken to be the same as that of whole numbers. Young children asked to add $\frac{1}{2} + \frac{1}{4}$ may respond $\frac{2}{6}$! It is not until later that they understand that the two numbers in the notation of fractions involve the division of one numerical representation by another, different numerical representation. Fractions are not about the division of portions in a cake! In other words, learning about fractions involves being able to use conventional mathematical terms about numerical relations, i.e., going beyond the knowledge implicit in earlier procedures and beyond operations on real-world entities. Thus, developing a broad theory about number involves fundamental theory changes similar to those discussed in chapter 2 with respect to language. The child's explicit theory of what a "word" is moves from thinking that words denote real-world objects and events to thinking of words in terms of the linguistic system in which they operate. Likewise, number is ultimately thought of in terms of the mathematical system in which it operates. But these theory changes are domain-specific and occur at different ages for the two domains. The domain specificity of number is, like that of language, also suggested by work on brain-damaged adults who show special patterns of number deficits, with the rest of their cognition intact (Sokol et al. 1989; Cipolotti et al. 1991).

Number in Nonhuman Species

In chapter 2 I suggested that, despite its extensive representational and problem-solving capacities, the chimpanzee cannot acquire language. Premack (1986) has provided an eloquent discussion of the extent of the chimpanzee's capacities. The chimpanzee can acquire a long list of lexical items (expressed in a visuomanual code or in an abstract geometric code expressed in plastic chips), which can be combined in interesting but limited ways. No species other than the human seems to be able to acquire a structured linguistic system. But what about number? Many species are capable of numerical discriminations and counting procedures. Are these equivalent to the human capacity?

This has been the subject of a great deal of controversy.[11] Even though the animal's capacity can be described in terms of elaborate mathematical models (MacNamara 1982; Kacelnik and Houston 1984), do we want to say that it is the equivalent of number in humans? Is a predator's ability to change its foraging strategies according to the exact distribution and density of prey merely proto-numerical? And what about laboratory tests? Animals' ability to discriminate between two and three objects is, according to Garnham (1991), one of the most firmly attested facts in the experimental literature on animal counting.[12] Or do we grant an animal knowledge of number only if it can explicitly manipulate a symbolic code? We did not make this restriction when attributing skeletal counting principles to human infants.

A distinction introduced by Gallistel (1990) seems particularly relevant at this point. We may attribute to animals and to the human neonate a counting process that maps from numerosities to *states of the representing organism*. By contrast, we attribute to toddlers and older children a counting process that maps from numerosities to *sets of symbols*. Does this mean that the human neonate's knowledge is the same as the animal's knowledge of number? Yes and no. Yes, because animals can discriminate numerosities and can adhere to the principles of one-to-one correspondence and item-indifference. Their numerosity discriminations may be like those of neonates and young infants. No, because the human child ultimately uses a symbolic system for counting involving the stable order principle. And no, because the human child, via its capacity for representational redescription, ultimately exploits its number knowledge to create one of the domains of mathematics.

Gallistel cites impressive results from the literature on animal number knowledge. For example, it has been shown that some species can discriminate large numerosities (e.g. 45 versus 50 pecks) that cannot be explained away by some low-level perceptual process (Rilling and McDiarmid 1965; Rilling 1967). One must invoke some mechanism that sequentially passes through an ordered series of states, the last of which represents the cardinal numerosity of the set. Moreover, animals count sets of heterogeneous items just as readily as sets of homogenous items (the item-indifference principle) and transfer the discrimination immediately to sets of stimuli not in the training set (Capaldi and Miller 1988; Fernandes and Church 1982). It has also been shown that animals can be taught to perform addition and subtraction operations with numerals (Boysen and Berntson 1989). However, animals, it seems, are often imprecise about representing numerosities because they base their judgments on magnitude. Rather than using number to represent magnitude, the animal uses magnitude to represent number.

Gallistel (personal communication) defines this difference with the following analogy: Suppose you counted by scooping up a cup of water for each item in a set and by emptying each cup into a cylinder.

Each additional cup (each count) would increase the level of the water in the cylinder. The cardinality of the set is then represented by the level of the water, after you have emptied the last cup (the last count) into the cylinder. Pouring a cup into the cylinder is equivalent to incrementing the count by one or taking another step in the counting sequence. The cup is not, however, a counting tag paired with an item counted. It is levels of water in the cylinder that are paired with items counted in this counting process, not the number of cups. These counting steps lack the order-indifference principle; i.e., it is impossible to pour water into the cylinder starting from the middle and then filling each end. The process is inherently ordered. It is equivalent to having to count objects only from left to right and never from right to left or starting from one of the middle objects. The animal's procedure violates the order-indifference principle, to which children adhere. Magnitudes generated by such a counting process show quite a bit of variability. To continue the cup analogy: The variability stems from the fact that the animal occasionally omits to scoop up a cup for an item (miscounts) or scoops up too many cups (overcounts). Also, the animal may not be careful in filling the cup each time, so that there is variability from one cup to the next.

Preverbal representatives of numerosities in the human neonate and young infant are, according to Gallistel, magnitudes of the above type. They are the number-relevant predispositions which the infant brings to the learning task. This type of variability may explain why infants seem to be precise with respect to very small numbers (Strauss and Curtis 1981, 1984) but cannot discriminate larger ones. However, it is abundantly clear that the human child goes well beyond these initial capacities.

The RR Model and Number Representation in the Human Child

We have seen that we must attribute to the human infant some innately specified processes that are sensitive to number-relevant inputs in the environment. These processes generate procedures to deal with number problems and allow for the storage of number-relevant representations. But since such capacities may hold for certain other species too, they do not suffice to account for the subsequent specificity of number in human children. The RR model posits that the number-relevant information available to very young children (and to other species) is implicit in procedures for processing environmental input. In the case of the human, and only the human, components of that knowledge subsequently become explicitly defined and available as data. This requires a process of redescription such that information about principles of ordinality and one-to-one mapping become available in the E1 format. It is on the bases of these redescriptions that mathematical knowledge is subsequently built.

However rich the innate specifications turn out to be, and particularly when initially there are parallels across species, it is clear that we must focus on the *representational status* of such knowledge in order to understand the nature of subsequent development. We end up, as before, with the need to go beyond the innate specification and to invoke an integration of aspects of nativism and constructivism.

Chapter 5
The Child as a Psychologist

Here is what I would have done if I had been faced with this problem in designing Homo sapiens. *I would have made commonsense psychology innate; that way nobody would have to spend time learning it!* (Fodor 1987, p. 132)

Young children are spontaneous psychologists. They are interested in how the mind can have thoughts and theories and in how representations mediate between the mind and the world. In order to engage in human interaction, to predict others' behavior, to understand their intentions/beliefs/desires, to interpret their statements/gestures/actions, to understand irony, to interpret utterances or facial expressions that are discrepant from actual feelings, and so forth, each of us relies on commonsense psychology or on a folk theory that enables us to ascribe mental states to ourselves and to others (Lewis 1969; Stich 1983; Olson et al. 1988). In this chapter we shall see how young normal children, but not autistic individuals, come to share our basic metaphysics of mind.

Throughout the preceding chapters, I noted that recent research and theorizing have challenged the Piagetian position. Yet, in every case, some of the most fundamental issues involved were first raised by Piaget, even though his theoretical answers are, for many, no longer viable. This chapter is no exception. As early as 1926, Piaget published research on children's concepts of dreaming and the externalization of internal representations (see Piaget 1929). His 1932 work focused on children's concepts of belief, intention, and lies. These have become "hot" subjects in the past couple of decades under the general banner of the child's "theory of mind" (Dennett 1971, 1978; Premack and Woodruff 1978). The epistemological positions with respect to theory of mind are, with the exception of Fodor (1983, 1987) and some of his followers (Leslie 1987), somewhat closer to Piaget's domain-general constructivism (see Broughton 1978; Chandler and Boyes 1982; Flavell

1988) than recent developments in other cognitive domains. Yet not surprisingly, as in each of the preceding chapters, I shall end up by arguing in favor of an integration of aspects of nativism and constructivism in the theory-of-mind domain too.

The Piagetian View of the Child as a Psychologist

For Piaget, theory of mind develops late as part of a domain-general process. He held (1929) that under 7 years of age children do not distinguish clearly between the mental and the physical, and that they confound activities such as thinking and dreaming with externalized actions such as speaking and acting. Piaget called this "childhood realism", and for some time the view was accepted in the developmental literature as an accurate characterization of young children's theory (or, rather, lack of theory) of mind. These conceptions have since come under serious attack, both experimentally and theoretically. It has now been shown that 3-year-olds already make a clear distinction between the mental and physical domains (Carey 1985; Estes et al. 1990; Chandler and Boyes 1982). And even infants treat human behavior as involving intentional agents quite distinct from objects in the physical environment (Leslie 1984; Premack 1990).

The Domain-Specific View: Infancy Prerequisites to a Theory of Mind

If, contrary to the Piagetian position, one adopts a domain-specific view of development, then one can expect to find prerequisites to the development of a theory of mind in infancy. What might these be? First, to even begin to attribute mental states to other human beings, the infant must recognize conspecifics and their behavior.

What Conspecifics Look Like

Do newborn infants have innately specified structural information that enables them to recognize members of their own species? Or, as Piagetian theory would have it, does the neonate have to learn everything about the characteristics of human faces, voices, and movements and slowly differentiate these from objects in the world? This question has been recently explored with respect to the relationship between imprinting and face recognition (Johnson 1988, 1990a). Johnson and Morton (1991) carried out a series of experiments on neonates and young infants on the basis of hypotheses drawn from a two-process theory of species recognition and imprinting in the domestic chick (Horn and Johnson 1989; Johnson and Bolhuis 1991; Johnson et al.

1985; Johnson and Horn 1988). The experiments explored the extent
to which face recognition in the human newborn is innately specified
or learned. Infants tracked, by means of head and eye movements,
various two-dimensional stimuli on a head-shaped board. The stimuli
included a face with normal configuration of eyes, nose, and mouth,
a "face" with three high-contrast blobs in the positions of the eyes and
the mouth, a "face" with the features scrambled, and the contour of
a face with a checkered pattern of optimal spatial frequency inside.
These are illustrated in figure 5.1. The details of these studies need
not concern us here.[1] But the conclusion is clear: neonates preferentially attend to stimuli with a face-like arrangement of elements. This
suggests that, at birth, infants possess some innately specified structural information about human faces. This does not preclude the need
for subsequent learning, however. On the basis of his work on chick
imprinting, Johnson (1990a, 1990b) proposes that specific subcortical
mechanisms particularly attentive to human faces ensure proprietary
input to cortical circuits, which rapidly become specialized.[2] This is
made possible by the huge amount of exposure to human faces that
the neonate and the young infant experience. The Johnson and Morton
theory posits two systems. The first is an orienting mechanism
("CONSPEC") functioning at birth and primarily mediated by subcortical
circuits. The other depends on a cortical mechanism ("CONLERN")
which gains control of behavior around 2 months and is "tutored" by
CONSPEC. In this way the infant's human-face recognition becomes
domain specific and progressively modularized and is no longer part
of general visuospatial recognition processes.

The fact that infants attend preferentially to faces at birth is important for their subsequent development of a theory of mind. Conspecifics and their behavior are of special interest to the infant mind, and
thus infants and toddlers pay particular attention to the range of
human behaviors: speech, gait, interactional patterns, and so forth.

Faces are not the only environmental cue to conspecific recognition.
For instance (as was discussed in chapter 3), infants are also sensitive

Figure 5.1
Face-recognition stimuli. (After Johnson and Morton 1991. Reprinted with permission
of the authors.)

to distinctions between animate and inanimate movement. They are particularly attentive to human movement. Premack (1990) argues that the infant is born with two innately specified predicates: a causal predicate, which constrains the perception of non-self-propelled objects, and an intentional predicate, which constrains the perception of self-propelled motion of biological beings (i.e., of agents capable of self-movement). Likewise, the research on the animate/inanimate distinction by Massey and Gelman (1988) showed that young children use potential movement as the basis for discriminating between photographs of animates and inanimates that they have not encountered before.

Aside from visual recognition of conspecifics, young infants also attend preferentially to human auditory input. We know from the work discussed in chapter 2 that at birth infants attend preferentially to human speech over other auditory input, and that by 4 days they distinguish certain properties of their mother tongue from those of other languages. Furthermore, later in development, when given a choice between two sources of sound that they can control by manipulating the buttons on two boxes, the 3–4-year-old prefers to listen to her mother's voice over other background noise in a canteen (Klin 1988, 1991). Interestingly, no such preference is shown by autistic children, who have deficiencies in the theory-of-mind domain. This suggests that preferential attention to human behavior is one prerequisite for the development of a theory of mind.

From birth, young infants process information about the human environment and information about the physical environment in different ways. This leads to the development of a theory of mind as distinct from a theory of physical phenomena. Whereas Piaget argued that it is only around age 7 that children differentiate the mental/biological from the physical/mechanical, Carey (1985), Brown (1990), and others now consider this fundamental distinction to be an innately guided process. This is Fodor's argument, too. He maintains (1987, p. 132) that the patterns of social interaction and attribution of intention manifest in our species (and others) could not have evolved without an innate component. For Fodor, this involves in the human case a biologically specified module for commonsense psychology (see also Leslie 1990). For the position I have been defending here, if commonsense psychology is modular, it can be thought of as a gradual process of *modularization* built up from these more basic attention biases which influence the storing of theory of mind-relevant representations.

All the recent empirical data and theoretical arguments point to a similar conclusion: Piaget was wrong in positing that the distinction between the mental and the physical does not occur consistently before age 7. Well before that age, the infant attends differentially to the mechanical and human worlds.[3] The infant comes to understand others as *subjects* (i.e. agents capable of self-initiated action), not, as Piaget argued, as "objects amongst other objects" (1952b).

As we shall see later in this chapter, autistic children do not develop a normal theory of mind. But this does not mean that they necessarily show any abnormalities in early face, voice, and movement *recognition*. However, they may not manifest *preferential* interest in such stimuli and treat them as equivalent to other objects in the physical environment. Recognition of conspecifics may start off quite normally in the autistic individual, but recognition of *intention* in the behavior of conspecifics and their *interactions* may be faulty or absent.[4]

How Conspecifics Interact

So far we've seen that faces, voices, and movements contribute to the infant's sensitivity to humans as special in the environment. These particular attention biases allow the infant to build representations that are prerequisites to the development of a theory of mind. But does social interaction play a formative role in the development of a theory of mind? Interaction has often been given a major explanatory role in language acquisition (Bruner 1975). The social-interaction approach to language came under heavy criticism from nativists. However, sensitivity to species-specific interaction patterns may, as Tager-Flusberg (1989) has suggested, turn out to be essential in another aspect of child development: the development of a theory of mind by the prelinguistic infant.

What aspects of early interaction could be involved? Mutual eye gaze and pointing to a specific referent (the "ostensive communication" discussed in chapter 2[5]) are nonlinguistic means of communicating by directing the attention of the addressee to something of interest. Slowly infants become capable of joint attention via eye contact. Note the term "joint attention"—eye contact alone can be much like attending to inanimate objects. Progressively, infants make use of gaze alternation (between the caretaker's eyes and a coveted object) to signal to the caretaker that they wish to obtain the object. It is the coordination between eye contact and pointing gesture that leads to ostensive communication (Butterworth 1991). Again, several studies indicate that autistic children are deficient in such coordination of eye contact and gesture (Dawson et al. 1990; Sigman et al. 1986; Mundy and Sigman 1989).

What are the functions of the early ostensive communications in the human infant? They are of two types: "proto-imperatives" and "proto-declaratives" (Bruner 1974–75; Baron-Cohen 1989b). Proto-impera-tives involve the use of pointing or eye gaze as the infant's means of trying to obtain an object by directing a nonverbal request at an inter-locutor who can reach the object for the child. If humans were mobile at birth, as many species are, the human infant would get the object herself or push the adult toward it. But its immobility forces the young infant to find other, *interactional* means of reaching certain goals. The pointing gestures therefore start out as instrumental requests (some-thing like "I want that toy").

However, these proto-imperatives rapidly become proto-declara-tives; that is, a point becomes the infant's means of making a nonverbal comment about the state of the world (something like "Look, that's a nice toy") rather than a request to obtain it. Of interest, again, is Baron-Cohen's (1989b) work showing that proto-declarative pointing to affect another's *attention* or *mental state* is neither used nor under-stood by autistic children; their competence is limited to proto-imper-ative pointing to affect another's *behavior.*

At numerous times throughout the book I have placed a great deal of emphasis on change provoked endogenously via maturation and representational redescription. I have stressed the role of the environ-ment in the epigenetic interaction between mind and input. But this is the first chapter in which I have anything to say about the socio-cultural environment. This is partly because a number of develop-mental theories, particularly as explanations of language acquisition,[6] have in my view given too much weight to social interaction at the cost of neglecting important endogenous factors. My stress on endog-enous factors in the RR model has been an attempt to redress that imbalance. Yet there are many different influences on development, and the child's sociocultural environment is an important one (Bates et al. 1979; Butterworth 1981; Bruner 1978; Cole 1989; Cole and Scribner 1974; Trevarthen 1987; Vygotsky 1962).

We need, of course, to distinguish between the role of culture in imparting new knowledge to children and the role of sociocultural interaction patterns in general. Theory-of-mind computations are not taught to the child. They develop spontaneously and unconsciously at first. But it is possible that social interaction plays a greater role in the theory-of-mind area than in any of the other areas, including language. There are several aspects of the child's commonsense psy-chology in which the knowledge is initially in the structure of the infant's interaction with conspecifics, rather than solely in the child's perception and representation of the world. Some recent work on infants' understanding and production of teasing and humor illus-trates this point nicely.

Reddy (1991) has made an extensive study of young infants' participation in humorous interactions with their caretakers. She claims that humor develops from a violation of expectation of the canonical outcome of an interactive event such as giving and taking. Of course, one can have a perception of violation that has nothing to do with humor (e.g. a violation of a physical principle, as we saw in chapter 3). But the creation of humor is not solitary. It is embedded in social interaction. Reddy shows that infants perceive events as humorous very early on. By 7–9 months, infants notice that in certain cases a behavior with a different goal happens to provoke a humorous interpretation by the adult, and they subsequently repeat the behavior only with humorous intent.

Take the following example from Reddy's observational data. An 11-month-old infant notices her great-grandmother snoring audibly with open mouth. The infant tries to imitate this, but draws her mouth to a small O-shape. The adults present laugh at this. Now, the infant's original intention was probably to understand the event by imitating it. Piaget has shown imitation to be a powerful device that young children use to explore their environments. But the adults' laughter lends to the infant's action a new and different interpretation. The infant notes this, laughs herself, and subsequently (for several days) reproduces the O-shaped mouth in interactive settings, now with the sole intention of producing humor. However, the adults' laughter is initially an essential component of the infant's representation of humor.

Reddy asserts that if we consider only the individual mind, as many cognitive developmentalists do, then knowledge about teasing and humor must be seen to exist *either* in the infant mind *or* outside it in the adult mind or the situation. However, if one sees the infant's mind also as part of an interactional context, as Reddy contends we must, then in some situations the child stores only one part of the knowledge and is crucially dependent on the total interactional framework (the child's representation, the actual event, the adult's laughter, and the adult's representation) in which the full knowledge is situated *between* minds. Here Reddy is grappling with a deep intuition that may well be true of early moments of knowledge acquisition. But my position is that, ultimately, knowledge *is* represented in individual minds. In infants' early generation of humor we have a particularly nice example of how epigenesis might work at the psychological level, in that the adult's external laughter serves as a crucial input to change and complete the child's representation, and is gradually incorporated into the child's internal representation to subsequently mark the humor explicitly.

Theory of Mind in Nonhuman Species

Earlier I discussed the distinction between affecting others' behavior and affecting their mental states. This distinction is clearly relevant to whether we attribute a theory-of-mind capacity to nonhuman species. Many species can do things to affect their conspecifics' behavior. In a discussion of the status of the notion of deception in other species, Premack (1988, pp. 161–162) provides a nice example. The plover, he notes,

> will fly from its nest to lead a potential intruder away from its fledglings; but it will not employ a comparable tactic in leading a competitor away from food, from a receptive mate, a piece of potential nesting material etc. In the plover, "deception" is an innate disposition restricted solely to protection of the young. Like other innate dispositions, it can be modified by learning. For example the bird can learn to distinguish the pseudo-intruder (who merely circumnavigates the nest) from the serious one (who heads directly for the nest), no longer bothering even to "deceive" the former, while steadfastly continuing to "deceive" the latter [Ristau 1988]. However, this does not change the fact that the bird's "deception" is an inflexible device that cannot be applied to any target except protection of the young. The bird is analogous to a human who could tell lies only about pilfering fudge; he could not tell lies about dirtying the carpet, breaking the lamp, taking money from his mother's purse, or about lying itself. We would look closely at such a "person", wondering whether it was a child or a robot.

The plover, then, can affect another's behavior by employing a procedure that at first blush looks like deceit. But the procedure is not applied outside the context for which it is genetically specified. Deceit in humans, by contrast, is not only aimed at affecting another's behavior in a multitude of situations; above all, it involves deliberately affecting another's mental states. However, the plover has only a bird brain! What about our close cousin, the chimpanzee?

Can it be shown that the chimpanzee can attribute mental states to others, given a carefully designed opportunity to display it? Via a series of ingenious experiments, Premack and Woodruff (1978) attempted to find out whether the chimpanzee has a theory of mind. Their results demonstrated that language-trained chimpanzees could generate intentional behaviors and establish a causal link between others' goals and their own actions but failed to attribute mental states to others and to represent the distinction between their own knowledge and knowledge of the other's different mental state. The chimpanzee does not go beyond trying to affect what another *does*; it does not try to affect what another *believes*. For Premack, one can attribute a theory of mind only to a species that does the latter.

Premack also carried out a series of experiments to see if chimpanzees understand deceit. He trained them to react differently to an experimenter who was generous and one who was not. The chimpanzee seemed to be able to use something like deceit in that she indicated the wrong hiding place to the experimenter who had been unkind. However, it turned out that deceit in the chimpanzee did not extend outside the experimental room. The animal had learned task-relevant sabotage that affected the behavior of others, but did not have a general capacity for deceit that affects the beliefs of others. Premack concludes that the capacity of the chimpanzee to engage in common-sense psychology is true only in the weakest of senses of a theory of mind.[7]

However, there are more naturalistic settings where one might want to impute more complex capacities to the chimpanzee. For example, what about the chimpanzee who suppresses his sexual cry? Does he do this to affect the beliefs of rival males so that they *think* he is doing something else, or merely to affect what they *do* (not attack him and compete for the female)? Premack (1991) argues that it is likely to be the latter, since the chimpanzee will have established a link between the sexual cry and the fact that competing male chimps will arrive on the scene. The suppression of the sexual cry does not have to be interpreted as a procedure for affecting the beliefs of other chimpanzees; it can be accounted for in terms of affecting their contingent behavior.

Gomez (1991) asked similar questions about the capacities of gorillas. He demonstrated that gorillas reared in a human environment understand that looking at others' eyes is a means of controlling attentional contact. They check that a human interlocutor is attending to the same goal as they are. Establishing joint attention to a goal (e.g. by checking that the other's gaze is directed to the same target) is equivalent to making sure that a stick is touching an object when one is using it as a tool to move the object. So joint attention to a goal does not necessarily imply imputing mental states to other minds. Rather, it can be considered as part of a causal link in an interactional process, because it involves understanding that attending to an object or an event is causally linked to others' subsequent actions with respect to that object or event. Joint attention to a goal is a kind of causality based, not on the transmission of mechanical forces through physical contact, but on the transmission of information by mental contact.

This allows the human infant, the gorilla, the chimpanzee, and perhaps the domestic cat, dog, and parrot (for readers who are still convinced their pet has a theory of mind!) to use proto-imperatives. But the use of proto-declaratives requires something more: a representational stance with respect to reality, in which the goal is to affect another's attention and/or thoughts rather than another's behavior.

Neither communication, interaction, social responsiveness, nor the understanding of others as agents suffices alone to account for the development of a theory of mind. They do help to ensure appropriate input to developing systems, but more is required. Humans, like a number of other species, are good ethologists—they recognize individuals, groups, and species, and they know who their conspecifics are and how to manipulate their behavior in interactional contexts. But with development humans become able to generate hypotheses about *why* their conspecifics behave and speak the way they do. From good ethologists, then, human children spontaneously go on to become good psychologists. And to do so, they need to represent the distinction between what the philosophy-of-mind literature calls "propositional attitudes" and "propositional contents."[8]

What Is Special about Theory-of-Mind Computations?

Although Piaget argued for domain-general processes, a number of developmentalists working in the theory-of-mind domain hold that there is something special about computations involving beliefs, desires, deceptions, intentions, and the like, in that they involve propositional attitudes toward propositional contents. A statement such as "There is a pencil on the table" has a propositional content which is either a true or false description of the world. By contrast, a statement such as "I BELIEVE that there is a pencil on the table" involves a propositional attitude (belief) toward that propositional content. Other propositional attitudes are expressed by mental-state verbs, such as "think", "hope", "claim", "pretend", "remember", and "know". Propositional contents express a true (or false) fact about the current state of the world (e.g., the existence of a pencil on the table). However, when the content is preceded by certain propositional attitudes (e.g. believe, think, hope, claim, pretend), then whether or not there is actually a pencil on the table is irrelevant to the truth value of the statement. There may actually be no pencil on the table, but I can still express the belief that there is one. So propositional contents describe (correctly or incorrectly) states of the world, whereas propositional attitudes express a mental state with respect to the world and do not necessarily entail the truth of the propositional contents on which they operate.[9] Mental-state verbs enable speakers to express the particular attitudes that they are taking toward particular contexts. In French, this is nicely differentiated in two forms for which English uses the single word "utterance". The French lexicon makes a contrast between "énoncé" (the utterance, with its propositional content) and "énonciation" (the act or process of uttering, with its propositional attitude).

In sum: Theory-of-mind computations are special in that it is difficult to find another area of human cognition in which the distinction between propositional contents and propositional attitudes is a crucial component. While language has an essential interactional component, it could function without the expression of propositional attitudes, although in a very impoverished way. It would simply express propositional contents and not the speaker's stance relative to them. The theory-of-mind domain involves, by its very nature, understanding the mental states of other minds—that is what is implied by the title of this chapter ("the child as a psychologist"). Theory-of-mind mechanisms and the types of representations that they generate may turn out to be domain specific par excellence.

The Toddler's Theory of Mind

Leslie has made a number of interesting suggestions about the beginnings of theory of mind in prelinguistic toddlers. Leslie (1987) uses notions identical to some found in the propositional-attitude literature,[10] but he calls them interchangeably "second order representations" or "meta-representations". The particularly interesting aspect of Leslie's theory is that it situates metarepresentational competence outside the realm of the *linguistic* encoding of mental-state verbs (such as "think", "believe", and "pretend"), and places it in the realm of *pretend play*—available to children as young as 18 months. Leslie argues that children's pretend play, verbal or not, involves the same distinction between propositional content and propositional attitude (though he uses different terminology) that is found in the subsequent use of mental-state verbs. In other words, he sees pretend play as the first nonlinguistic behavioral manifestation of the underlying structure of the toddler's theory of mind. He argues that all the psychological structures of pretense are innately specified, so that when the child is first exposed to examples of pretense she can immediately interpret it. Later in the chapter, I shall take a somewhat different position, since the constraints on pretense are only gradually relaxed.[11]

Leslie suggests that the structure of young children's pretend play should be understood as the computation of a three-term relation among an agent (usually the child herself), a primary representation (the actual objects being played with), and a decoupled, secondary representation of the content of the pretense. This contrasts sharply with Piaget's arguments that young children represent events as "schemes" in which agent, event, and object form an undifferentiated amalgam. For Leslie, it is the notion of a decoupled representation that is specific to theory of mind.[12] The decoupling allows the child to treat the pretend content separately from the normal relations that the representation of the real object or event entertains. Thus, when a 3-year-old picks up a block of wood and declares "Right, this is the car, vroom, vroom, vroom, toot, toot!", the pretend computation involves PRETEND [(Agent = child)(Primary Representation = a mental structure representing the fact that the object on the table is a block of wood)(Decoupled Representation = a copy of the previous mental structure but cordoned off from veridical descriptions and standing for "the car")]. The primary and decoupled representations involve different and separate levels of processing and obey distinct causal and logical inferential constraints. Thus, pretending that a simple block of wood has a steering wheel, a horn, and four wheels in no way detracts from toddlers' understanding of the real properties of the block of wood and of real cars, nor does it change their representations of such properties. It is the decoupled (temporary) representation that is "tampered" with—not the primary representations, which continue to entertain their normal representational relationships. And the decoupled representation involves a distinction between a propositional attitude and a propositional content: [I pretend that] [this block of wood] [it is a car]. As with our earlier example of the pencil on the table, it is irrelevant to the truth value of the resulting statement of the propositional attitude PRETEND (and of BELIEVE, THINK, CLAIM, etc.) that the block of wood is not actually a car. Some propositional attitudes (e.g. KNOW, REMEMBER) do, of course, entail the truth of their propositional contents.

Leslie situates the onset of the ability to pretend somewhere between 18 and 24 months of age—exactly the time at which Piaget maintained that the symbolic function (which includes pretend play, but also the onset of language, mental imagery, and deferred imitation) starts to become part of the toddler's cognitive competence. For Piaget these are domain-general developments resulting from the culmination of sensorimotor intelligence. Olson et al. (1988) also suggest that the onset of a more general symbolic capacity may be an important element in the 18-month-old's development of a theory of mind—a position close to Piaget's. For Leslie, however, the propositional attitudes underlying the structure of pretend play are modular. Leslie

(1987; 1990) posits the onset at 18 months of a metarepresentational module which is genetically coded and triggered by maturation in the brain. It is this static nativist stance involving genetic coding rather than epigenetic change, eloquently expressed by Fodor in the epigraph at the beginning of this chapter, that I have challenged throughout the book. Theory of mind does not have to be a genetically specified, encapsulated module as Leslie argues. It is true that *some* genetically specified predispositions are likely to be involved, but such a claim should not automatically negate the *epigenetic* influence of the socio-cultural environment on the development of the child's theory of mind. Furthermore, although theory-of-mind computations may end up being domain specific, this does not necessarily mean that they form a module in the full Fodorian sense of the term, although pro-gressive modularization may occur.

Is Language Essential for Distinguishing Propositional Attitudes from Propositional Contents?

In most analyses, the language of mental-state verbs is an essential component of propositional attitudes. However, we have just seen how Leslie posits language to be unnecessary for the propositional structure of pretend play. Premack (1988) has also argued that lan-guage is not a necessary condition for theory-of-mind computations, although he suggests that it amplifies subsequent possibilities. There is in fact an intimate relationship between the subsequent develop-ment of theory of mind and language. Gerhart (1988) has shown that once children become more sophisticated linguistically, they use dif-ferent linguistic markers within pretend play than for their nonpretend comments on the play. And many languages make special use of temporal markers for pretend play. In French, for example, the child uses the imperfect past tense to set up present pretend play: "Toi tu étais la maman, et moi j'étais le bébé" (You were [are] the mummy and I was [am] the baby"). Of course, as Piaget stressed (1951), pretend play is usually contemporaneous with the onset of language, but Leslie's point is that *complex* linguistic constructions involving mental-state verbs appear much later than the equivalent structural complex-ities of pretend play. Pretense can be described with the same prop-ositional structure that underlies mental-state verbs. It is in these crucial ways that the structure of pretend play differs from that of normal functional play, which is to be found in the infant prior to 18 months and in many other species. Clearly, then, the use of complex mental-state verbs is not essential to the onset of theory-of-mind computations.

Although language is not necessary for early manifestations of propositional attitudes, it is subsequently intimately related to the development of theory of mind. The RR model posits that it is not the language capacity per se that explains development, but rather the redescriptive processes which allow for re-representation of knowledge in different (often linguistic) representational formats. However, the theory-of-mind domain may be one area where the translation into natural-language terms (e.g., the use of mental-state verbs such as "pretend that", "think that", "believe that", and "know that") is an essential part of the redescriptive process. Work on autistic individuals' capacity to distinguish between knowing and guessing in themselves and others (Kazak et al. 1991) indicates that it is highly correlated with their level of language ability. Furthermore, Zaitchik (1991) has shown that if 3-year-olds, who fail traditional theory-of-mind tasks, are merely *told* about the true location of an object, but do not actually see it being hidden, they are able to predict that a story character who holds a false belief will look in the location where he thinks the object is rather than where the child knows it to be.[13] But, interestingly, the opposite case also exists. Norris and Millan (1991) have recently shown that children of 4 who have no difficulties with a traditional theory-of-mind task, which is both visual and verbal, have considerable problems with a totally nonverbal version of the same task presented on film. These different results suggest that when a domain is represented preferentially in a given representational format (e.g., the linguistic encoding of mental-state verbs), and when the environment provides direct input in that format (as in Zaitchik's study), children can set up privileged representations. Language, then, may not be necessary for the beginnings of a theory of mind. But language and multiple representations are very important for subsequent development.

The Child's Developing Belief/Desire Psychology

Propositional attitudes in pretend play involve attributing counterfactual identities, emotions, and events to the self, to pretend playmates, and to objects: "Right, I'm the mother, you're the baby, and you're crying because we're going too fast in this car." But beyond these early competences in toddlers, the propositional contents and attitudes that older children can express and understand become more complex. Baron-Cohen (1991) has shown that PRETEND and WANT are simpler propositional attitudes than BELIEVE. Indeed, each may have its own initial developmental path. Children may also be able to express more complex propositional contents when using the propositional attitude PRETEND. This is likely to be the case, because 3-year-olds have a lot of difficulty dealing with quite simple propositional contents that involve false belief.

Consider the following experimental setup for testing false belief, based on seminal work by Wimmer and Perner (1983): The child watches a scene in which the experimenter and a boy called Maxi are in a room together. The experimenter hides a piece of chocolate under a box in front of Maxi. Maxi then leaves the room momentarily, and while he is absent the experimenter moves the chocolate to another hiding place. The child is then asked where the chocolate really is and, crucially for the task, where Maxi will look for it upon his return. In other words, the child has to distinguish between what she knows to be true of the current state of the world and what she knows to be Maxi's current mental state. She also has to know that Maxi's behavior will be a function of his *internal representations*, not of the external reality.

Another typical theory-of-mind experiment, designed by Perner et al. (1987), involves showing the child a Smarties container and asking the child what is inside. The child typically replies "Smarties." The child is next shown that the typical candy tube actually contains a pencil. She is then asked what her classmate, who has not yet seen the actual contents, will respond when asked what is in the tube. The response can either be based (incorrectly) on the current state of the world or (correctly) on the current belief state of the classmate.

These are simple yet stringent tests of the child's ability to impute mental states with content to others. Children of age 3 fail both of the above tasks and claim that the protagonist will behave in accordance with the real-world situation. They do not understand that he will behave on the basis of his false belief. But 4-year-olds are successful. The minimal criterion for possessing a theory of mind is, according to Dennett (1971), successfully dealing with circumstances in which an individual cannot rely on her own knowledge in order to assess another's mental state. In our first example, the child holds a true belief about the new hiding place of the chocolate. However, Maxi entertains a false belief. He will act on the basis of his false belief and thus look in the box where the chocolate was, and not where the child knows it to be now. To answer correctly the question of where Maxi will look for the chocolate, the child must know that others have thoughts and beliefs, true or false depending on their current knowledge, and that they act on the basis of their mental states rather than the real-world situation. The child also has to keep the representations of her own belief about the current state of the world separate from that of the deceived protagonist's false belief. She has to differentiate between propositional attitudes (Maxi believes that the chocolate is . . .) and propositional contents (the present location of the chocolate is . . .). At the age of 3, children assign a single truth value to a veridical description of the current state of the external world and expect Maxi to act on the basis of the same veridical description. At 4, they can hold in mind the representations of both the veridical description and the protagonist's false belief in the form of a propositional attitude operating over a propositional content.

The RR Model and Changes in Children's Theory of Mind

As was mentioned above, Leslie argues that the propositional-attitude stance is available to 18-month-olds in the structure of the representations sustaining their pretend play. There is nothing in his theory, however, to explain why the propositional-attitude stance that allows for PRETEND is not also available to 3-year-olds in their inferences concerning BELIEVE and THINK. Leslie's theory of pretense does not address the question of how information about agents, objects, and events becomes data structures (i.e., explicitly defined representations over which propositional attitudes can operate). One solution to this problem, in the form of representational redescription of perceptual input into image schemas was discussed above in chapter 2.

It is worth speculating on how the RR model might help in explaining the developmental progression of theory of mind. The RR model argues that, in order for components of a procedure to be manipulable, the procedure must have first reached behavioral mastery. Only then can its components be redescribed in the E1 format. Pretend play involves the violation of veridical descriptions of reality as well as the manipulation of *explicit* representations of agents, primary representations of play objects, and decoupled representations of those objects in their pretend roles. According to the RR model, this requires (first) behavioral mastery over veridical representations of reality and (subsequently) re-representations at level E1 or higher. However, young children also often announce linguistically their intention to pretend: "I pretending!" At first blush, this would suggest that they have already represented in explicit form (E2/3 format) the distinction between propositional attitudes and propositional contents. Yet, if this were so, why would 3-year-olds fail to use such distinctions in false-belief tasks? It is plausible that the 2–3-year-old can deal with the propositional attitude PRETEND more easily, not because she already uses level E2/3 representations, but because it involves *observable externalized marking* (change of voice, change of intonation contour, exaggerated movements, laughter, etc.), which keeps the distinction salient in her mind. Recall that in earlier chapters, particularly chapter 2, we saw how children mark externally in their productions distinctions to which they have become sensitive. According to the RR model, this requires the E1 format. And Gerhart (1988) has shown that children use different linguistic markers and intonation patterns in pretend play than in their nonpretend comments on the play. In other words, they mark and sustain *externally* the internal distinction with which they are operating.

Thus, although toddlers may announce "I'm pretending", and although they must have E1 representations of the three terms of the pretense computation (agent, primary representation, decoupled representation) over which the propositional attitude PRETEND can operate, the distinction between propositional attitudes and propositional contents does not have to be represented in the E2/3 format and thus be available to conscious access. It does have to be available as a data structure in the E1 format, though. The 4-year-old subsequently comes to grips with the fact that nonobservable (non-externally-marked) propositional attitudes, such as BELIEVE and THINK, are predictors of a protagonist's behavior rather than observable states of the world. When 4-year-olds can make successful inferences on the basis of another's false belief, they are able to justify this in verbal reports. This necessitates the E2/3 format.

Numerous authors have now shown that by age 4 children distinguish explicitly between propositional contents and propositional attitudes. They can justify how they themselves can hold true or false beliefs that can change, and how others can hold beliefs different from their own and act in accordance with those beliefs (Gopnik and Astington 1988). They grasp the active role of the mind in fixing belief (Chandler and Boyes 1982; Wellman 1988) and the representational nature of belief (Perner 1991; Olson 1988; Flavell 1988; Forguson and Gopnik 1988; Astington 1989). They are able to predict other's actions predicated on false beliefs (Perner et al. 1987; Wimmer and Perner 1983) and recall the sources of their own beliefs (Gopnik and Astington 1988; Gopnik and Graf 1988; Wimmer et al. 1988). They can call the information given into question rather than respond automatically. They recognize appearances discrepant from reality, intentions discrepant from action, facial expressions discrepant from feelings, and how point of view and perception influence belief formation (Flavell et al. 1981; Olson et al. 1988). This impressive array of abilities suggests that from age 4 on, the distinction between propositional attitudes and propositional contents is explicitly represented in the E2/3 format.

Should Theory of Mind Be Set in a Broader, Domain-General Context?

So far, I have argued that theory of mind involves domain-specific computations distinguishing propositional attitudes from the propositional contents over which they operate, stored at different levels of explicitness. Perner, one of the pioneers in the theory-of-mind domain, posits a more general change in metacognitive abilities at around 4 years whereby children come to understand explicitly that it is internal representations that mediate between the mind (their own and others') and the world (Perner 1988, 1991).

Perner postulates three steps in the child's development of commonsense psychology. First, the infant has at its disposal an innate sensitivity to the behavioral expressions of mental states (expressions of happiness, sadness, anger, and so forth in the eyes, faces, and body postures of conspecifics). Perner contends that a sensitivity to the *behavioral* expressions of mental states during early infancy does not require the attribution of internal mental states but only veridical descriptions of the behavioral state of conspecifics. He maintains that at this first level infants only represent observable behavior but that they are capable of changing these representations via a "single updating model."[14] That model allows infants to attend to and represent changes in the behavioral expressions in others' and their own inner experiences of pleasure, sadness, anger, etc. At this first level, then, the infant understands only the external behavioral expressions of emotional states, not their status as internal mental states.

The second level of commonsense psychology involves for Perner the young child's understanding of mental states as relations to real-world and hypothetical situations rather than simply to behavior. This, according to Perner, results in the child's moving from a "behavioral theory of emotional states" to a "mentalist theory of behavior." Rather than a single veridical description of reality, at this point children have at their disposal multiple alternative models of the same reality, which they can hold simultaneously in short-term memory.[15] For Perner, multiple models involve the establishment of a relationship between two propositional contents, but not yet between a propositional content and a propositional attitude. Perner et al. (1987) explain the counterfactual nature of pretense without invoking propositional attitudes. They claim that the establishment of a relationship between two propositional contents suffices to explain pretense: one propositional content describing the real situation and the other describing the imagined (nonveridical) situation, both of which operate on the same level. These alternative models are kept in short-term memory and used to evaluate the real situation. Different protagonists (real and imagined) are mapped selectively to the situation described by each of the alternative models and thereby kept apart.

However, according to Perner, entertaining alternative models is not sufficient for an understanding of the distinction between "I think that the cup has tea in it" (a belief involving a propositional attitude) and "I think of the cup having tea in it" (a pretend thought only involving propositional contents). Perner's point is not that 2–3-year-olds are solely reality-based. Rather, it is that they understand the differences between (e.g.) "think", "want", "pretend", and "hate" by virtue of alternative models of how these words make people act differently. Recall Leslie's rather different formulation that pretense, like belief, involves two distinct levels obeying separate inferential and causal principles: the level of a propositional attitude (PRETEND/BELIEVE that) and the lower level of the propositional content X. But Perner contends that multiple models at the same level of propositional contents suffice to explain the child's understanding of pretense and also to explain a number of other contemporaneous developments: invisible displacements, mirror image of self, and empathy. This involves for Perner, then, a domain-general change, not a change specific to the theory-of-mind domain. Likewise, for Perner 3-year-olds try to deal with false-belief problems by holding simultaneously in memory the actually perceived situation and the situation described by the false sentence, and then looking at the mismatch between two propositional contents. To understand false belief properly, however, requires more than the assignment of standard truth values because a false belief is characterized not only by its being false but also by the fact that the holder of the belief deems it to be true. This more complex computation is what is required by a propositional attitude—which is why, according to Perner, it is not available before age 4.

A third level comes into play, at age 4, when children are able to make use of what Perner calls "meta-models." These models involve metarepresentation, and are necessary for understanding a number of contemporaneous developments: false belief, misrepresentation, and the fact that mental states are internal representations. Perner claims that it is at this point that the child first comes to distinguish propositional attitudes and propositional contents. For Perner, at 4 children reach an understanding of the very nature of representations; that is, the child learns that a past belief is her *representation* of the world at that time, even if the past model misrepresented the world. Thus the child finally builds a "representational theory of mind" which can be applied to her reasoning about both commonsense psychology and the physical world. The 4-year-old knows that people act, not according to alternative factual and counterfactual situations, but according to their *mental representations* of situations. She also knows that her perception of objects is a function of the distinction between appearances and reality. Perner holds that although children may develop a concept of representation by the age of 3, it is not till they are at least 4 that they incorporate their concept of representation into their theory of mind and thereby understand false belief. Perner sees these developments as parts of a broader, domain-general change with respect to the capacity for metarepresentation, rather than a domain-specific change in the capacity to use and understand propositional attitudes.[16]

So both Perner and Leslie claim that a fundamental change occurs at around 18 months. For Leslie this involves a new mechanism allowing for new representations: propositional attitudes. For Perner, no new representational power is yet invoked; rather, Perner argues for more computational power, in that alternative models of the world can now be held simultaneously in short-term memory and mapped onto different elements in normal and pretend play. For Leslie the mechanisms available at 18 months for pretend are the same as those used at 4 in false-belief tasks. Perner, by contrast, invokes a second fundamental change at 4 years that enables the child to represent representations (i.e., create metarepresentations), and thereby to use, inter alia, propositional attitudes. Neither author discusses the issue of how representations become progressively explicit, which I addressed via the RR model in a previous section.

There is, in my view, something right in these different theories. Baron-Cohen (1989a, 1991b) is right to situate the beginnings of a theory of mind in the proto-declaratives of early infancy, and Leslie is correct to keep the two levels of processing separate not only for belief but also for pretend play (since both seem to involve the operation of propositional attitudes over propositional contents). It is this important distinction that makes theory-of-mind computations highly specific and not part of a domain-general development of representation in general. The distinction between propositional contents and propositional attitudes is, I submit, a classic case of domain specificity. But, in contrast to Leslie, Perner is right to focus on possible changes around 4 years in this domain and to see theory of mind as ultimately incorporating a causal theory of knowledge[17] rather than solely focusing on the extension of the same structure available in pretend play at 18 months to the understanding of false belief at 4 years.

Furthermore, within the framework of the RR model, I argue that the general process of representational redescription operates on the domain-specific representations of theory-of-mind proto-declaratives, just as it does in other domains of cognition, to turn them into data structures available to other processes (such as propositional-attitude operators). And at each level of redescription, the development of an explicit theory of mind can call on other parts of the cognitive system, while automatic theory-of-mind computations can continue to operate domain-specifically. But domain-specific theory-of-mind computations interact with processes that are relevant to all domains: e.g., marking representations temporarily (state of the world at time 1/ belief at time 1, different state of the world at time 2/belief at time 2, etc.),[18] or building representations that can be held in mind for a few seconds for later processing without being affected by other ongoing processing of the input.[19] Thus, false belief does not only involve creating representations that sustain propositional attitudes; it also involves maintaining such representations in short-term memory and marking their time relationships.

Is Theory of Mind Just Like Any Other Theory-Building Process?

The distinction Perner draws between the 3-year-old's mentalist theory of behavior and the 4-year-old's representational theory of mind stresses an important point absent from Leslie's formulations: that theory-of-mind computations subsequently incorporate a more general metarepresentational stance that goes beyond the propositional attitudes peculiar to theory of mind and incorporates a causal theory of knowledge. Leslie argues that metarepresentation is specific to theory-of-mind computations only and, together with Frith, has sought in the autistic individual's deficit in the theory-of-mind domain a substantiation of this, by attempting to demonstrate that the specific deficit in autism is the lack of the capacity for metarepresentation (Leslie and Frith 1987). Leslie suggests that all other computations take place on the basis of primary representations.

However, many see metarepresentation as a more domain-general capacity. Moreover, Frith suggests that, even in the autistic case, a more general deficit is probably also involved.[20] What, in fact, autistic individuals seem to lack specifically is not a general capacity for metarepresentation, but the specific capacity to set up representations sustaining propositional-attitude structures specific to the theory-of-mind domain. It is the propositional-attitude stance that leads to an understanding of what is specifically mental about human intentionality—what speakers intend, rather than merely the words they use (Sperber and Wilson 1986). Autistic individuals tend to take language literally rather than understanding the pragmatics of intentionality (Frith 1989). They respond "Yes" to "Can you pass the salt" instead of seeing an indirect request for the salt to be passed. But the deficit does not necessarily imply a general lack of a metarepresentational capacity. Nothing in our discussion of children's building of theories about language, mathematics, and physics involved propositional attitudes. They are a domain-specific subset of the more general capacity for metarepresentation, which seems to permeate all domains of cognition. Sensitivity to domain-specific inputs in early childhood is followed in many microdomains by explicit theory-building activities. Now, it could be that autistic individuals have a general deficit in theory-building, but that seems unlikely in high-functioning subjects and remains to be tested empirically.

Thus, on the one hand, theory of mind is unlike other theory-building activities; it specifically involves representations and mechanisms that sustain the computation of propositional attitudes. On the other hand, it is like other theory-building activities; it involves inferences based on unobservables (mental states, such as belief), a coherent set of explanations of causal links between mental states and behavior which are predictive of future actions (because Maxi thinks the chocolate is still in the basket and doesn't know it has been moved, he'll look for it in the basket), a growing distinction between evidence and theory (understanding the reliability of different sources of knowledge about mental states and behavior contingent thereupon), and a clearly defined mentally represented domain over which the causal explanations operate.[21]

When discussing pretend play, I stressed the importance of externalized markers which act as a sort of cognitive prop to sustain the internal processes. We are one of the only species to make use of various forms of externalized marking to extend memory and to communicate. So let us now look at the child as a notator, and explore how the use of cultural tools bypasses our biological constraints.

Chapter 6
The Child as a Notator

Verba volant, scripta manent.

Rats and chimpanzees are highly intelligent, yet they do not draw. And this is not due simply to their lack of manual dexterity. Yet, pop your head through any kindergarten door, browse through any book on the human record from as far back as the neolithic and paleolithic periods, or visit peoples devoid of contact with Western culture and you will be struck by the pervasiveness of the human tendency to create notations of various kinds—to draw, to engrave, to paint, to sculpt, to make maps, and to invent systems for written language, for number notation, for music notation, and so forth.

Many species generate internal representations, but there is something about the architecture of the human mind that enables children and adults also to produce external notations, that is to use cultural tools for leaving an intentional trace of their communicative and cognitive acts. Humans have a "print-out facility" (Wilks 1982) for creating notations of various kinds. I shall use the term "notation" to refer to these external depictions, and "representation" to imply something internal to the mind. Of course, individuals of a number of nonhuman species, such as mollusks and insects, leave external traces of their spatial displacements which allow them to return to their point of departure (Gallistel 1990). But, to my knowledge, this always occurs via excretions from the animal's body and not via some form of tool external to the body. Moreover, the trace is always left on the actual physical location of the displacement. It is not intentional or communicative. In no way does it resemble the human print-out facility.

What if we look much higher on the evolutionary scale? Take the chimpanzee, an intelligent species which makes use of tools for certain purposes and which has rich communicative and representational abilities. Yet, as far as I could ascertain, the chimpanzee never uses tools to purposely leave a permanent trace of its intentional acts as a form of external memory or communication.

The human print-out facility can be expressed either iconically (as in drawings) or non-iconically (as in alphabetic writing). Maps, memory aids, and diagrams fall somewhere between the iconic and the non-iconic. There is considerable debate (Freeman 1987) regarding the extent to which children's drawings and other notations can be used as data about internal representations (Kosslyn et al. 1977; Laszlo and Broderick 1985; Olson and Bialystok 1983). That debate concerns children's knowledge of spatio-geometric relations. This chapter has a different purpose. Here I shall use the notational domain to probe the constraints that children impose on different notational systems. I shall also use the development of notational competence to explore internal representational change (both microdevelopmental and macrodevelopmental) in the human mind.[1]

Does Precedence Imply Derivation?

According to present archaeological evidence, modern writing systems are derived from systems that appeared about 5000 years ago. Notation of quantity probably dates back even farther. Drawing, engraving, and painting predated these systems, but precedence does not necessarily imply derivation, either historically or ontogenetically (Karmiloff-Smith 1990b; Tolchinsky-Landsmann and Karmiloff-Smith 1992). Indeed, even the simplest precursor of writing included some nonpictorial signs. And it is now generally accepted that the systems of written language and number are not mere extensions of drawing (Schmandt-Bessarat 1977, 1978, 1981).

An analogy can be made to human sign languages. Because they are realized in a visuomanual mode, some of the signs do have iconic components; that is, they bear some resemblance to the reality that they encode. The sign for the verb "to drink" in many sign languages, looks to a nonsigner like an imitation of the act of drinking. But the sign becomes very schematic in fast communication and thus loses much of its iconicity. Nonetheless, its etymological source is iconic. However, the syntax of sign languages and a large proportion of the signed lexicon bear no resemblance whatsoever to the meanings and relations that they encode. They are purely arbitrary and abstract, just as in spoken languages (Klima and Bellugi 1979). Likewise with the historical development of writing. Although some early signs bore analogy with what they depicted, many early signs were arbitrary abstract notations. But what about ontogeny? Since drawing predates writing in child development, are we to conclude that writing derives from drawing? Are drawing and writing simply parts of general notational development?

Notation from a Domain-General Perspective

The Piagetian view of drawing and writing is that both are rooted in, and develop from, a common semiotic function at the culmination of the period of sensorimotor development. There is no need to reiterate here the arguments marshaled in previous chapters for rejecting a totally nonsymbolic period during infancy (Mandler 1988). Symbolic representation seems to be available to the young infant and doesn't emerge only at the end of the so-called sensorimotor period. But drawing and writing develop *after* infancy. So here a case might be made for domain-general development through which these competences come into being. Indeed, Ferreiro (1982) and Ferreiro and Teberosky (1979) have favored the Piagetian domain-general framework for exploring the preliterate child's "reading" and "writing."

Working with Spanish- and French-speaking children, Ferreiro devised a series of tasks to capture what preliterate children's hypotheses might be with respect to the written form. She asked nonreaders to guess what was written on a page, which of two words went better with a picture, and so forth, and found that preliterate children initially expect written text to be a more or less faithful reflection of the drawing on the same page. Thus, if there is a picture of a dog, they expect any writing underneath it to say "dog" and not "cat". Given a choice of two written strings and two pictures, one of a tiny butterfly and the other of a dog, these young children match the shorter written string with the butterfly (because it is small) and the longer string with the dog (because it is bigger). And the same string can be moved under another picture of an elephant and will then be considered to say "elephant" (see also Bialystok 1992).

Ferreiro and Teberosky argue that young children initially confuse drawing and writing and that both are rooted in what Piaget calls the semiotic function. This domain-general view of notation contrasts with the domain-specific view that we are about to consider. In this chapter, the term "domain specific" will take on a slightly different connotation, or rather, a double connotation. On the one hand I shall use it to distinguish the notational domain from other domains such as language and physics. On the other hand, I shall use it to refer to the separate development of each microdomain (drawing, writing, or number notation), the term "microdomain-specific" being rather long winded. The domain-specific approach to notation posits that each symbolic system follows its own developmental path.

A Domain-Specific Approach to Notation

In the previous chapters, we first considered innate constraints on a given domain, and then explored subsequent representational change. In this chapter there is relatively little to say about infancy, because the notational domain has not hitherto attracted the attention of infancy researchers. But, given our interest in the functional architecture of the human mind at birth and the effects of early constraints on subsequent learning, it seems essential to determine whether differentiations obtaining between the non-iconic systems of writing and number and the iconic system of drawing in any way reflect perceptual constraints, such as differentiation of shapes of elements and strings. Thus, even in the absence of a substantial body of data, my ongoing research with Slater and Tolchinsky-Landsmann on the young infant's sensitivity to different systems of notation deserves a brief mention, since it will pinpoint the issues that I deem to be important.

Let us take as a working hypothesis that the domain-specific view is valid with respect to infants' initial differentiations of notation systems. We know from the research of Gibson (1970), Slater (1990), Slater and Morison (1991), and many others that visual perception (orientation discrimination, perception of shape, size constancy, etc.) is already highly organized at birth. We also know that in Western cultures the infant's environment is permeated with notational inputs. Do infants simply attend to all notational inputs in the same way, or are they sensitive to distinctions between the systems? In chapter 4 I pointed out that toddlers apply one set of principles to number names and a quite different set to object labels. There is reason to suppose that infants might distinguish between these two domains in their visual processing also, on the basis of other constraints.

In collaboration with Slater and Tolchinsky-Landsmann, I am undertaking a series of experiments to determine whether the infant is sensitive to differences between the writing and number systems, on the one hand, and these systems and line drawings, on the other. Our pilot studies will use the infant habituation paradigms described in chapter 1. Infants of 10–18 months will be presented with a set of single letters or strings (words) until they reach habituation criterion. They will then be measured for renewed attention to numbers and/or line drawings. Our prediction is that 10-month-old infants will discriminate between drawing and the other two systems and, later in infancy, between number and written-language notations.

This infancy research is, of course, still in its infancy! But our intention is to carry out the experiments cross-culturally (using environments in which notational systems are far less pervasive than our own) and cross-linguistically (comparing different numeral systems [Arabic, Roman] and different orthographic systems [English, Hebrew, Chinese]). I stated in chapter 2 that infants distinguish human languages from other auditory input at birth, and their mother tongue from other languages at 4 days. It is possible that similar developments hold, but considerably later in infancy, for written systems. In other words, infants may initially make a perceptual distinction between all written systems and drawing, and subsequently differentiate the writing system of their own environment from the writing systems of other cultures. I of course do not mean by this that there are innate predispositions specifically for differentiating writing and number notation from drawing. What I am suggesting is that 5000 or 6000 years ago culture cashed in on some salient perceptual distinctions to which human biological constraints were already sensitive. It is also possible that the structure of the actual process of writing has a particular spatial frequency or periodicity—i.e., that writing can be defined by its "wavelength" and thereby clearly differentiated from drawing. These perceptual distinctions could lead the infant to be sensitive to different types of notational inputs and to store them in ways relevant to each microdomain.

Preliterate and Prenumerate Children's Notational Competence

Since we are far from having complete results from the infancy studies, the question remains open as to whether different notational systems are first all processed as a single domain and only subsequently differentiated into writing, number, and drawing or whether they are processed domain specifically from the outset. My hunch is that the latter will obtain. However, it is already clear from the spontaneous productions of preliterate and prenumerate toddlers that they do not process notational systems in a domain-general fashion. Indeed, preliterate children differentiate between drawing and writing even if their "drawings" are not much more than circular scribbles and their "writing" wiggly horizontal lines. But they are adamant about the distinction: "That's a dog" (a circular scribble unrecognizable to anyone but the budding artist) "and that says 'Fido'" (equally unrecognizable, but a horizontal squiggly line). We have been looking at this issue in an experiment with toddlers (Karmiloff-Smith 1990b; Tolchinsky-Landsmann and Karmiloff-Smith 1992) in which preliterate and predrawing children were asked to "draw" a dog and "write" its name. When children objected that they didn't know how to draw or write, we encouraged them to pretend to be doing so. Figure 6.1 shows two toddlers' productions in which distinctions between pretend drawing

Figure 6.1
Two toddlers' drawings (top) and writings (bottom) of 'dog'.

and pretend writing are clear cut. Moreover, video tapes show that preliterate toddlers lift the pen much more frequently when pretending to write than when pretending to draw.[2] The toddler goes about the processes of writing and drawing differently, even though the end products sometimes turn out similar. It is essential to distinguish between product and process, because toddlers' notational products may at times appear domain-general to the observer whereas their notational intentions and hand movements bear witness to a clear differentiation that they have established between the two systems.

In contrast to the dearth of data concerning infants' perception of different notational systems, research has been very active with respect to children beyond infancy but prior to formal schooling (Ferreiro 1982; Tolchinsky-Landsmann 1986; Tolchinsky-Landsmann and Levin 1985, 1987; Hughes 1986; Sinclair et al. 1983). Most of these studies have concentrated on a single notational domain and concluded that early on children confound notational systems and drawing. Tolchinsky-Landsmann and I have taken a different stance. First, our focus is on the comparison between notational domains. Second, we draw a distinction between notations as referential-communicative tools, as studied in the above-cited research, and notations as domains of knowledge in which each notational micro-domain is a formal problem space for children. Do young children impose different constraints on written language and number notation when these are focused on as domains of knowledge?

We presented children with a series of cards to be sorted into those which were "good for reading" and those which were not. Another set was used for a similar task concerning number notation. The set of cards contained real words, strings of either identical or different letters, single letters, single numbers, mixtures of letters and numbers, mixtures of letters and drawings, and so forth. Children's sorting behavior made it possible to determine their conceptions of each notational system.

It was found that well before they are able to read and write, young children abide by a number of constraints which govern their acceptance of what counts as a legal member of the written language system and a different set of constraints for the number system (Tolchinsky-Landsmann and Karmiloff-Smith 1992). These constraints, implicit in the sorting behavior, show that children do not confound drawing with notation and that they make clear-cut distinctions between the two notational domains. Thus, drawings as well as cards with mixtures of systems are rejected for both written language and number notation. Single elements are accepted for number but rejected for writing. Likewise, repetition of identical elements is accepted for number but rejected for writing. By contrast, linkage between elements is accepted for writing but not for number notation. Finally, children impose a limited range for the number of elements that can form a written string (between three and nine), but no such constraint holds for number notation.

In other words, children as young as 4 do *not* confuse writing, number notation, and drawing; they impose different constraints on each system. Are these constraints merely implicit in the representations sustaining their sorting behavior, or are they explicitly represented and therefore available for purposeful manipulation?

The RR Model and Early Notational Skills

To follow up the sorting tasks, we used a technique devised for a drawing study (Karmiloff-Smith 1990a). Children of 4–6 years were first asked to write a word, a letter, and a number. They were then asked to "write a word that doesn't exist" ("a pretend word" or "a word from another planet"—we meant to convey to the children that we wanted them to violate the constraints on normal writing).[3] In the same way, we also asked for a letter and a number that don't exist.

The technique was successful at differentiating different levels of explicitness of children's representations. Some 4-year-olds simply reproduced their normal notational efforts. They could not yet purposefully manipulate the procedures they used for sorting. Their representations were still at level I. However, a few other 4-year-olds and the majority of the 5- and 6-year-olds were capable of violating certain constraints on writing and number notation. The representations sustaining their sorting behavior had already been redescribed into E1 format. For a word or letter that doesn't exist, the 4- and 5-year old subjects produced drawings or mixtures of systems, or strings of identical letters (see figure 6.2). The 6-year-olds who could already use the conventional written system proposed words that could not be pronounced (last example in figure 6.2). For a number that doesn't exist, the youngest subjects again proposed drawings and mixtures of systems (see figure 6.3). In contrast with writing, they did not propose a string of identical numbers, because this is a legal number string. Older children (last example in figure 6.3) tended to produce extremely long numbers ("too long to exist") or ones with a large proportion of zeros.

In general, this series of studies suggests that, however limited young children's knowledge of writing and number is, they develop a spontaneous sensitivity to *different* characteristics of their notational environments before formal schooling. In other words, they go beyond simply responding to the notational environment in a global, domain-general fashion. This was evident from the sorting behavior, which showed clear-cut differentiations between writing, drawing, and number notation. Initially the knowledge is only implicitly represented in the level-I format, but our subsequent experiment shows that with development children can violate the criteria which their earlier sorting activities obeyed. Such deliberate violations (which remind us of pretend play discussed in chapter 5) require explicitly defined representations (i.e., at least at level E1).

Biology versus Culture: The Paradox of Notational Systems

Let me summarize the story so far. It may turn out that, after a certain amount of exposure to their notational environment in general, 10–

Figure 6.2
Children's productions of nonletters and nonwords. Left column: normal words. Right column: words that do not exist.

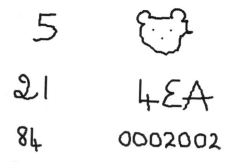

Figure 6.3
Children's productions of non-numbers. Left column: normal numbers. Right column: numbers that do not exist.

18-month-old infants may be sensitive to differences between various notational systems. This is certainly true of toddlers who produce differences in the hand movements by which they pretend to write and draw, even if at times the products of their attempts are almost indistinguishable. Preschoolers sort written language, written number, and drawing in accordance with different constraints on each system. Slightly older children are able to purposely violate the normal constraints on these systems when asked to write words and numbers that don't exist. Development in the notational domain seems to involve system-specific constants.

But arguing for the domain specificity of these systems leads us to a paradox. In the case of language, it makes sense to take a constraints view of the infant's sensitivity to proprietary input for *spoken* language. We saw in chapter 2 that infants are sensitive to distinctions between linguistic and nonlinguistic auditory input and between their mother tongue and other languages, and that they are sensitive to differences in word order, intonation contours, phrase structure, and subcategorization frames for different types of verbs and their argument structures. For many, these early sensitivities suggest some innately specified constraints on language. Hundreds of thousands of years of evolution were needed for spoken language to become biologically constrained. But the use of cultural tools for writing dates back only 5000 or 6000 years. Most consider this to be minute in terms of evolutionary time. It is thus implausible to invoke an innately specified bias for writing.[4] Yet, just as language can be selectively impaired (e.g. in cases of adult brain damage) or selectively spared (recall the example of Williams Syndrome children mentioned in chapter 2), so writing and drawing can be selectively impaired or spared. Several cases of hyperlexics have been reported (Cossu and Marshall 1986) (otherwise severely mentally retarded children who read accurately and rapidly, albeit without understanding), idiot-savant drawers (Selfe 1985), and hypergraphics (Marshall 1980, 1984). Moreover, writing and drawing are processed in different hemispheres of the brain. Marshall argues for the existence of a writing module, a reading module, and so forth, implying prespecified biological constraints on each system. My argument is that, if these systems turn out to be modular in adults, they are due to a process of modularization—that is, they are products of learning during childhood.

My guess is that the distinction between drawing and other conventional notational systems introduced in recent evolutionary time by human cultures capitalized on distinctions particularly relevant to human attention and production mechanisms, such as sequentiality, directionality, iconicity or noniconicity, and periodicity of movement. Infants faced with various types of notational input would have a head start for attending to them differentially, because their minds are structured such that sequentiality, directionality, iconicity, periodicity, etc. are relevant to them. This would then enable them to store examples of the production or of the product of each system separately, output them distinctly, and gradually represent each microdomain of notation in its own right.

Using the Notational Domain to Probe the RR Model and Microdevelopmental Change

Research in the notational domain goes beyond the questions raised in previous chapters, where it was established that representational change does indeed occur macrodevelopmentally. Here I address microdevelopmental change, i.e. change that occurs within the confines of an experimental session.

If, as I argue, representational change is pervasive in human development, then there is no a priori reason to limit it to the macrodevelopmental time scale. It should be possible to establish its occurrence also on the microdevelopmental time scale. A rather simple experiment suggested that this might be the case. Children between the ages of 5 and 7 were shown a model railway formed of straight and curved pieces of track (figure 6.4) and were asked to draw it. They had no difficulty complying with this instruction. They were then instructed to build a circuit similar to the original one by asking the experimenter for the pieces of track needed. This again was a simple task for them. Next, they were asked to draw again the original circuit, which remained visible. Surprisingly, a number of 5-year-olds were

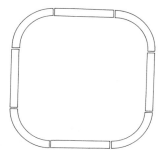

Figure 6.4
Railway-circuit stimuli. (From Karmiloff-Smith 1979c. Reprinted with permission of Editions Médecine & Hygiène.)

incapable of reproducing a correct shape similar to their original drawings. Rather, as can be seen in figure 6.5, they now depicted in their drawings their new internal representations of the task. The shapes that they drew depicted the straight and curved sections of track separately. In children's original drawings, the different shape components remained implicitly represented, while the goal was a global drawing task. But after the child had to ask for each type of track (i.e., use a linguistic code), the separate elements were represented explicitly. It was these new explicit representations that were accessed during the second drawing attempt, despite the existence of the model.[5] I went on to look at such microdevelopmental issues in a more complex experimental situation.

The RR model postulates that change occurs after behavioral mastery, i.e., after a consistently stable state is reached. To explore representational change at the microdevelopmental level, I needed a task for which subjects already had competence, but for which they needed to generate a novel solution. If the experimental session were long enough, could one observe microdevelopmental changes that were indices of a process of representational redescription? Would changes merely be exogenously driven? Or would they be along similar lines to those observed macrodevelopmentally when, over a period of years, children go beyond successful goal attainment? In previous chapters we saw several examples of macrodevelopmental change. Now to explore microdevelopmental change.

The study involved the creation of an external memory device (Karmiloff-Smith 1979b). Only subjects who already had full competence in the notational task were tested. However, the task was designed such that subjects had to create on-the-spot, novel solutions based on

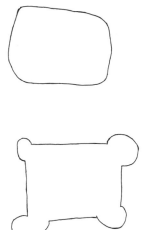

Figure 6.5
Children's drawings of railway circuits. Top: initial drawing. Bottom: second drawing. (From Karmiloff-Smith 1979c. Reprinted with permission of Editions Médecine & Hygiène.)

that competence. Children were shown a 12-meter roll of wrapping paper on which a route from a house to a hospital was traced. There were 20 bifurcation points at which one of the branches of the route led to a cul-de-sac and the other permitted the child to continue toward the target. The task was to "drive" a patient in a toy ambulance from the house at the start of the roll along a winding route to the hospital. As the child "drove" the ambulance, the experimenter unrolled the wrapping paper and rolled up the already completed segments (figure 6.6). The child could not see in advance of a decision at each bifurcation which of the branches led on toward the hospital, and had to backtrack if, when the paper was further unrolled, she found herself in a cul-de-sac. The patient was not in the ambulance during the practice run, "in case he might bleed to death." Children love such scenarios! In this first run, if the child chose a road leading to a cul-de-sac she was allowed to backtrack. But since the patient would be in the ambulance during the second run, children were encouraged during the practice run to mark something down on a piece of paper which they could use later to avoid cul-de-sacs on subsequent runs. Paper and colored pencils were provided for the notetaking. Some of the bifurcations were marked with figural indices (trees, people, and the like); others had topographic indices such as zigzags along one of the branches. If

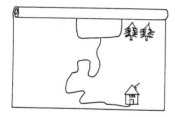

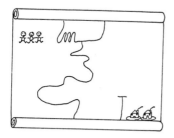

Figure 6.6
Stimuli for map task. Top: initial state of route. Bottom: state of route halfway through. (From Karmiloff-Smith 1979b. Reprinted with permission of Ablex Publishing Corporation.)

notated, these were usable as landmarks for the decoding phase. Some of the bifurcations, however, were not identifiable on the basis of figural or topographic indices.

In other words, the problem children faced was to create a notational system that could be used as an external memory trace to help to drive the patient along the correct branches of the bifurcations. The form(s) that the child's notations could take was left entirely open. There was no "right" answer. Children could use the figural and topographic indices as clues, simply mark left or right, or invent an idiosyncratic solution. I was not interested in *which* notation children would use. I had purposely chosen an age group (7–12 years) in which, from previous work on symmetrical relations (Piaget and Karmiloff-Smith 1990), I already knew that a variety of useful systems was within the children's competence. My focus was on whether children might change their adequate notations as they proceeded with the lengthy task.

The results of the study were rich. Some children drew miniature maps reproducing every detail of the route; others' maps were schematic. Some used left/right systems, writing out "turn right" and "turn left" or "R" and "L". Others simply drew each bifurcation separately, without details of the roads joining them, and then used arrows, different colors, thickening, or cross-hatching to mark which branch of the fork was a cul-de-sac and which led toward the hospital. Some used linguistic notations, writing instructions about landmarks such as "turn towards the trees", "not the side of the windows [in the experiment room]", and "take the zigzag side". The detailed results can be found in Karmiloff-Smith 1979b and 1984. The examples below give a sense of changes that were made *after* the child had already devised an adequate system of notation.

Built into the design of the map task was the falsifiable hypothesis that internal constraints, and not solely external ones, motivate representational change. This is a key prediction from the RR model. Throughout the book, I have held that failure via exogenous factors is neither the sole nor even the main motivation for change. My argument is that change is also consequent upon internal stability. Two types of change were possible in the ambulance experiment: one exogenous, the other endogenous. Let us look at each in turn.

Imagine that you have chosen to write instructions indicating figural indices (e.g. "take the branch where the man is standing", "don't take the side with the pond") or to draw the figural indices next to the bifurcations. You will be forced to change such a system on encountering a bifurcation bare of any such indices. In such a case, your change would be generated by an *exogenous* cause. If one were interested in the child's ability to make flexible use of different strategies, one's analysis could focus on that type of change. Just as with language development, some changes are indeed generated by external constraints, such as misinterpretations or corrections from addressees. But in the language case we saw that there were other changes that had nothing directly to do with external pressures. Often children introduce changes after their linguistic output is already correct. In the map task, too, children generate a notational system adequate for all the bifurcations, and yet make alterations to it in mid-route. One must then invoke *endogenous* causes, because failure or inconsistency of the notational system cannot be adduced to explain the changed behavior. The experiment was specifically designed to allow for both types of change, but our interest here is in endogenously provoked changes.

Take the example of children who drew abstractions, merely marking each bifurcation in sequence on the page, as in figure 6.7. This is a perfectly adequate and economical notation for succeeding on every bifurcation throughout the task. The order of decisions for each bifurcation is encoded implicitly in the sequence of drawings children made on the lines of the note paper (and sometimes even explicitly by adding

Figure 6.7
Part of a typical solution to the map task. (After Karmiloff-Smith 1979b.)

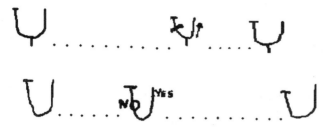

Figure 6.8
Two children's micro-developmental changes in productions for the map task. Left to right: initial phase, later phase, and still later in each child's protocol. (After Karmiloff-Smith 1979b.)

numbering). None of the figural or topographical features are included in the child's notational system. Hence no exogenous problem is posed by bifurcations that don't have these features. The child could continue to use the same notational system throughout, because it reproduces the essential decision-point information only. So, just as we asked why our child linguists don't simply continue using correct forms but go beyond adequate output, here, too, in the notational domain, we can ask: Why don't children simply continue with their adequate, economical method of notation?

Interesting microdevelopmental changes reveal themselves as the child proceeds with the task. Take another look at figure 6.7. It is easy to ascertain that the notation is adequate to convey which branch leads toward the hospital, and which one leads to a cul-de-sac. But after using such adequate notations for a number of bifurcations, children suddenly introduce redundant information, as can be seen from two children's solutions in figure 6.8. These examples illustrate different surface notations, but they are both very similar at another level of abstraction. In each case, the child started with a series of reproductions of the bifurcation—a solution that could have been used throughout. Subsequently, however, both children altered their economical notational solution during a few bifurcations. One added an arrow on the correct branch and put a cross through the incorrect one. The other added "Yes" on the correct branch and "No" next to the incorrect one. In both cases, the additional information was totally redundant, in that the original system carried all the information necessary for subsequent decoding.

There were many other microdevelopmental changes of this nature made to already-adequate notation systems. After using the new, redundant notations for a few bifurcations, children revert to the initial, more economic one. Why do children make these changes?

First, one must establish that the changes were not exogenously provoked by external pressures due to the difficulty of encoding a particular bifurcation. Several findings demonstrate that they were not. First, when different children introduced changes, these did not always occur at the same bifurcation. Some notations were changed at, say, bifurcation 7, others at bifurcation 10. None, however, were changed during the early productions for bifurcations 1–6. It seems that children needed to consolidate their task-specific solution before change was introduced. Second, there was nothing about the particular bifurcations where changes took place that precluded the continued use of the initial system. Third, the changes that children introduced, although superficially different, all involved spelling out information that was implicit in the earlier system. Another reason for making changes could have been that, although from the observer's point of view the initial system was adequate, perhaps the child considered the initial system to be inadequate in some way. This, however, is implausible, since no child went back to add the new information to previously notated bifurcations. Clearly children considered their earlier notations adequate for subsequent use. So why were redundant modifications introduced?

My view is that as the original system becomes consolidated and automatized for a particular task—and in this task behavioral mastery can be reached rapidly, because the components of the solution are already within the child's competence—the child moves from mere goal-directed activity of a data-driven type to focusing on the components of the internal representation. These are then explicitly represented internally. And, fortunately for the researcher, this sometimes induces children to spell out in their externalized notations the change in internal representations. I coined the term "metaprocedural processes" for such operations. In other words, the procedures originally used as a means of reaching a goal now become input to other metaprocesses, which redescribe them and represent their component information explicitly in E1 format. Recall, also, the similar process that occured in the 5-year-olds' second drawings of the railway circuit. The notion "metaprocedural" implies neither conscious focus nor verbally statable knowledge. But it does mean that the child is operating at a different level from the earlier purely goal-oriented activity. The new behavior indicates that the child is explicitly spelling out components of the knowledge implicit in earlier solutions.

The Importance of Behavioral Mastery

To observe microdevelopmental change in notations, several criteria have to be met. First, one must use subjects who already possess full notational competence. If Perner (whose theory was discussed in the previous chapter) is right about the radical change beyond age 4 in children's understanding of the representational mind, then it should be impossible for young children to really understand notational tasks. And indeed it may be. In some studies, although the youngest subjects were able to generate notations for a memory task, they frequently made no use of their notes during the decoding phase. It is as if they do not understand the function of notations even when they can produce them. This was true, for instance, of 5-year-olds in a study of musical notation (Cohen 1985).

Second, even for older subjects, the solving of the actual task to be notated (map reading, percussion instrument playing) must be well within the child's competence if endogenous representational change is to be observed microdevelopmentally. Thus, with a similar notational design but using more complex problem-solving tasks, Bolger (1988) did not find endogenous changes in the notations of 8-year-olds; however, the tasks chosen were difficult for these subjects, so although they did manage to solve them before the notational part of the experiment they had clearly not reached behavioral mastery in the problem-solving part (Bolger 1988; Bolger and Karmiloff-Smith 1990). This suggests that for notational efficacy, for adaptation of a notational message to others (Li and Karmiloff-Smith 1990a, 1990b), and for subsequent representational change, behavioral mastery at the problem-solving level is a prerequisite. This parallels the situation that Shatz (1983) has shown to obtain for spoken language. Only after children have reached behavioral mastery in certain aspects of language can they adapt those aspects to the communicative needs of different addressees.

Constraints on Representational Redescription

We have seen that representational change occurs both macrodevelopmentally and microdevelopmentally. That representational redescription is part of human development seems plausible. Yet some important questions remain unaddressed. Why does representational change take developmental time? What are the constraints on representational change—i.e., on the child's capacity to operate on the knowledge components embedded in earlier, efficiently functioning procedures? How can the researcher devise empirical studies that might serve to address these issues? And how can a developmental perspective help us to take a more subtle look at constraints on representational change in general? Let us now turn to a study in which I attempted to explore the RR model in more depth.

When procedurally embedded knowledge becomes available as a data structure in E1 format to other parts of the cognitive system, logically there are many formats in which such knowledge might be represented. They could immediately be totally flexible or they could retain a certain rigidity. I set out to explore the status of the initial redescriptions and to see whether, at the first level of redescription, the new representation is specified as a relatively fixed list, partially embodying a constraint that is inherent at the procedural level. If that were so, it would restrict inter-representational flexibility. Later in development, via further redescription, such sequential constraints might become increasingly relaxed, yielding an internal representation specified as a structured yet flexibly ordered set of manipulable features.

The issue of constraints on representational redescription was tested in a drawing experiment involving children between the ages of 5 and 11 years. In keeping with the research strategy described throughout the book, I chose a minimum age at which children were already successful at producing drawings of houses and men. At this age, they also have adequate conceptual knowledge about the objects to be drawn. In other words, all subjects had already reached behavioral mastery of the chosen drawing procedures.

The subjects were asked to draw a house and then, after that drawing was removed, to draw "a house that doesn't exist." The same procedure was used with regard to drawing a man. Recall the similar experiment involving "writing a word that doesn't exist" that was discussed earlier in this chapter. In that study, the point was to probe the core boundaries which children establish between drawing, writing, and number by examining how they can violate them. The rationale behind the experimental design in the present drawing task was not focused on the content of the drawings per se, but attempted to pinpoint general constraints on representational change.

Over time in early childhood, children build procedures for drawing a house and a man. This may well involve a laborious developmental process, but by around 4–5 years of age children can run these procedures efficiently and in a relatively automatic way. When children are asked to draw a house, for example, they do so rapidly and well. If they are asked to draw a house that does not exist, they are forced into operating on their internal representation. As long as one uses subjects who have no difficulty in the actual planning and execution of the drawing itself, then an analysis of the types of modification that they produce makes it possible to capture essential facets of the constraints on representational flexibility.

We have already seen that behavioral mastery is a prerequisite for passing from procedurally encoded representations to the first level of representational redescription. The drawing study focused on subjects who had already reached behavioral mastery. Indeed, the analysis did not concentrate on whether or not children were successful on the task. The vast majority of children are. All 54 subjects produced adequate drawings of "existent" houses and men, and only five failed to produce depictions of "nonexistent" houses and men. So success is not a problem. The important question here is whether there are developmental differences, not in success rates, but in the *type* of change introduced. And, if there are such differences, are they informative about constraints on representational change?

Several types of change were observed, as figures 6.9–6.14 show. They involved the shape of the whole, the shape and size of constituent elements, the deletion of elements, the insertion of new ones, changes in position and/or orientation, and the insertion of elements from other conceptual categories.

The criteria for a "house that does exist" were a rectangular shape, a roof, a door, a window, and optionally a chimney, curtains, various numbers of windows, and features such as a doorknob. A "house that doesn't exist" might have the roof, the door, a window, or a chimney in the wrong position or orientation, or might lack an essential feature such as a door, or might have an unusual shape (say, a circle) or an unusual feature (such as eyes or wings). A "man that doesn't exist" might have an unusual number of features, such as two heads; adding a hat would not count. Additions had to violate household or manhood in some way while retaining other core aspects of the concept. A house with a second chimney did not constitute a "house that does not exist"; however, one with a pair of eyes or one with an absurdly placed chimney did. The same went for deletions. Deleting a hat or a walking stick in the second man-drawing was not considered a violation of manhood and was therefore not considered a successful drawing of a "man that does not exist"—in contrast with deleting the eyes or the mouth or adding extra ones.

In figure 6.9 we have examples of changes in the shape and/or size of elements with the contour outline unchanged. Figure 6.10 provides examples of changes in the shape of the whole. Figure 6.11 illustrates deletions of elements, while figure 6.12 shows insertions of new elements. Drawings from subjects who changed the orientation or the position of elements (or the whole) are shown in Figure 6.13. Figure 6.14 shows examples of elements inserted from other conceptual categories.

The full results are reported in Karmiloff-Smith 1990a. Children of all ages, from 5 to 11, changed the shapes and sizes of elements or the shape of the whole, and they deleted essential elements. However, very few children below age 8 inserted elements, changed position or orientation, or made cross-category insertions.

A second experiment was carried out to verify whether the absence of certain changes made by otherwise successful 5–7-year-olds was merely due to a lack in inventiveness (i.e., whether they simply had

Figure 6.9
Changes to shape of elements. Left: child, age 4 years, 11 months. Right: child, age 8 years, 6 months. (From Karmiloff-Smith 1990a. Reprinted with permission of Elsevier Science Publishers B.V.)

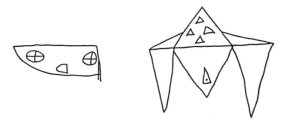

Figure 6.10
Changes to contour. Left: child, age 4 years, 11 months. Right: child, age 8 years, 6 months. (From Karmiloff-Smith 1990a. Reprinted with permission of Elsevier Science Publishers B.V.)

Figure 6.11
Deletions. Left: child, age 5 years, 3 months. Right: child, age 9 years. (From Karmiloff-Smith 1990a. Reprinted with permission of Elsevier Science Publishers B.V.)

Figure 6.12
Insertions of elements from same category. Left: child, age 8 years, 7 months. Right: child, age 9 years, 6 months. (From Karmiloff-Smith 1990a. Reprinted with permission of Elsevier Science Publishers B.V.)

Figure 6.13
Changes in position or orientation. Left: child, age 9 years, 8 months. Right: child, age 10 years, 11 months. (From Karmiloff-Smith 1990a. Reprinted with permission of Elsevier Science Publishers B.V.)

Figure 6.14
Insertions of elements from other categories. Left: child, age 8 years, 3 months. Right: child, age 10 years, 9 months. (From Karmiloff-Smith 1990a. Reprinted with permission of Elsevier Science Publishers B.V.)

not thought of making insertions and cross-category changes) or whether a deeper reason lay behind this. A different group of 5-year-olds were first tested with the same experimental technique. Those children who were successful on both drawings but whose changes were limited to size, shape, and deletion were then asked to draw "a man with two heads" and "a house with wings." In other words, they were explicitly instructed to introduce the types of change typical of the spontaneous productions of older subjects.

As the first young subject began to draw a second head, I was reminded of T. E. Huxley's lament: "the great tragedy of science: the slaying of a beautiful hypothesis by an ugly fact." But the first subject, and all but one of the seven others tested, first went on laboriously and very slowly to draw two bodies, two arms and two legs on each body, etc. And they kept starting again because they were dissatisfied with their results. They had some difficulties even in simply copying a model provided by the experimenter. By contrast, when 8–10-year-olds spontaneously drew a man with two heads (interrupting sequential order to insert a new subroutine for drawing a second head), they drew a single body with the speed of their usual drawing procedure. Moreover, when the 5-year-olds were asked to draw "a house with wings" (a spontaneous cross-category response also typical of older subjects' solutions), they all performed rapidly and successfully.

When younger subjects in the follow-up experiment were given specific instructions, why were they able to draw a house with wings rapidly although they found it difficult to draw a man with two heads? There are two reasons, and both are relevant to the RR model. The first concerns inter-representational flexibility and why our instructions made it easier for young children to add features from other representations. The second concerns constraints on sequence suggesting why the house with wings is easier than the two-headed man.

In the original study, older children spontaneously drew houses with wings, faces, and so forth. They moved flexibly between different representational categories—something the younger subjects did not do easily. In the follow-up study, the experimenter supplied the cross-category reference for the addition of wings, thus allowing the younger children to access the other representational category and add it after the house-drawing procedure was completed.[6] Older children were able to spontaneously move flexibly across representational categories without the suggestion from the experimenter.

The second reason concerns constraints on sequence. The reason why children easily draw a house with wings is that wings can be added at the end of a house-drawing procedure that has been run through in its entire sequence. In contrast, to comply with the instructions to draw a man with two heads, the child has to interrupt the normal sequence of the man-drawing procedure and insert a subroutine. A large number of studies in the developmental literature outside drawing have shown this to be difficult for young children. The 5-year-olds in my study also experienced such difficulties, whereas the older children spontaneously introduced subroutines into their rapid drawing procedure. But then again, the younger children retained their ability to draw a normal man rapidly. As children start to render explicit their level-I representations, they do not overwrite them. These are still available for certain goals. But it is the redescribed E1 representations that are manipulated for different goals.

Implicit Representations and Their Procedural Status

Throughout a lot of my past work, and in the above discussion of the drawing study, I argued that representations sustaining behavioral mastery in any domain were first in the form of procedures. A procedural representation *as a whole* is data to a system, but the component parts of a procedure are implicitly defined and not available as data. I used this procedural definition to further explore the details of representational redescription, concluding that redescriptions of procedural knowledge initially embody sequential constraints. I now no longer entirely agree with myself. Let me explain why.

First, I was using the notion of a compiled procedure in a much looser way than is intended in the artificial intelligence literature. Technically speaking, a compiled procedure is one that has been modified from a high-level language into a lower-level code for speed of execution of the procedure *as a whole*. It is the equivalent of giving something a name, then only calling the name and no longer having any access to the component parts. In this sense, a compiled procedural representation is an unanalyzable whole that is run in its entirety, with the components no longer accessible. In the drawing study, my use of the notion of procedure was meant to capture something close to this. I was grappling with something like the distinction in classical artificial intelligence between an ordered stack and a flexible array and arguing that development involves repeatedly changing representations from the former to the latter.

It turns out that the sequential constraint on the first level of redescription is, particularly in domains like drawing, considerably weaker than I originally predicted. Subsequent researchers[7] have demonstrated that young children can interrupt their drawing routines. The question is why? Post factum, is drawing the best domain in which to probe the question of constraints on representational change? It seems not. Drawing and all forms of *external* notation leave a trace. They also take far more time to execute, compared to the milliseconds of spoken language output, perception, and so forth. An interruption in an ongoing drawing leaves a trace of where the drawing was cut off, and it acts as a potent cue about where to continue. I nonetheless remain convinced that representational change does exhibit initial sequential constraints, but that one may need to explore them in areas (such as counting, music, and spoken language) where no external notation is involved.

But whether early drawing routines are compiled procedures in the technical sense of the term or not, the conclusion that can be drawn from the drawing area as well as from many other domains of research that we have explored throughout the book is that, if they are not directly encoded linguistically, new representations start by being in the level-I format. In other words, the knowledge that they contain is merely implicit to the system.

RR and the Progressive Relaxation of Sequential Constraints

That at the procedural level skills are sequentially represented has been widely discussed (Bruner 1970; Dean, Scherzer, and Chabaud 1986; Fuson, Richards, and Brians 1982; Goodnow and Levine 1973; Greenfield and Schneider 1977; Huttenlocher 1967; Kosslyn, Cave, Provost, and von Gierke 1988; Lashley 1951; Premack 1975; Restle 1970; Cromer 1983; Gilliéron 1976; Goodson and Greenfield 1975; Greenfield, Nelson, and Salzman 1972; Greenfield and Schneider 1977; Piaget and Inhelder 1948). This long list of references demonstrates that sequential constraints have been clearly documented across a number of different domains. For example, in seriation tasks children can at first only add elements to the end of a series. Subsequently they add elements to the beginning of a series, and only later still can they introduce new elements within an already formed series. This applies both to the performance of simple seriation tasks by toddlers (Greenfield et al. 1972) and to the performance of complex seriation tasks by older children (Gilliéron 1976; Piaget and Inhelder 1948). Thus, a sequential constraint seems to operate at different moments in development and across a variety of tasks outside the notational domain. Seriation tasks are particularly diagnostic of representational redescription, in my view. Thus, when a toddler can interrupt a highly learned routine and insert a cup in the middle of a sequence of nesting cups, we can conclude that the representations underlying the earlier routine have now been explicitly represented in the E1 format.

Exogenously Driven and Endogenously Driven Change

I have argued that, in notation and in other domains, certain aspects of change are endogenously driven. Freeman (1980) offers a somewhat different explanation for the fact that drawings of men, houses, and so forth remain "formula-driven" (i.e., stereotyped). He argues that drawing is a non-communicative act and that there is thus rather limited scope for ongoing social interaction to alter the course of the drawing.

Although drawing is not always communicative, it is an intentional act. However, even if drawings are changed by feedback (which is doubtful), feedback is only given exogenously on the drawing *product*, not on the drawing *process*. Thus, the child has to build up and change sequential representations *endogenously*. Of course, Freeman is right in stressing that children and adults continue, in normal circumstances, to produce formula-driven drawings if they are not artists. But such externalized depictions are not necessarily informative about potential internal capacities. According to the RR model, the formula-driven drawings continue to be generated by level-I representations, whereas other levels of explicit representation are called upon for other tasks. My drawing study shows that, given appropriate instructions, even young children can demonstrate that their formula-driven drawing procedures have undergone representational redescription such that changes can be introduced. There is an essential difference between external drawing behavior (the formula-driven depictions produced by non-artist children and adults) and internal representations (which, as my study and previous research suggest, undergo developmental changes with respect to accessibility and flexibility). Much as children go beyond behavioral mastery of language, change in drawing is also endogenously driven and not subject only to external, communicative influences.

This is not to deny that external influences on children's drawing can be effective. Recall that I am not arguing that change is always endogenously provoked; rather, I am arguing that it often is, and that when exogenously initiated it still involves subsequent *internal* change. Indeed, drawing experiments in which change has successfully been induced exogenously (Cox 1985; Davis 1985; Freeman 1980; Pemberton and Nelson 1987; Phillips et al. 1985) have shown that there is only modest (if any) generalization of the results of drawing training. Pemberton and Nelson (1987) trained young children on various draw-a-man skills and found only "modest evidence that some generalization of the new drawing skills carried over to house drawing." Likewise, successful training in drawing a cube did not transfer to drawing a pyramid, nor vice versa (Phillips et al. 1985). Cox (1985) successfully trained children to change from object-centered to viewer-centered depictions, but, as she points out herself, "the training procedures merely create a new entry in the child's repertoire for producing specific graphic outputs, given specific prompting inputs." As Freeman argues, when exogenous training is used, children do not induce a general solution to a projection problem; they merely build a separate structural description. In terms of the RR model, they simply add a new, independently stored representation, which will have to undergo representational redescription and explicitation—an endogenously provoked process—before becoming data available for generalization and more flexible uses.

In noting the importance of endogenously driven processes that generate developmental change, we should not lose sight of the role of the environment. One reason for my placing so much emphasis on internal factors is that many developmentalists use failure-driven models of development in which all change is generated by the external environment. The RR model invokes an endogenous success-driven view of change that is generated by internal stability and representational reorganization. But, to reiterate, endogenous factors are not the sole generators of change. The integration of nativism and constructivism I have defended throughout the book requires that *both* innate predispositions and environmental influences on brain development in the neonate and the older child be seen as crucial.

Chapter 7

Nativism, Domain Specificity, and Piaget's Constructivism

The invocation of innate influences in no way implies a commitment to immutability. (Marler 1991)

Throughout the chapters on the child as a linguist, a physicist, a mathematician, a psychologist, and a notator, several recurrent themes have emerged to suggest that Piaget's constructivism is not necessarily incompatible with innate predispositions or with the domain specificity of development. They all entail constraints on the way in which the mind functions as a self-organizing, self-redescribing system, from infancy and throughout development.

When the RR model was originally conceived, I made no commitment one way or the other with respect to the initial architecture of the infant mind. The model focused on the process of representational redescription in older children. As a model of representational change, it would stand unaltered even if it turned out that there were no innate predispositions or domain-specific constraints on development. However, with the spate of infancy research since that time, it seemed important to take a stand on infancy in this book. Moreover, as more is understood about the knowledge available to young infants, the question of the *representational status of infant knowledge* comes to the fore. I have argued throughout that, when first acquired, knowledge is stored in the level-I format (i.e., implicitly), and that a crucial aspect of development is the redescription of that knowledge into different levels of accessible, explicit formats.

The fact that I took a stand with respect to infancy had other implications, too. It highlighted the existence of domain-specific constraints on development. Let me also reiterate the distinction drawn in the book between "domain" and "module". From the point of view of the child's mind, a "domain" is the set of representations sustaining a specific area of knowledge (language, number, physics, and so forth) as well as the various microdomains that it subsumes. A "module" is an information-processing unit that encapsulates that knowledge and the computations on it. Considering development as domain specific does not necessarily imply modularity. In other words, the storing and the processing of information may be domain specific without being encapsulated, hard-wired, of fixed neural architecture, mandatory, and so forth. Fodor is probably right that there are perceptual modules, in his strict sense of the term. But I have argued that to the extent that the mind is modular, this is the result of a gradual process of modularization, and that much of cognitive development is domain specific without being strictly modular.

Finally, integrating infancy into the RR model turned out to be crucial with respect to the more general epistemological framework within which the whole of the discussion of the book has taken place (i.e., an attempt to reconcile aspects of nativism and Piaget's constructivism). At times it became apparent that Piaget's view required the addition of innate domain-specific predispositions in infancy; at other times, Piaget's epigenetic/constructivist view turned out to be a vital complement to the nativist framework.

Domain Specificity and Piagetian Theory

As we have seen throughout, Piagetian theory posits that minimal domain-general processes are available to the neonate, with no domain-specific predispositions. The theory also calls for a lengthy period during which all representations have only sensorimotor status. By contrast, throughout the book we have seen that the neonate and the young infant either already have or rapidly acquire domain-specific principles which constrain the way in which they compute different classes of input. The domain-specific attention biases mean that only certain inputs are computed. This implies more than simply an attention to relevant data. It means that selection, attention, and coherent domain-specific storage of different inputs can take place *before* much learning has occurred (Feldman and Gelman 1987). To some degree, then, the infant mind anticipates the representations that it will need to store for subsequent domain-specific development. The infant is not faced with totally undifferentiated and chaotic input, as the Piagetian view would have it. Now, future research may lead to reinterpretations of the present infancy data, but I remain convinced that we will have to invoke *some* innately guided domain-specific predispositions which constrain the architecture of the infant mind.

Invoking domain-specific constraints on development does not negate the existence of some domain-general mechanisms. The infancy tasks that we explored in each chapter make it very clear that infants can call on complex inferential processes. The work discussed in several chapters suggests that young infants go well beyond sensorimotor encodings and make use of domain-general processes such as representational redescription to encode sensorimotor input into accessible formats. Thus, domain-general processes sustaining inference and representational redescription operate throughout development and are likely to be innately specified. But invoking general *processes* that are the same across different domains is not equivalent to invoking domain-general *stages of change*.

The *function* and the *process* of representational redescription are, I have hypothesized, domain general in that an equivalent process operates in the same way in different domains and microdomains. But representational redescription recurs at different times throughout development. Although the process is domain general, the structure of the changes over which representational redescription operates is constrained domain specifically. In other words, it is affected by the form and the level of explicitness of the representations supporting particular microdomains at a given time. It does not involve an across-the-board structural change à la Piaget.

Yet I am left with a lurking feeling that there may turn out to be *some* across-the-board domain-general changes also. One such change seems to occur around 18 months of age. This holds for several domains, particularly with respect to holding two representations simultaneously in mind and representing hypothetical events in general (Meltzoff 1990; Perner 1991) rather than theory-of-mind computations in particular (Leslie 1987). Eighteen months is the point at which Piaget too called for a change in representational structure which allowed for the onset of pretend play, language, mental imagery, etc. The precise way in which Piaget accounted for such a change in terms of the closure of a purely sensorimotor period is likely to be wrong, but the conviction that something fundamental occurs around 18 months may turn out to be well founded.

The other age at which an across-the-board, domain-general change may occur is 4 years. The age of 4 does not correspond to a stage change in Piagetian theory, but it has turned out to be an age at which fundamental changes seem to occur across various domains. Moreover, this age also seems to be roughly the point at which the human child begins to differ radically from the chimpanzee. As Premack (1991, p. 164) has put it, "a good rule of thumb has proved to be: if the child of three and a half years cannot do it, neither can the chimpanzee."

Piaget's explanation of such changes in terms of an overarching modification in logical structure is likely to be wrong. In my view, the more plausible assumption for any across-the-board developmental change and for cross-species differences is that they may be related to specific types of brain development. Thus, if it turns out that across-the-board, domain-general changes do occur, we may be able to use them as a diagnostic for fundamental neural changes in the brain. This of course remains an open question, but the flourishing new field of developmental cognitive neuroscience may soon provide some relevant answers. However, even if some across-the-board changes were to hold, it is important to recall that their effects would be manifest somewhat differently across domains, since they would interact with domain-specific constraints. Development will not turn out to be *either* domain specific *or* domain general. It is clearly the intricate interaction of *both*—more domain general than is presupposed by most nativist/modularity views of development, but more domain specific than Piagetian theory envisages.

Domain Specificity and Abnormal Development

At several points throughout the book, I have alluded to abnormal development. Nature, alas, often presents the scientist with experiments of its own, in which different capacities are either spared or impaired. Such cases not only warrant study in their own right, they also help us to gain a deeper understanding of normal development and the issue of domain specificity.

In chapter 5 I mentioned the fact that autistic children appear to have relatively normal development in a number of domains, yet are seriously impaired with respect to theory of mind. Even autistic subjects with relatively high IQs fail false-belief tasks that normal 4- and 5-year-olds, and Down Syndrome children with much lower IQs, find easy. It remains unclear whether the autistic deficit is informational (i.e., the inability to construct representations of mental states in others) or resource-limited (i.e., the inability to hold in mind one representation of the state of the world, and time-mark it, so that later the necessary inferences can be made about another's previous mental state and the present state of the world).[1] If the autistic deficit is representational, this would suggest domain specificity. If it is computational, then whether or not it is domain specific depends on demonstrating that the computations impaired in theory of mind (maintaining representations in memory, time-marking and comparing different representations, etc.) are indeed available for all the *other* domains of the autistic individual's cognition.[2]

Another syndrome that helps us to probe the issue of domain specificity is Williams Syndrome (WS), which presents a different cognitive profile than the purported single deficit in autism. Many WS individuals have one or two domains relatively intact (e.g., language and face recognition [Bellugi et al. 1988; Udwin and Yule 1991]) although most of their cognition (number, problem solving, planning, etc.) is severely impaired. For a start, although WS children and adults are often extremely good at face-recognition tasks, they are very impaired on other spatial tasks. This fact suggests that face recognition is domain specific and is not simply part of general visuospatial skills. Whether this reasoning can be extended to the normal case depends, of course, on whether the processes of modularization for face recognition in WS subjects are the same as those in the normal population.

Individuals with Williams Syndrome are often surprisingly good at language production and comprehension. And, despite IQs in the 50s range, they even show some metalinguistic awareness (Karmiloff-Smith 1990c). Not only did two WS subjects perform at ceiling on the simple, partially on-line metalinguistic tasks discussed in chapter 2; they also showed high levels of success on off-line metalinguistic tasks. These metalinguistic capacities stand in sharp contrast to their very poor performance on other simple tasks involving number and visuospatial skills. Metacognition is exceedingly rare in retarded children. Its existence in WS individuals indicates that some forms of metacognition may not be as domain general as is normally presumed.

The domain specificity of language or of face recognition is also implied by research with various groups of previously normal brain-damaged adults. Aphasics, for instance, are severely impaired in aspects of their language, but can often perform normally on other cognitive tasks (Shallice 1988; Tyler 1992). Prosopagnosics are severely impaired in face recognition (either with respect to faces in general or, more commonly, in the recognition of individual faces), but seem to have no difficulty recognizing other spatial input (Bornstein 1963; Farah 1990).

Together with the examples from abnormal development, those from adult neuropsychology point to the domain specificity of language and face recognition. However, I know of no cases of adult brain injury where a deficit in the full set of theory-of-mind computations has been demonstrated. There are, none-the-less, cases of right-hemisphere patients in whom fluent syntax and semantics co-exist with a peculiar lack of pragmatics (Gardner 1985). Such patients appear to be unable to take into account the status and/or prior knowledge of their addressees; for example, they are overfamiliar toward complete strangers. It would be particularly informative to test the domain-specificity of theory of mind in these patients. By using the theory-of-mind tasks devised by Perner and his colleagues (discussed above in chapter 5), it would be possible to ascertain whether the

patients' pragmatic deficit is also accompanied by a failure to understand false belief in others. Such a result would support the contention
that theory of mind is domain specific.

Although there are some persuasive indications of domain specificity of theory-of-mind computations from the developmental literature
on autism, a substantial contribution from domain-general processes
is not yet ruled out. In favor of the latter is the fact that both Williams
Syndrome and Down Syndrome children who succeed on the theory-
of-mind tasks that normal 4-year-olds pass still fail on more complex
theory-of-mind tasks which require the intelligence of a normal 7–9-
year-old. By contrast, in the domain of language, the WS subjects can
use complex syntax which is not apparent in normal speech before
7–9 years. Thus, theory of mind may turn out to involve more of a
contribution from domain-general processes than language.

One type of abnormal development that does seem to indicate
across-the-board, domain-general deficits is Down Syndrome. To
probe this further, Julia Grant and I carried out an in-depth case study
of a 9-year-old Down Syndrome boy, M.G. M.G. was repeatedly tested
on a large number of the experiments reported in the various chapters
of the book. One striking result was the inconsistency of his successes;
for most microdomains, M.G. never seemed to achieve a consistent
level of behavioral mastery. For example, in one session he would
produce a drawing of a house which looked like that of a 6-year-old;
a week later, his productions might look more like those of a 2-year-
old; and so on, inconsistently, across the testing sessions. Furthermore, although M.G. quickly learned to balance both the evenly and
unevenly weighted blocks of the task discussed in chapter 3, and
showed immense pleasure at repeating his success in every testing
session, he seemed to relearn each time. Never did we witness any
signs of even the beginnings of the geometric-center theory emerging
in his behavior. Thus, although able to perform quite well, this Down
Syndrome child rarely achieved full behavioral mastery, and when he
did he never went beyond behavioral mastery in the microdomains in
which he showed success. In other words, there were no indications
that M.G.'s internal representations had undergone any form of
redescription.

The same was true of subject D.H., a 17-year-old girl who suffers
from spina bifida and internal hydrocephaly, is severely retarded, but
has very fluent language output. Despite the latter, she performed
rather poorly on our very simple partially on-line metalinguistic tests,
which 4–5-year-olds find very easy. D.H. could not do the off-line
metalinguistic task at all, although some of the Williams Syndrome

subjects who had equally low IQs and equally fluent language as D.H. could do it.

The case of M.G., the Down Syndrome child, indicates that behavioral mastery is a necessary condition for representational redescription. He did not reach a consistent level of behavioral mastery in the microdomains in which we tested him. But the case of D.H. suggests that, although behavioral mastery may be a necessary condition for representational redescription, it is not a sufficient one. Despite her very fluent language, D.H. was unsuccessful in all our tasks aimed at measuring the first signs of representational redescription.

Whatever mechanism we invoke to explain the general process of representational redescription, it may be lacking or deficient in many retarded individuals. By contrast, some Williams Syndrome children with IQs in the 50s not only achieve the first level of redescription (they perform at ceiling on our partially on-line task) but also demonstrate some metalinguistic capacities (Karmiloff-Smith 1990c; Karmiloff-Smith, Klima, Bellugi, Grant, and Baron-Cohen 1991). This is consistent with the hypothesis that redescription has taken place at higher levels. It suggests that an across-the-board normal level of intelligence is not a necessary prerequisite for the process of representational redescription to occur in a *particular* domain. The metalinguistic capacities of WS individuals suggests that metacognitive processes can occur domain-specifically if all the mental capacity is focused on one or two domains only.

In general, then, in-depth neuropsychological studies of abnormal development should allow us to generate more precise hypotheses about the extent to which normal development is domain general and the extent to which it is domain specific.

What Is Left of Piagetian Theory?

Since I have repeatedly argued against stages and in favor of the domain specificity of development, you may wonder what, if anything, I think is to be salvaged from Piaget's theory. In order to address this, I must return to a more general epistemological level of discussion.

Piaget's view of development is rooted in an epigenetic and constructivist stance in which both mind and environment play essential roles at all times. The nativist position, by contrast, places the main burden of explanation on prespecified structures in the mind. Nativists argue that development follows similar paths because all normal children start life with the same innately specified structures. The role of the environment is reduced to that of a mere trigger. But the fact that development proceeds in similar ways across normal children does not necessarily mean that development must be innately specified in detail, because it is also true that all children evolve in species-typical environments (Johnson and Morton 1991). Thus, it is the interaction between similar innate constraints and similar environmental constraints that gives rise to common developmental paths. Moreover, despite my arguments for some innate domain-specific predispositions, I recognize with Piaget that the brain has far more inherent plasticity than the nativist position presumes. The case of the congenitally deaf, discussed in chapter 2, is a particularly good example of how an area of the brain destined for auditory processing can be reconfigured to compute visuospatial input in linguistically relevant ways.

Research with other species also demonstrates the brain's plasticity. In studies of the rat, for example, Greenough et al. (1987) have shown that the brain's losses and gains of synapses are functions of different types of experience.[3] Thus, when placed merely for exercise in a treadmill, the rat shows an increase in blood capillaries in the cerebellum, but a decrease in synapses (due to pruning of existing neural pathways, because of the lack of stimulation other than physical exercise). However, when the rat is placed in a rich environment that challenges it to learn, substantial increases in dendritic growth and synaptic connectivity are generated.[4] Piaget would have embraced these findings as concordant with his own early work on mollusks,[5] for this is precisely the way in which he envisaged the epigenetic dynamics of change, as opposed to the nativist's view of genetic unfolding. The major difference between Piaget's position and the one I have adopted here is my insistence that there are *some* innately specified, domain-specific predispositions that guide epigenesis. Young infants have more of a head start on development than Piaget granted them.

Piaget's constructivism incorporates a process of "equilibration" based on a notion of internal conflict between systems at different levels of development. The RR model, by contrast, calls for success-based change. Indeed, many of the studies discussed in the book, and new data from Siegler (1989a, 1989b), show that change follows success, not only failure. In other words, children explore domain-specific environments beyond their successful interaction with them. This is not equivalent to Piaget's notion of "abstraction réfléchissante" generated only when the system is in disequilibrium. Such a view would imply that a system in a state of equilibrium would never spontaneously improve itself or explore new possibilities. Yet we know that change can occur without conflict, and that conflict does not automatically give rise to change. I have always posited something that many find counterintuitive: that representational change is generated when *stability* occurs in any part of the system dynamics.

This is not to deny the importance of instability, failure, conflict, and competition as generators of other types of change (Bates and MacWhinney 1987; Thelen 1989). It is worth reiterating this point. Competition can occur on line between different processes and cause behavioral change. But the hypothesis I have developed throughout the book is that competition leading to representational change can take place only after each of the potential competitors has been consolidated (i.e., is stable in its own right). In chapter 3, for example, we saw that counterexamples are not taken into account (do not have the status of a counterexample) until the child's theory about a particular microdomain has been consolidated. Similar examples are to be found in the history of science and in children's strategies of scientific experimentation (Klahr and Dunbar 1988; Kuhn et al. 1988; Kuhn and Phelps 1982; Schauble 1990),[6] as well as across the various domains of knowledge discussed throughout the present book.

So, does Piagetian theory retain any role in developmental theorizing? To me the answer is clearly affirmative. Theories of cognitive development (and recent connectionist modeling of cognitive development [McClelland 1991; Parisi 1991],[7] which I will discuss in the next chapter) continue to draw inspiration from Piaget's *epistemology*—his general stance with regard to the rich and constructive interaction between child and environment and his quest to understand emergent properties. It is the details of his *psychological* description of across-the-board stage-like changes in logico-mathematical structure that are no longer viable. I believe that it is possible to retain the essence of Piagetian theory while doing away with stage and structure. Beilin (1985), however, takes the opposite stance. He argues that stage and structure are core elements of Piaget's theory. Previously, I tended to agree. However, the process of writing a book makes one reexamine one's own positions more thoroughly. I am now convinced that the true essence of Piaget's theory lies in his epistemology, in his more general quest to understand epigenesis and emergent forms. But the problem with Piaget's theory (as indeed with the RR model) is that it is underspecified in comparison with, say, theories expressed as computer models. I now turn to this issue.

Chapter 8

Modeling Development: Representational Redescription and Connectionism

The principal virtue of computational models . . . is unattainable in more traditional verbal formulations of developmental theories. (Klahr 1991, p. 21)

One of the aims of this book is to persuade cognitive scientists of the value of a developmental perspective on the workings of the human mind. Yet at the heart of much of the work in cognitive science is the use of computer models to test psychological theories. It is therefore essential to devote a little space to a discussion of how the RR model might be relevant to attempts to express developmental theories in the form of computer simulations.

Soft-Core and Hard-Core Approaches to the Modeling of Development

What type of model is the RR model? Throughout the book, I have described the RR model in verbal terms. It is, as Klahr (1991) has put it, at the soft-core end of the modeling of cognitive development, the hard-core end being the implementation of theories as computer programs.

Klahr's opposition captures an important distinction between a focus on general principles of development and a focus on the specification of precise mechanisms. Klahr argues that the very process of simulating development in the form of computer programs leads to insights about the mechanisms underlying developmental change, whereas verbal descriptions always grossly underspecify the mechanisms. I agree. But soft-core and hard-core approaches should not be considered mutually exclusive.

In my view, soft-core modeling often leads to a broader intuitive understanding of general principles of change, whereas both the information-processing use of the flow chart and the symbolic approach to computer simulation run the serious risk of reifying into one or more boxes or single-named operators what is in fact the product of a highly interactive system. Nonetheless, at the hard-core end of modeling there have been a number of interesting attempts to express developmental theories in various information-processing terms—for example, in the form of scripts (Schank and Abelson 1977; Nelson 1986), of developmental contingency models (Morton 1986), and within the framework of self-modifying production systems (Klahr et al. 1987).[1] In this chapter, however, I shall take as my main example some recent connectionist simulations, since they seem to be the closest to the spirit of epigenesis and constructivism. They also address the problem I have raised with respect to stage theories, in that they demonstrate that by incremental learning one can obtain stage-like shifts in behavior without the need for qualitatively different structures and mechanisms (McClelland 1989).

Although the connectionist framework has come under severe criticism (Pinker and Mehler 1988) and has been called "a return to Associationism in high tech clothing" (Jusczyk and Bertoncini 1988) and "a revamping of the order from noise approach championed by Piaget" (Piatelli-Palmarini 1989), a growing number of cognitive developmentalists see in it a considerable theoretical potential for explicating the more general tenets of Piaget's epistemology (Bates 1991; McClelland 1991; Bechtel and Abrahamsen 1991). Moreover, a number of features of the RR model, developed quite independently in the 1970s and the early 1980s, map interestingly onto features of recent connectionist simulations.

After presenting some of the main features of the models, I shall go on to explore the extent to which connectionist simulations can and cannot capture what I deem to be crucial to a model of developmental change. To the extent that they can, connectionism would offer the RR model a powerful set of "hard-core" tools from the mathematical theory of complex dynamical systems (van Geehrt 1991). And to the extent that connectionist models fail to adequately model development, the RR model suggests some crucial modifications.

The Basic Architecture of Connectionist Models

In contrast with the von Neumann conception of a computer model, in which states in the computer are processed as symbols specifying a set of sequential operations, many connectionist networks involve parallel distributed processing (PDP). When I first learned about PDP models of development, I decided that PDP stood for "preposterous developmental postulates." But as my own understanding of the models deepens,[2] and as the developmental versions of the models take increasing account of the processes of real children's learning, I have come to recognize their potential for developmental cognitive science. I have thus changed the **P** from "preposterous" to "promising." I will not enter into a detailed discussion of connectionism here, since there are excellent works entirely devoted to the topic (Rumelhart and McClelland 1986; McClelland and Rumelhart 1986; Clark 1989; Bechtel and Abrahamsen 1991). Rather, I shall take from connectionist modeling those aspects that are of particular relevance to our discussion of the RR model. But first a brief description of the basic architecture.

The most common type of connectionist network is composed of a large number of simple processing units, each of which takes varying degrees of activation and sends excitatory or inhibitory signals to units to which it is connected. The architectures of these networks are typically composed of an input layer, one or more layers of hidden units corresponding to the network's evolving internal representations, and an output layer, with a vast network of connections between layers. In general, the hidden layers have fewer units than the input layer, which causes the representation of the information from the input to be compressed. Figure 8.1 illustrates a typical three-layer network.

Not all connectionist networks function with fully distributed representations. When localist representations are used, the status of the

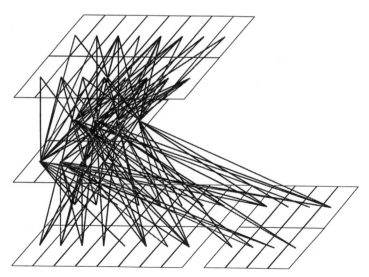

Figure 8.1
Three-layer network.

network's input is more like that of the symbols in a von Neumann architecture. In the fully distributed systems, the network's knowledge is not a static data structure situated in particular units, as in traditional programs; rather, it is stored across strengths of the connection weights between units via a simple nonlinear transformation (e.g. a logistic function) of the input. The activation of any particular unit is a continuous function of the net input to that unit. The initial weights on the connections between layers are usually random, and during learning the weights on connections change constantly as a function of the learning algorithm. A frequently used learning algorithm is "backpropagation," which involves the fine tuning of activations resulting from the sum of the squared difference between the target and the feedforward-computed activation levels of the outputs. Other learning algorithms involve fully interactive connections (McClelland 1990; Movellan and McClelland 1991). The hidden units develop representations progressively as learning proceeds. Ultimately, when learning is complete, activation levels and connection strengths tend to settle into a relatively stable state across the entire network.

Instead of the prespecified, discrete sequential steps typical of previous work in artificial intelligence programs, connectionist networks involve massively parallel systems dynamics. Processing elements exhibit nonlinear responses to their inputs. This has consequences for both representation and learning.

First, representations can be continuous and graded, reflecting fine-grained subtleties, and when appropriate they can also exhibit binary and categorical properties (Elman 1991).[3]

The second consequence for learning goes right to the heart of the Piagetian view of the process of development, which is that the same process of assimilation and accommodation of new information operates continuously. However, in contrast with Piaget's stage view, McClelland (1989) and others have shown that networks will exhibit stage-like transitions, not because of discrete changes in structure or learning algorithm, but as a result of slow incremental learning until at some point a small change produces an important modification in output. In other words, a huge number of simple local interactions can result in complex global effects, without the need to invoke any form of executive control (a homunculus) over and above the systems dynamics. Connectionist networks are particularly good examples of how one can get a surprising amount of order emerging from random starting states without any changes in architecture.

Another telling (albeit noncognitive) analogy is the Belousov-Zhabotinskii autocatalytic chemical reaction described in Thelen (1989).

When bromate ions are put into a highly acidic medium in a shallow glass dish, concentric ringed patterns start to emerge which have an amazingly ordered appearance (Madore and Freedman 1987). Thelen stresses that it is impossible to describe the emergent patterns in terms of the random competitive behavior of individual ions, because they are so huge in number. The different patterns do not preexist in the chemicals. They emerge as the product of complex random interactions of the constraints inherent in the chemicals, the constraints imposed by the shape and texture of the container, those created by the temperature of the room, and so forth. In other words, the resultant patterns are the emergent property of systems dynamics—nothing more, nothing less. Thelen argues that the order we witness in embryogenesis and ontogenesis can also be thought of in terms of properties emerging from systems dynamics. And likewise, it seems, for connectionist networks.

Let us now explore some of the ways in which connectionist approaches to the modeling of development are relevant to the recurrent themes that have arisen throughout the book. As I mentioned earlier, the RR model was developed before I had any knowledge of the connectionist framework. However, some of the intuitions I was grappling with at the time (behavioral mastery, the status of implicit representations, and so forth) turn out to be surprisingly close to some of the basic tenets of the connectionist approach. For example, many of the details of phase-1 learning, which leads to behavioral mastery and level-I representations, may turn out to be captured particularly well in a connectionist model. However, as we shall see, the very aspect of development that this book has focused on—the process of representational redescription—is precisely what is missing thus far from connectionist simulations.

Nativism and Connectionism

Most researchers of the connectionist persuasion take as their research strategy a non-nativist view. This makes it possible to explore the extent to which developmental phenomena can be simulated from a tabula rasa starting state—i.e., from random weights and random activation levels, with no domain-specific knowledge. This has led some to interpret the results of connectionist modeling as strong evidence for the anti-nativist position. However, there is nothing about the connectionist framework that precludes the introduction of initial biased weights (i.e., weights that are the equivalent of innately specified predispositions) rather than random weights. Indeed, this has been the solution taken by a number of modelers, although often more for technical than for theoretical reasons. Since we know, for instance, that infants are sensitive to symmetry, shape, and ordinality, there would be nothing inherently nonconnectionist about building such predispositions into the starting state of a network learning some other task.

Various ways of simulating developmental change have been proposed. One is to start a network with a small number of hidden units and, as "development" proceeds, to recruit more and more units or an extra hidden layer to compress the data even further (Schultz 1991 a,b). This is rather like the neo-Piagetians' notion that processing capacity increases with age. Other researchers have suggested the equivalent of "maturational" change, such that the network would start by using contrastive Hebbian learning and, with "maturation," come to use backpropagation (Bechtel and Abrahamsen 1991). Incremental learning has also been used, such that the network first sees only part of the input at a time, rather than the whole input set in one go (Elman 1991; Plunkett and Marchmann 1991). These are all domain-general solutions to developmental change. However, we are beginning to witness an increasing tendency on the part of connectionists to explore the ways in which domain-specific constraints might shape learning. This, in my view, is likely to be a future focus for connectionist models of development.

Domain Specificity and Connectionism

It might seem that connectionist models deny, either implicitly or explicitly, the need for domain-specific learning. However, as we shall see in a moment, domain specificity slips in subtly through the back door!

In chapter 1 I discussed a distinction drawn by Fodor between resource encapsulation and informational encapsulation. For Fodor, modules are informationally encapsulated; he is neutral about their resource encapsulation. In terms of domain specificity, this translates into stating that domains are specific from a representational point of view but may employ general learning algorithms. In favor of domain generality, connectionists stress that their models use the *same* learning algorithms for different categories of input presented to different networks. But no single network has been presented with an array of inputs from *different* domains (e.g. language, space, physics). Networks used to simulate language acquisition (which will be discussed in detail in a later section) see only linguistic strings (Elman 1991). The same network could not be used for learning about a physics task without totally upsetting the language learning that has already taken place unless it continues to be trained also on the original set. In other words, the fact that each network is dedicated to a specific type of input, in a specific learning task, turns out to be equivalent to domain specificity (or modularity) in the human. Infants seem to process proprietary, domain-specific inputs separately, and so do networks.

Networks are not necessarily resource encapsulated. The same learning algorithm can be used within many different networks. However, single networks are informationally encapsulated. Interestingly, although they are informationally encapsulated, networks are not "modules" in the sense of the distinction I drew in chapter 1 between modules and a process of modularization. In fact, networks mimic the process of modularization because, with few or no built-in biases, it is only as learning proceeds that they *become* increasingly like special-purpose modules. Initially, a network could be trained to process physics or linguistic input data. But after learning (say) linguistic data, the same network becomes incapable of learning physics data without undoing all the learning it had achieved for the initial input set. At one level of description, then, networks are just as domain specific as many instances of human learning. We may end up requiring multiple networks with different learning algorithms.

Let us now look at some of the specific features of the RR model and how they relate to the connectionist framework.

Behavioral Mastery and Connectionism

Throughout the book I have repeatedly argued that behavioral mastery is a prerequisite for representational change. We saw, for example, in the block-balancing task in chapter 3 that children remain competent block-balancers for a couple of years before they change to the geo-metric-center theory. Recall, too, the examples in chapter 6 on the child as a notator. Microdevelopmentally, in the map-generation task, no children introduced changes to their systems very early in the task. Changes occurred only after 7 or 10 bifurcations—that is, after the original task-specific solution had been consolidated. Similarly, in acquiring grammatical gender, children first consolidate each of the systems (the morphophonological, the syntactic, and the semantic) separately; only later does one system constrain another (Karmiloff-Smith 1979a). In each case, a period of behavioral mastery seems to precede representational change. However, an analysis of hidden units during learning in a connectionist network reveals some representation of subsequent change *before* it is observable in the output. This suggests that change may start to occur prior to full behavioral mastery.

So what is behavioral mastery? I believe that the intuition underlying the notion of behavioral mastery maps rather well onto the connectionist notion of a network's having settled into a stable state. At some point during the learning process within a network, weights tend to stabilize such that new inputs no longer affect their settings. Whereas this is the *endpoint* of learning in a connectionist model, in the RR model it is the *starting* point for generating redescriptions of implicitly defined level-I representations.

Implicit Representations and Connectionism

It has often been difficult to convey, particularly to developmental psychologists, precisely what I meant by "level-I implicit representations." As I mentioned in chapter 1, researchers have often used the term "implicit" to explain away efficient behavior that appears "too early" for the tenets of a particular theory. But no definition of "implicit" has yet been offered. And "explicit" is usually confounded with access to verbally statable knowledge. Throughout the book, I have argued for a more complex picture of representational change than such a dichotomy would suggest. I have posited several levels of redescription beyond the level-I representations.

Some recent connectionist simulations of language learning are particularly illustrative of the status of level-I representations within the RR-model view of development. Elman's work (1991) is a particularly elegant example.

Elman's network attempts to simulate the young toddler's task of learning structure-dependent relations from English-like input strings. The network is fed one word at a time and has to predict the next input state, e.g. the next word in a string. The difference between this predicted state (the computed output) and the actual subsequent state (the target output) is fed back at every time step. But the network is recursive. A context layer, a special subset of units that receive no external input, feeds the results of previous processing back into the internal representations. In this way, at time 2, the hidden layer processes both the input of time 2 and, from the context layer, the results of its processing at time 1. And so on recursively. It is in this way that the network captures the sequential nature of the input. The architecture of the network is shown in figure 8.2.[4]

Elman's input corpus consists of sentence-like strings that differ according to number agreement between subjects and verbs (e.g. "boy hears."/"girls see."), whether verbs are transitive or intransitive ("boy chases girl."/"boy walks."), and levels of embedding of relative clauses ("boys who chase girl see."/"girls who boy chases walk."), and so

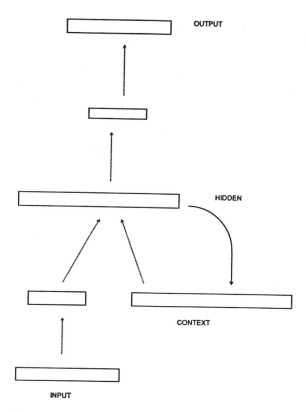

Figure 8.2
The Elman recurrent network. (From Elman 1989. Reprinted with permission of the author.)

forth. The full stop at the end of each string plays a role equivalent to that of the exaggerated intonation contours that mark constituent structure in the "motherese" inputs to young children. Each noun and each verb in Elman's network appears in a variety of different grammatical roles across the input strings. Thus, identical inputs are processed differently, depending on the current state of the context units (e.g., "boy" after a relative clause marker versus "boy" after a transitive verb). Note that although the network is given presegmented words (a task the child must accomplish in acquiring language), the network is never given information about sentential role, grammatical category, or number agreement. Such categories must be inferred by the network, during learning, from several simultaneous sources: the statistical regularities across the input sequences, the information fed back into the hidden units from the context units, and the backpropagated information about the differences between the network's predictions of the next input and the actual input.

To train the network, Elman tried various forms of incremental learning, initially inputting simple strings and then, after a certain amount of learning, providing longer strings with relative clauses. He also varied the "short-term memory" of the network, in that initially it could scan only two or three items in a sequence but later it could scan longer strings. With incremental learning, as the network's processing increases, new representations continue to be constrained by the earlier learning on short strings which contain the major generalizations required for later learning.

Connectionist models have been criticized for the way in which the inputs they represent follow from the modeler's own rule-based knowledge (Lachter and Bever 1988). Though this may be true for some models, Elman uses arbitrary localist input vectors for the representation of all his inputs. Thus, "boy" and "boys" are arbitrarily different, as are all nouns and all verbs. No part of the representation gives any indication of an overlap of grammatical function or meaning. Each input vector is simply a long string of zeros, with single ones at different arbitrary points. Grammatical function must be progressively inferred and represented in the hidden units as learning proceeds.

Elman's network receives inputs that are actually weaker in representational potential than those that the child receives.[5] However, paradoxically, despite the difference with normal input to the child, this feature of Elman's model turns out to be true to the spirit of the RR model. Indeed, I have argued that, despite the potential information that exists in the structure of the input (e.g. the phonological and semantic overlaps between "boy" and "boys"), children's representations are *initially* stored independently of one another (Karmiloff-Smith 1979a).

The full details of the learning process of Elman's network need not concern us here; we are interested in the *status* of the representations that the network progressively builds. First, Elman shows that, as with most connectionist networks using nonlinear functions, a long initial period is essential to learning. At first, the network's predictions are random. However, with time the network learns to predict, not necessarily the actual next word, but the correct *category* of word (noun, verb, etc.), as well as the correct subcategorization frame for the next verb (transitive or intransitive) and the correct number marking on both noun and verb (singular or plural). This cannot be done by mere association between adjacent surface elements. For example, while in the case of the simple strings a network could learn to always predict that strings without an "s" (plural verb) follow strings with an "s" (plural noun), it cannot do so for embedded relative clause strings. Here a plural verb may follow a singular noun (e.g., "boys that chase *girl see* dog"). In such cases, the network *must* make *structure-dependent* predictions. Thus, the network progressively moves from processing mere surface regularities to representing something more abstract, but without this being built in as a prespecified linguistic constraint.

Do these impressive results allow us to conclude that the network really knows about the linguistic categories of noun/verb, singular/plural, transitive/intransitive, and different levels of embedding? Yes and no. No, because neither this network nor another network could directly use this grammatical knowledge for other purposes (see below). But yes, it does know about these grammatical categories in the sense that it now has what the RR model would call level-I representations of them. Let us look at the status of the network's implicit knowledge.

There are various ways of scrutinizing the internal representations of a network during and after learning. One is to analyze the weight spaces of its hidden units. This can by done by cluster analysis or, more dynamically, by principal-component analysis of multiple trajectories through the activation space (Gonzalez and Wintz 1977). In Elman's example, as learning progresses, each string is internally represented as a trajectory through weight space. Representations of the whole set of input sentences can be recorded by freezing the weights and saving the patterns on the hidden units. The set of trajectories this creates in the *N*-dimensional weight space of the network shows that certain categories tend to line up in specific ways orthogonal to others. One can then create phase-state portraits of the rotation of axes, picking out the most significant principal components.

For example, uses of "boy" as subject are on one trajectory through weight space with other sentence subjects, whereas uses of "boy" as sentence object line up slightly differently but nearby. Likewise, uses of "girl" in subject position line up with uses of "boy" in subject position. On another dimension of the activation space, "boy" and "girl" in all their grammatical roles line up with all other words that we call nouns. These are further away from the patterning of all the verbs. Elsewhere in activation space, verbs break down into trajectories separating transitives from intransitives. And so forth. These different trajectories are derived from representations in the hidden units which share overlapping activation levels. They are the product of the overall system dynamics that take place while the network is learning the input set.

Explicit Representations and Connectionism

This seemingly impressive grammatical knowledge is only implicit in the system's internal representations. This does not mean that it is not represented. As in the case of early learning in the child, I would argue that it is represented in level-I format. But it is we, as external theorists, who use level-E formats to label the trajectories through weight space as nouns, verbs, subjects, objects, intransitives, transitives, plurals, singulars, and so on. The network itself never goes beyond the formation of the equivalent of stable level-I representations. In other words, it does not spontaneously go beyond the behavioral mastery that allows it to perform efficiently. It does not redescribe the representations that are stored in its activation trajectories. Unlike the child, it does not spontaneously "appropriate" the knowledge it represents about different linguistic categories. It cannot directly use the higher-level, more abstract knowledge for any other purpose than the one it was designed for or engage in internetwork knowledge transfer. Another network would need to be called to exploit the products of its learning. This does not occur *spontaneously* after a certain threshold of stability has been reached. The notion of nounhood always remains implicit in the network's system dynamics. The child's *initial* learning is like this, too. But children go on to spontaneously redescribe their knowledge. This pervasive process of representational redescription gives rise to the manipulability and flexibility of the human representational system.

Now, it is not difficult to build a network, inspired by the RR model, that would redescribe stable states in weight space such that the implicit information represented in trajectories could be used as knowledge by the same or other networks. But this would seem to entail a change in the architecture of the network, involving perhaps the creation of special nodes not implicated in other aspects of the on-line processing. Furthermore, the RR model suggests that what is abstracted during the redescriptive process involves a loss of detail and a gain in accessibility. Thus, one would not want the entire trajectories of the network to be redescribed, but rather the *product* of the most important ones. (This would be equivalent to redescribing the phase-state portraits of the principal-component analysis.) And the RR model postulates that redescribed knowledge capturing abstract notions such as "verb" and "noun" must be in a *different* format than the original level-I representations. In other words, redescriptions would have to be in a representational format usable across networks which had previously processed *different* representations at the input level. Hence the need for representational redescription into level-E formats—simple copies of level-I representations would not be transportable from one network to another, because they would be too dependent on the specific features of their inputs.

In chapter 2, there was a particularly relevant example of what such a process might look like in the human case. When 3–6-year-olds were asked to repeat the last word that the experimenter had said before a story was interrupted, some of the youngest subjects (3–4 years old) could not do the task at all despite lengthy modeling and help from the experimenter. Their fluent language and their lack of segmentation errors suggest that they did represent formal word boundaries for the majority of words they used and understood, but they were not yet ready to go beyond behavioral mastery. There were other children (4–5 years old) who could not do the task immediately but who, with one-off modeling for a few open-class words, were able immediately to extend the notion of "word" to all open-class and closed-class categories. Their level-I representations were ready for level-E1 redescription generated from outside. However, slightly older children (5–6 years) who had never had a grammar lesson had spontaneously undergone the redescriptive process on their own. They showed immediate success, even on the practice story. Finally, 6–7-year-olds' representations showed signs of having undergone further redescription into the E2/3 format; these children were able to consciously access their knowledge and to provide verbal explanations as to what counts as a word and why. I deem this process of *multiple* redescription of knowledge that becomes increasingly accessible to different parts of the system an essential component of human development and one that connectionist modelers need to take into account.

Finally, I discussed in chapter 2 a case where representational re-description does not seem to occur at all. This case involved knowledge about on-line computations of discourse constraints (decisions in ex-tended discourse about when to pronominalize, when to use full noun phrases, and so on). Such decisions depend not only on the structure of the language per se but also (and above all) on the on-line construc-tion of a particular discourse model. It may be that, by exploring in connectionist networks the difference between stable representational states and those that are relevant only to on-line dynamics and should not be stored, we may be able to further explore the constraints on representational redescription in humans. Furthermore, we know from the developmental literature on metalinguistic awareness, and on metacognition in general, which features of learning become avail-able to conscious access and in what order. We could use connectionist simulations to explore the extent to which different features are in-volved in multiple mappings and which become more explicitly rep-resented in the hidden units.

What Is Missing from Connectionist Models of Development?

Although connectionist models have potential for developmental theorizing, they have several shortcomings. One concerns the input presented to networks. With some exceptions, up to now connection-ists have not really modeled development; they have modeled *tasks*. This becomes particularly apparent if we look at the example of the balance scale that is so popular in all kinds of computer modeling, connectionist or other (Schultz 1991 a and b; McClelland and Jenkins 1990; Langley 1987; Siegler and Robinson 1978; Newell 1991). The models have focused on children's performance on the balance-scale task, not on how they learn about physical phenomena in general. It is a fact that many children come to a balance-scale experiment with no experience of balance scales. But that doesn't mean that they bring no relevant knowledge to the task. They may focus on weight in tasks using the traditional balance scale because weights are what the ex-perimenter more obviously manipulates. But in the block-balancing task discussed in chapter 3, many young children ignore weight and focus solely on length. Children come to such tasks having already learned something about how rulers fall from tables, how children balance on see-saws, and so forth. But a see-saw is not a balance scale. It does not have a neat line of equidistant pegs on which children of absolutely equal weight can be placed one on top of another! Devel-opment is not simply task-specific learning. It is deriving knowledge from many sources and using that knowledge in a goal-oriented way.

Thus, in my view, far richer input vectors are needed if we are to model the ways in which real children learn in real environments.

To be fair, precise modeling necessarily involves simplification, which is why I argued for the complementary role of soft-core approaches. Moreover, certain connectionist simulations of the balance scale were not focused on the physical issue. McClelland's (1989) work on the balance-scale task, for example, was principally aimed at demonstrating that networks can produce stage-like behavior from incremental learning. But if we are to model the content of children's learning in specific microdomains, then our models must reflect the complexities of the child's interaction with the world. And, as was suggested in earlier sections of this chapter, the starting point of learning in networks does not have to be random. It could include some initially biased weights as a result of evolution and/or earlier learning.

It seems plausible that connectionist models can indeed lend precision to an account of what I have called phase-1 learning—the phase that results in behavioral mastery (i.e., the period of rich interaction with the environment during which level-I representations are built and consolidated). However, there is much more to development than this. I have intimated at various points that connectionist simulations stop short of what I deem to be certain essential components of human development. Indeed, as I discussed in some detail in the previous section, up to now connectionist models have had little to say about how to move from implicit representations to explicit ones,[6] an essential process called for by the RR model. How could a network appropriate its own stable states? Clark (1989), Dennett (1978), and McClelland (1991) have argued that all that would have to be added to a connectionist network is another network that uses the equivalent of public language, implying that the only difference between implicit and explicit knowledge is that the latter is linguistically encoded. However, I have provided examples of children's knowledge that is explicitly represented but which they cannot articulate linguistically. The RR model posits a far more complex view of multiple levels of representational redescription, of which language is but one—and not necessarily the most important—manifestation. Finally, the fact that most connectionist models blend structure and content makes it difficult to exploit knowledge components. Yet we saw, particularly in chapter 6, that children extract knowledge components from the processes in which they are embedded, re-represent them, and use them in increasingly manipulable ways.

It remains an open question how representational redescription might be modeled in a connectionist network. Can it be done simply by adding layers to the architecture of a single network, or by creating, say, a hierarchy of interconnected networks? Should a node, external to the on-line processing, be gradually fed with information from the developing internal representations when hidden units reach a certain threshold of stability? Or will we have to opt for hybrid models containing both parallel distributed processing and more classical sequential manipulation of discrete symbols (see discussions in Karmiloff-Smith 1987, 1991; Clark and Karmiloff-Smith 1992; Schneider 1987)? As connectionist networks become more complex, I think that the issue of whether something is truly "hybrid" will lose relevance. Future developmental modeling must, in my view, simulate *both* the benefits of rapid processing via implicit representations and those gained by further representational redescription—a process which, I posit, makes possible human creativity.

There'll Be No Flowcharts in This Book!

Since the 1970s, when I introduced the notion of representational redescription and metaprocedural operators, I have been constantly questioned about precise mechanisms. I would run off and draw a flowchart or two, with separate boxes for a "stability detector," an "analogy scanner," a "redescriber," a "consciousness operator," and so forth. These would rapidly find their way to the wastepaper basket. Then, if I dared to present a flowchart during an informal talk, I was immediately interrupted and subjected to questioning about how each of the metaprocedural operators knows when to apply itself. Back to the drawing board, and yet another flurry of flowcharts and calculations of the ratio between positive exemplars and counterexamples. But apart from a couple of moments of madness when I actually published something that fell awkwardly between a flowchart and an information flow diagram (Karmiloff-Smith 1979a, 1985), I have always sensed that the questions were at the wrong level for the intuitions I was grappling with. Consciousness for me was not a "box" or a separable operator; it was, and is, an emergent property of the reiterated process of representational redescription. It is my view that the types of construct that arise within dynamical systems theory, and its implementation in connectionist models of development, may turn out to be at the right level for more precise future explorations of the RR model.

Chapter 9
Concluding Speculations

It is less illogical than it first appears to speak of instincts for inventiveness. (Marler 1991, p. 63)

Perhaps the title of this chapter has made you smile! There was more than a small dose of speculation in each of the other chapters, too. But, along with the collection of experimental and observational data, theorizing and speculation are essential parts of the developmental perspective on cognitive science.

I started the book by distinguishing between the representations that sustain complex behavior and the things that a given species can do with that complexity. My argument has been that, far more pervasively than even its near cousin the chimpanzee, the human mind exploits its representational complexity by re-representing its implicit knowledge into explicit form. Thereby the knowledge becomes usable beyond the special-purpose goals for which it is normally used. I claim that this is rarely if ever true of other species.

Recall David Premack's example of the plover, discussed in chapter 5 above. To keep competitors at bay, the plover displays a complex set of behaviors that, in human terms, would be called deceit. But these behaviors are not available even for other closely related purposes.

What about the chimpanzee, with whom we share close to 100 percent of our genetic makeup? Do chimpanzees, like children, play with *knowledge*, just as they play with physical objects and conspecifics? According to discussions I have had with Premack, there are no obvious indicators of representational redescription in the behavior of the chimpanzee. There are numerous examples of how the chimpanzee goes beyond a specified task; for example, when the task is to assemble the pieces of a puzzle of a chimp face, a chimpanzee might, after succeeding, add extra pieces as decoration to form a hat or a necklace (Premack 1975). But Premack could recall no case of a chimpanzee's spontaneously analyzing the components of its successful behavior in the way a child does. It is, of course, not immediately obvious how we would recognize representational redescription in the chimpanzee if it did exist. The higher levels of redescription (into, say, linguistic format) are obviously ruled out. But we know that in many instances children develop explicit representations which lie between the implicit representations and the verbally reportable data. In the child, level E1 of representational redescription frequently follows behavioral mastery. The chimpanzee, by contrast, seems to be content to continuously repeat its successes; it does not go beyond behavioral mastery. Yet throughout the book we have seen that human children spontaneously seek to understand their own cognition, and that this leads to the sort of representational manipulability that eventually allows them to become folk linguists, physicists, mathematicians, psychologists, and notators.

My speculation is that either the process of representational redescription is not available to other species or, if it is (perhaps to the chimpanzee), the higher-level codes into which representations are translated during redescription are very impoverished. It is plausible that "language-trained" chimpanzees will show signs of representational redescription. But this would be due, not to the existence of a language-like code per se, but to the possibility of redescription into any other more explicit code (Karmiloff-Smith 1983).

The RR model is fundamentally a hypothesis about the specifically human capacity to enrich itself from within by exploiting knowledge it has already stored, not by just exploiting the environment. Intra-domain and inter-domain representational relations are the hallmark of a flexible and creative cognitive system. The pervasiveness of representational redescription in human cognition is, I maintain, what makes human cognition specifically human.

This is, of course, a challenge to ethologists and one I look forward to pursuing in the future. What indices should we be seeking in other species? What machinery would we have to add to the plover, the ant, the spider, the bee, or the chimpanzee to make the process of representational redescription possible?

Figure 9.1 is a caricature of the difference between humans and other species that I have in mind. It illustrates that level-I representations exist as cognitive tools allowing an organism (human or nonhuman) to act on the environment and be affected in turn by it. The second part of the figure is not meant to suggest that, in the human, knowledge goes in one ear and out the other! Rather, it is a reminder that, in the human, *internal representations* become objects of cognitive manipulation such that the mind extends well beyond its environment

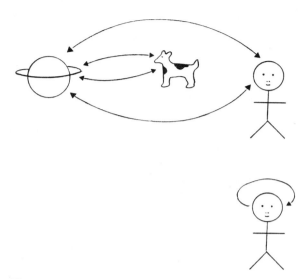

Figure 9.1
Two types of learning.

and is capable of creativity. Let me go as far as to say that the process of redescription is, in Marler's terms, one of the human instincts for inventiveness.

I hope to have convinced you that the flourishing new domain of cognitive science needs to go beyond the traditional nativist-empiricist dichotomy that permeates much of the field, in favor of an epistemology that embraces both innate predispositions and constructivism. And cognitive science has much to gain by going beyond modularity and taking developmental change seriously. Understanding the mind of the developing child should be an essential component of both teaching and research in cognitive science.

I began the book with a quote from Fodor. Let me end it with another: "Deep down, I'm inclined to doubt that there is such a thing as cognitive development in the sense that developmental cognitive psychologists have in mind." (1985, p. 35)

Now that you have come to the end of this book, I sincerely hope that, deep down, you disagree!

Notes

Chapter 1

1. See also Marr's (1976) discussion of the principle of modular design.
2. Fodor 1985, p. 37. This is a point also discussed by Caplan (1985), who argues that input systems are encapsulated because of the nature of the representations that they compute, not because of any special-purpose feature of their processing.
3. See also Logan 1988; Posner and Snyder 1975; Shiffrin and Schneider 1977.
4. In fact, Fodor (1985, p. 35) specifically denies not just the relevance of cognitive development but the very existence of development as most cognitive developmentalists conceive of it.
5. See Marr's (1982) discussion of modularity in terms of varying degrees of modularity. See also Shallice 1988 for suggested modifications to Fodor's strict definition of a module.
6. Another definition of "innate" comes from Pylyshyn (1987, p. 117): "This is what people mean, or should mean, when they claim that some cognitive state or capacity is *innate*: not that it is independent of environmental influence, but that it is independent of rule governered construction from representations of relevant properties of the environment. In other words, it is not systemically related to its environmental cause solely in terms of its semantic (or, informational) content."
7. Karmiloff-Smith 1986. For a more recent discussion of the nature of innate specifications, see Johnson (in press) and Johnson and Morton 1991.
8. Suggestive data do exist from studies of adult brain activity using positron emission tomography scans which show, for instance, that different areas of the brain are activated according to whether subjects see real words (which they acquired during childhood when learning to read) or newly encountered nonwords—see Peterson et al. 1989 and Posner et al. 1988. To my knowledge, as yet no such work exists with respect to infants.
9. See Beilin 1989, Gruber and Voneche 1977, and Gold 1987 for excellent overviews of Piaget's theory. For neo-Piagetian, domain-general theories, see Case 1978, Fischer 1980, Halford 1982, and Pascual-Leone 1976, 1987; these authors argue for across-the-board changes in memory or computational power. For a new contrasting view, see M. Anderson 1992.
10. Fodor (1983, p. 33) uses the term "constructivism" differently from Piaget. For Fodor it is a form of empiricism: "Specifically, if mental structures can be viewed as assembled from primitive elements, then perhaps mechanisms of learning can be shown to be responsible for effecting their construction . . . real convergence between the motivations of classical associationism and those which actuate its computational reincarnation: Both doctrines find in constructivist analyses of mental structures the promise of an empiricist (i.e., non-nativist) theory of cognitive de-

velopment." Piaget argued that his constructivist genetic epistemology—the notion that new cognitive structures are emergent properties of a self-organizing system—was an alternative to both nativism and empiricism.

11. Boden 1982; Karmiloff-Smith 1979a, 1986, 1991; Mandler 1983. For discussions see Feldman and Gelman 1987 and Gelman, Massey, and McManus 1991.

12. Since Piaget's theory of cognitive development is rooted in the notion of a biological continuum (see e.g., Piaget 1967), implicitly—even if not explicitly—Piaget must have attributed *some* specifically human attributes to the neonate mind, without which it would be difficult to see how the human infant could differ so radically from other species or what sort of evolutionary theory Piaget had in mind.

13. See Keil 1986 for a discussion of domain-specific developmental change, Mounoud 1986 for a theory in terms of repeated developmental phases, and Carey 1985 with respect to fundamental knowledge reorganizations within domains.

14. See Gelman 1990b and the whole of volume 14 (1990) of the journal *Cognitive Science*, which is devoted to the issue of domain-specific constraints on development. See particularly the excellent discussion by Keil in that volume on the differences between domain-general and domain-specific theories.

15. Before birth, too, there is organization. According to Turkewitz and Kenny (1982), the onset of different sensory systems during embryogenesis is sequential, resulting in independence among prenatal developing systems. Initial postnatal organization thus arises as an emergent property of these sequential onsets. Constraints on sensory input are therefore adaptive and advantageous as a basis for neural organization and subsequent perceptual development.

16. See also Johnson-Laird 1982 and Marshall 1984.

17. See also Maurer 1976 and Meltzoff 1990.

18. See Johnson 1988 and Johnson and Karmiloff-Smith 1992 for critical discussions of various selectionist theories of genetic specification.

19. Thelen (1989) argues persuasively that, in fact, in an epigenetic system there is no formal difference between exogenous (external) and endogenous (internal) sources of change in which the action of the organism plays a crucial role.

20. Rubik's Cube is composed of tiny movable squares of six different colors. The goal is to move the squares, by articulated blocks which move in all directions, until each side of the cube is composed of a single color.

21. The movement from laborious practice to automaticity or proceduralization has been much discussed in the literature on adult skill learning. See, e.g., Anderson 1980, Logan 1988, Posner and Snyder 1975 and Shiffrin and Schneider 1977.

22. See J. Campbell 1990 for a discussion of the importance of introducing the notion of re-representation to current AI modeling.

23. I should like to thank Jean Mandler for having had the patience to constantly raise, when commenting on my papers, the issue of direct linguistic encoding, until I finally started to listen to her!

24. Sarah Hennessy, a PhD student at CDU, showed how children have quite elaborate linguistically encoded information about mathematical principles and yet, for a lengthy period of time, violate these principles when doing mathematical calculations.

25. See E. Clark 1987 and Marshall and Morton 1978 on the importance of mismatch between output and input in early language learning.

26. The following anecdote amusingly illustrates my point. I once agreed to teach the developmental part of a European Science Foundation Summer School in Sociolinguistics. I naturally felt obliged to devote one of my lectures to mother-child interaction (with some exceptions, a predominantly atheoretical area about which

I am not overly enthusiastic), and to make certain points clear I had to imitate the exaggerated prosodic features of mother-child discourse. After the lecture, a student came rushing up to me exclaiming: "That was just wonderful! So expressive! One can tell you love babies." And I heard the cognitive scientist (not the mother) in me retort vehemently: "I *HATE* babies!" My lovely daughters will forgive me, they know exactly what I mean.

27. See also Meltzoff 1990.

28. But see Rutkowska 1991 for a different view, as well as Keil's 1991 response.

29. See, e.g., Gelman and Coley 1991; Keil 1979, 1989; Carey 1985; Mandler 1988; Mandler (in press); Markman 1989.

Chapter 2

1. Atkinson 1982; Chomsky 1986; Bloom 1990; Hyams 1986; Pinker 1984, 1987, 1989; Roeper 1987; Valian 1986, 1990.

2. Piaget 1955b; Schlesinger 1971; Slobin 1973; Bowerman 1973; Sinclair 1971, 1987; Bates and MacWhinney, 1987; Bruner 1974/5, 1978; Greenfield and Smith 1976; Bates et al. 1979; Golinkoff 1983; Schaffer 1977. There is an interesting paradox about language learning which does not seem to be true of other domains of knowledge. Newport and her collaborators (Johnson & Newport 1989; Newport and Supalla, in press) argue that whereas skill increases over the course of development in most domains of learning, the ability to acquire a native language is at its peak early in life but subsequently declines. Anyone who has tried to learn a second language in adulthood recognizes this. Yet the general problem-solving abilities of adults are considerably greater than those of 4-year-olds. The most obvious conclusion is that the acquisition of a native tongue is a maturationally constrained, domain-specific ability, since calling on domain-general processes to acquire a second language in adulthood does not lead to native-like acquisition. But not all researchers take such a stance. Newport (1990) argues that because general cognitive processing abilities are *less* developed in young children, they perceive and store only a limited number of component pieces of form and meaning. By contrast, adults store larger segments, focusing on whole-word mappings. This puts the young child at an advantage over older children and adults for those aspects of language learning that require componential analysis (e.g., complex morphological structure). In other words, having less cognitive processing capacity enables the child to acquire the component parts of the linguistic system that remain opaque to the adult. Newport shows that, irrespective of length of exposure to a second language (e.g., 30 years or more), acquisition that took place between 3 and 7 years of age ends up being indistinguishable from that of native speakers, whereas persons whose learning started at later ages show decreasing proficiency in subtle gramaticality-judgment tasks. The "less is more" hypothesis is an interesting one; however, since 7-year-olds are far more advanced cognitively than 3-year-olds, Newport's argument predicts that it should be more difficult to acquire a second native-like language at 7 than at 3. To my knowledge, this is not the case. One can acquire several languages in a native-like fashion, as long as the learning takes place early during the period before puberty. (Obviously, to acquire the second language in a native-like fashion, the child must be immersed in a natural language-learning environment and not be learning the language in a formal school-like situation.) For Newport's domain-general argument to hold, she would have to show decreasing proficiency, perhaps on more difficult linguistic judgment tasks, between 3 and 7. She would also have to reconcile these arguments with those made in earlier papers (e.g., Newport 1981)

in which she showed that children learning ASL first produce holistic signs which they subsequently break up into their morphological parts. I discuss this later in the chapter.

3. It is also difficult to fit the notion of a critical period for language acquisition (Lenneberg 1967) into the Piagetian notion that language is simply the outcome of sensorimotor intelligence. A critical period implies a biological predisposition present only at certain maturational periods. This is true not only for second-language learning, as mentioned in the previous note, but also for first-language learning. Newport (1990) tested this in a detailed study of congenitally deaf but otherwise normal adults for whom ASL was the primary language. These adults varied in the age at which they were first exposed to ASL—ranging from birth through childhood. The native signers started their ASL learning in the crib, i.e., within the family atmosphere of their deaf, ASL-signing parents. The others were born to hearing parents who did not know sign language. The so-called early learners were first exposed to ASL by deaf peers between the ages of 4 and 6 when they entered a residential school for the deaf. The third group ("late" learners) were first exposed to ASL by deaf peers between ages 14 and 26. When tested, all the adults had been exposed to ASL, for periods between 40 and 70 years. Yet, although all the adults had become fluent users of ASL, Newport found a consistent relation between the age at which they were first exposed to the language and their capacity to produce and comprehend the complex morphology of ASL verbs. The results suggest a long-lasting effect of maturational state on the acquisition of a primary language.

4. Note that these arguments would hold even if one were to reject the Chomskyan syntactic model of principles and parameters (Chomsky 1981, 1986; see also discussion in Roeper 1987) in favor of, say, lexical-specification models (Bresnan 1982; Gazdar 1982) or universal implicatures (Hawkins 1983), provided that these were deemed to be innately specified. The point here is not to argue for Chomsky's model but to stress that some *specifically linguistic* predisposition, in interaction with linguistically relevant input, is essential to explain how language acquisition gets off the ground.

5. For a fuller description and critical discussion of the Piagetian school's position on language acquisition, see Karmiloff-Smith 1979a, pp. 3–19.

6. See discussion in Marshall 1980, 1984.

7. See Gleitman and Wanner 1982 for a full discussion.

8. Different languages do this somewhat differently, and use different devices to do it (Bowerman 1989; Choi and Bowerman 1991).

9. Eilers et al. 1984; Eimas et al. 1971; Fernald and Kuhl 1981; Fowler et al. 1986; Kuhl 1983; DeMany et al. 1977; Spring and Dale 1977; Sullivan and Horowitz 1983.

10. See also Seidenberg and Petitto 1987.

11. See Mandler 1988 for a discussion of the symbolic character of these early signs.

12. See also Soja et al. 1985.

13. See also Taylor and Gelman 1988.

14. In her critique of the constraints view, Nelson (1988) missed this important point. However, her arguments do highlight the need for constraints theorists to provide more precise formulations of the constraints they invoke.

15. See Maratsos and Chalkley 1980 for a discussion of several abortive attempts to reduce syntactic categories to semantic categories, but see Braine 1991 for a subtle recent revival of the semantic-bootstrapping hypothesis.

16. See also Golinkoff and Hirsh-Pasek 1990.

17. Most psycholinguistic experimental tasks call for a metalinguistic stance on the part of subjects, be they children or adults. And once representations are dealt with

metacognitively, they are indeed open to domain-neutral cognitive constraints. One must therefore be wary of drawing conclusions about the early cognitive basis of language from psycholinguistic experiments on later language. Although experiments do indeed sometimes show that language is constrained by cognition, this is often because the experiments themselves do not engage normal language processing but actually call on domain-general metacognitive constraints.

18. Berthoud-Papandropoulou 1978; Bialystok 1986a, 1986b; Clark 1978; Tunmer et al. 1983.
19. See Tyler 1988 for a discussion of the on-line/off-line distinction as it applies to aphasic adults.
20. This was based on an off-line task designed by Berthoud-Papandropoulou (1978, 1980).
21. See also Gerken et al. 1987.
22. For details see Karmiloff-Smith 1979a, pp. 170–185.
23. Although they temporarily take the indefinite article to mean preferentially "one" rather than "a," if one adds the expression "I want to play"—e.g., "Prête-moi un ballon, je veux jouer" ("Lend me a ball, I want to play"), then the 5–7-year-olds will again succeed like the 3-year-olds. The addition seems to underline the non-specific reference function of "a ball" rather than "one ball." (See Karmiloff-Smith 1979a, p. 175.
24. See Karmiloff-Smith 1979a, pp. 64–86, for full details.
25. E.g., Maratsos 1976 and Warden 1976 for English, Karmiloff-Smith, 1979a for French.

Chapter 3

1. Spelke's proposal challenges Marr's (1982) notion of object perception in which the three-dimensional representation is formed subsequent to a two-dimensional analysis, yielding a 2½-dimensional sketch. For Spelke, object segmentation occurs *after* perception of the distance and the motion of three-dimensional objects, thereby obviating some of the problems occurring when object boundaries are sought in lower-level representations of two-dimensional visual array. See Spelke 1990 for a more detailed, thought-provoking discussion, and Rutkowska 1991 for a different view.
2. Motion also seems to be an essential factor for early attention biases and perceptual processes. For example, Vinter (1984, 1986) showed that for imitation to be provoked in the newborn the model must be dynamic (e.g., involve the movement in and out of the tongue). Vinter replicated Meltzoff and Moore's (1977) findings for neonates using movement, but it was not until 8–9 months that Vinter's infants imitated tongue protrusion on the basis of a stationary model with tongue already protruding. Likewise, Johnson and Morton (1991) have shown that neonates are selectively attentive to moving faces over other visual stimuli, but that this does not hold at certain ages if the face stimulus is stationary.
3. Not all researchers agree with this interpretation; see, e.g., Stiles (personal communication) and Rutkowska 1991.
4. See Leslie 1988 for discussion.
5. See Karmiloff-Smith 1984 for a reinterpretation of the data.
6. See also S. Gelman and Coley (in press); S. Gelman and Markman 1986; Keil 1979, 1989, 1990.
7. Other authors (Klahr and Dunbar 1988; Kuhn et al. 1988; Moshiman 1979) have taken a domain-general view of scientific discovery in the child in which the child moves from considering data to theorizing. The phase concept underlying the RR

model argues for domain-specific developments in the relation between theory and data.

8. See discussions of the notion of "theory" in Carey 1985, Perner 1981, and Wellman 1990.

Chapter 4

1. See also Gruber and Voneche 1977.
2. Of course, if one sets up a situation with, say, eggs and egg cups, this makes the one-to-one matching much simpler for the child, who can then ignore cardinality. See Gold 1978, 1985, and 1987 for subtle discussions of this and a number of other Piagetian themes.
3. Beilin 1989; Tollefsrud-Anderson et al. (in press).
4. Gelman 1982; Gelman and Cohen 1988; Gelman and Gallistel 1978; Gelman and Greeno 1989; Gelman and Meck 1986; Starkey, Spelke, and Gelman 1983, 1990.
5. See Sophian and Adams 1987, Starkey and Cooper 1980, Strauss and Curtis 1981, 1984, and Starkey et al. 1980 for similar studies.
6. Why infants usually consistently respond intermodally over a wide range of input types to matches, yet sometimes to differences, is still not clear (see Spelke 1985 for discussion). What is important is the consistency of their responses either to matches or mismatches in any given task.
7. Moreover, Siegler has shown that in all cases prior to the discovery of new strategies, children were successfully solving the number task. Siegler shows that children *discover* a new strategy after a period of success without external pressure for change. But they start to *generalize* new strategies after encountering difficulties. Often, too, he found that successful trials preceding the discovery of new strategies involved long pauses and/or strange mutterings. These could be indications that something like representational redescription is occurring internally. What Siegler's new studies show is that a system has to reach stability—what I have called behavioral mastery—before the child can develop new strategies. Siegler's new findings seem particularly relevant to the RR model. (See also Resnick and Greeno 1990.)
8. This early differentiation also seems to hold for written notations of numbers and letters well before the child can read (Tolchinsky-Landsmann 1991; Tolchinsky-Landsman and Karmiloff-Smith, in press). Moreover, in recent experiments (Karmiloff-Smith, Grant, Jones, and Cuckle 1991) we have shown that children are willing to accept that "table," "think," and "ceiling" are words but reticent to accept "three" and other numbers as words. As one 5-year-old put it: "Three is a sort of word, but not really a word, it's a number."
9. The counting of pregrouped sets yields two numbers: the within-group count (six cowry shells for each group) and the between-group count (total number of groups). The product of these two numbers would seem to be multiplication.
10. The same holds for language in the absence of environmental input (Curtiss 1977).
11. See Davis and Perusse 1988 and peer commentaries.
12. See also Capaldi and Miller 1988.

Chapter 5

1. See Johnson and Morton 1991 and a condensed version in Morton and Johnson 1991.
2. See also Johnson et al. (in press).

3. There remain dissenting views on this. Frye et al. (1983) claim that young infants do not distinguish the human and nonhuman worlds.

4. Adrien et al. (1991) provide an interesting account from a study of home movies in which they find hints of differences in the autistic infant at a very young age.

5. Bruner 1974–75. See also Leslie and Happé 1989.

6. See, for example, Bruner 1974–75 and 1978.

7. See Premack 1988 for a particularly illuminating new discussion of the issue of whether nonhuman species have a theory of mind.

8. This distinction was brought into developmental discussions of theory of mind by Wellman (1983) and Wimmer and Perner (1983). See also Gopnik and Astington 1988 and in press. I shall use the philosophy-of-mind distinction between propositional contents and propositional attitude throughout most of this chapter to avoid lengthy discussion about differences between Vygotsky's notions of "second order representation," Leslie's use of "second order" and "meta-representation," Perner's use of "meta-representation" and "meta-models," my own use of "meta-representation" and "meta-procedural operators," Flavell's use of "meta-cognition," and the numerous other uses of these terms to be found in the developmental literature over the past couple of decades.

9. It might be that a domain-general metarepresentational capacity is applied to protodeclaratives, which are domain-specific, with propositional-attitudes arising as emergent products.

10. See Astington and Gopnik 1991 for a discussion of this important distinction, which a number of developmentalists are now using.

11. Bates (1979) and Nicholich (1977) have shown that young children able to pretend to drink from an empty cup will not yet make a doll or another person pretend. It also seems that young subjects are able to pretend with real objects earlier than with no object.

12. Perner (1991) argues that temporal terms like "tomorrow" are also decoupled. Neil Smith points out that all deitic terms (tomorrow, here, there, etc.) cannot be represented in a language of thought and therefore must have a special representational status different to verbs like believe and think.

13. Interestingly, in problem-solving situations such as the Tower of Hanoi young children can sometimes solve a task linguistically (giving verbal instructions to an experimenter) although they have difficulties in actually performing the solution (Klahr and Robinson 1981).

14. By this Perner seems to have in mind something analogous to the representations supporting behavioral mastery in the RR model, i.e., independently stored representations which can be added to but which are not linked to other representations. I have called these simply "representational adjuncts" (as opposed to representational redescriptions and restructuring).

15. This new development postulated by Perner is reminiscent neo-Piagetian theories of growth in the capacity of the short-term memory (Case 1989).

16. See Zaitchik 1990 for a similar position. Freeman (1990) argues persuasively against broadening the notion of theory of mind.

17. See also Wimmer et al. 1988.

18. This is involved in causality and planning. DasGupta and I are exploring these time-marking and planning processes in normal 3- and 4-year-olds.

19. Rolls (1991) suggests that this is the role of the hippocampus. It goes beyond the purported specificity of theory-of-mind computations.

20. Frith (1989 and previous papers) argues that autism also involves a more general deficiency having to do with what she calls "central coherence." This does not seem

to require metarepresentation. See further discussion of abnormal development in chapter 7 below.
21. See Carey 1985, Perner 1991, and Wellman 1990 for a full discussion of the definition of a theory.

Chapter 6

1. It is important to note that the use of the term "representation" differs according to the focus of study (for discussion, see Mandler 1983 and Sperber 1985). In the traditional literature on drawing, "representation" is usually employed to refer to the externalized form that children put on paper (i.e., the depiction) as well as the physical representation of space in the form of maps and models (Blades and Spencer 1991; Liben and Downs 1989). Throughout this book, "representation" is used solely in the sense of something internal to the child's mind; "notation" (and occasionally "depiction") is used to refer to the external product.
2. I should like to thank Rochel Gelman for letting me view the videotapes from one of her as-yet-unpublished studies, during which I noticed this revealing difference.
3. See Tolchinsky-Landsmann and Karmiloff-Smith (in press) for full details.
4. But see McManus 1991 for arguments in favor of a gene for reading.
5. For more details of the experiment, see Karmiloff-Smith 1979c.
6. Recall the arguments about end points and cardinality in Chapter 4.
7. I'd like to thank Fiona Spencer from Open University, Ceri Evans from Oxford University, and a group of Italian students working under Anna-Emilia Berti at Padova University for sending me the results of their student projects.

Chapter 7

1. See Frith 1989, Leslie 1990, and Rutter 1987 for a full discussion of autism.
2. See DasGupta and Frith (in progress) on causality, and DasGupta and Karmiloff-Smith (in progress) on problem solving and planning.
3. See also Changeux 1985, Piatelli-Palmerini 1989, and Johnson and Karmiloff-Smith 1992.
4. Since reading Greenough's work, I now optimistically read about tricky issues like consciousness when working out on my exercise bike!
5. We do not, however, have to buy into Piaget's (1967) notion of a phenocopy passed on to future generations.
6. The same has been shown to hold in children's acquisition of grammatical gender (Karmiloff-Smith 1979a) and in their acquisition of arithmetic skills (Siegler and Crowley 1991; Siegler and Jenkins 1989).
7. Interestingly, both Piaget and the connectionists focus on sensorimotor nonsymbolic input/output relations, and both initially avoided the term "representation." The authors of the first volumes on connectionism prided themselves on having systems dynamics with "no representations." I always thought that the so-called hidden units were in fact the network's representations. More recently, connectionists themselves have begun to refer to this level as the layer of internal representations.

Chapter 8

1. See also the use of production systems to model development by Siegler (1989) and Newell (1991). Also of interest are hybrid parallel processing/sequential production

system approaches such as those of Anderson (1983), Just and Carpenter (1992), and Thibadeau et al. (1982), who incorporated the notion of production strength into production-system modeling.

2. I should particularly like to thank Elizabeth Bates, Jeff Elman, and Jean Mandler, of the University of California at San Diego, for persuading me to attend the Neural Network Modeling Course for Developmental Psychologists, financed by the MacArthur Foundation. The hands-on experience of connectionist modeling I gained through that course increased my appreciation of the developmental possibilities of PDP networks. Cathy Harris and Virginia Marchmann were terrific instructors. I'd also like to thank Jay McClelland and all his collaborators at Carnegie-Mellon University for encouraging me to pursue further my initial forays into the modeling of development.

3. But see the lengthy challenge of this by Pinker and Prince (1988) and Pinker (1989).

4. See also Servan-Schreiber et al. 1988.

5. It is not clear whether it would have been easier or more difficult for the network to learn if overlaps in the semantic and grammatical relationships across words had been represented in distributed form.

6. Some relevant attempts have been brought to my notice recently, including Hinton's reduced descriptions; Pollack's RAAMs; Mozer and Smolensky's skeletonization; Jacobs, Jordon, and Barto's task decomposition through competition between different networks; Touretsky's chunking; and McMillan's projection of a set of symbolic rules.

Bibliography

Adrien, J. L., Faure, M., Perrot, A., Hameury, L., Garreau, B., Barthelemy, C., and Sauvage, D. 1981. Autism and family home movies: Preliminary findings. *Journal of Autism and Developmental Disorders* 21: 43–49.

Andersen, E. M., and Spain, B. 1977. *The Child with Spina Bifida*. Methuen.

Anderson, J. R. 1980. *Cognitive Psychology and Its Implications*. Freeman.

Anderson, M. 1992. *Intelligence and Development: A Cognitive Theory*. Blackwell.

Antell, E., and Keating, D. P. 1983. Perception of numerical invariance in neonates. *Child Development* 54: 695–701.

Ashmead, D. H., and Perlmutter, M. 1980. Infant memory in everyday life. In M. Perlmutter (ed.), *New Directions for Child Development: Children's Memory*, vol 10. Jossey-Bass.

Astington, J. W. 1989. Developing theories of mind: What develops and how do we go about explaining it? Paper presented at meeting of Society for Research in Child Development, Kansas City.

Astington, J. W., and Gopnik, A. 1991. Developing understanding of desire and intention. In A. Whiten (ed.), *Natural Theories of Mind: Evolution, Development and Simulation of Everyday Mindreading*. Blackwell.

Atkinson, M. 1982. *Explanations in the Study of Child Language Development*. Cambridge University Press.

Au, T. K., and Markman, E. K. 1987. Acquiring word meanings via linguistic contrast. *Cognitive Development* 2: 217–236.

Baillargéon, R. 1986. Representing the existence and the location of hidden objects: Object permanence in 6- and 8-month-old infants. *Cognition* 23: 21–41.

Baillargéon, R. 1987a. Object permanence in 3.5- and 4.5-month-old infants. *Developmental Psychology* 23: 655–664.

Baillargéon, R. 1987b. Young infants' reasoning about the physical and spatial properties of a hidden object. *Cognitive Development* 2: 170–200.

Baillargéon, R. 1991. Reasoning about the height and location of a hidden object in 4.5- and 6.5-month-old infants. *Cognition* 38, no. 1; 13–42.

Baillargéon, R., Graber, M., Devos, J., and Black, J. 1990. Why do young infants fail to search for hidden objects? *Cognition* 36: 255–284.

Baillargéon, R., and Hanko-Summers, S. 1990. Is the top object adequately supported by the bottom object? Young infants' understanding of support relations. *Cognitive Development* 5: 29–53.

Baillargéon, R., Spelke, E., and Wasserman, S. 1986. Object permanence in five month old infants. *Cognition* 20: 191–208.

Baron, J. 1973. Semantic development and conceptual development. *Cognition* 2: 299–318.

Baron-Cohen, S. 1989a. Are autistic children 'behaviorists'? An examination of their mental-physical and appearance-reality distinctions. *Journal of Autism and Developmental Disorders* 19: 579–600.

Baron-Cohen, S. 1989b. Perceptual role-taking and proto-declarative pointing in autism. *British Journal of Developmental Psychology* 7: 113–127.

Baron-Cohen, S. 1991. Precursors to a theory of mind: Understanding attention in others. In A. Whiten (ed.), *Natural Theories of Mind: Evolution, Development and Simulation of Everyday Mindreading.* Blackwell.

Baron-Cohen, S., Leslie, A. M., and Frith, U. 1985. Does the autistic child have a "theory of mind"? *Cognition* 21: 37–46.

Baron-Cohen, S., Leslie, A. M., and Frith, U. 1986. Mechanical, behavioural and intentional understanding of picture stories in autistic children. *British Journal of Developmental Psychology* 4: 113–125.

Bates, E. 1979. *The Emergence of Symbols: Cognition and Communication in Infancy.* Academic.

Bates, E. 1991. Developmental psychology and connectionism. Talk given at meeting of Society for Research in Child Development, Seattle.

Bates, E., Benigni, L., Bretherton, I., Camaioni, L., and Volterra, V. 1979. *The Emergence of Symbols: Cognition and Communication in Infancy.* Academic.

Bates, E., and MacWhinney, B. 1987. Competition, variation and language learning. In B. MacWhinney (ed.), *Mechanisms of Language Acquistion.* Erlbaum.

Bechtel, W., and Abrahamsen, A. 1991. *Connectionism and the Mind: An Introduction to Parallel Processing in Networks.* Blackwell.

Beilin, H. 1985. Dispensable and core elements in Piaget's research program. *Genetic Epistemologist* 13: 1–16.

Beilin, H. 1989. Piagetian theory. *Annals of Child Development* 6: 85–131.

Bellugi, U., Marks, S., Bihrle, A. M., and Sabo, H. 1988. Dissociation between language and cognitive functions in Williams Syndrome. In D. Bishop and K. Mogford (eds.), *Language Development in Exceptional Circumstances.* Churchill Livingstone.

Berthoud-Papandropoulou, I. 1978. An experimental study of children's ideas about language. In A. Sinclair, R. J. Jarvella, and W. J. M. Levelt (eds.), *The Child's Conception of Language.* Springer-Verlag.

Berthoud-Papandropoulou, I. 1980. *La réflection métalinguistique chez l'enfant.* Imprimerie Nationale (Geneva).

Bever, T. G., Mehler, J., and Epstein, J. (1968). What children do in spite of what they know. *Science* 162: 921–924.

Bialystok, E. 1986a. Factors in the growth of linguistic awareness. *Child Development* 86: 498–510.

Bialystok, E. 1986b. Children's concept of word. *Journal of Psycholinguistic Research* 15: 13–32.

Bialystok, E. 1992. Symbolic representation of letters and numbers. *Cognitive Development* 7, no. 3.

Bialystok, E. 1993. Metalinguistic awareness: The development of children's ideas about language. In C. Pratt and A. F. Garton (eds.), *The Development and Use of Representation in Children.* Wiley.

Blades, M., and Spencer, C. 1987. Young children's strategies when using maps with landmarks. *Journal of Environmental Psychology* 7: 201–217.

Bloom, L. 1970. *Language Development: Form and Function in Emerging Grammars.* MIT Press.

Bloom, L., Lifter, K., and Broughton, J. 1985. The convergence of early cognition and language in the second year of life: Problems in conceptualization and measurement. In M. Barrett (ed.), *Children's Single Word Speech*. Wiley.

Bloom, P. 1990. Syntactic distinctions in child language. *Journal of Child Language* 17: 343–355.

Boden, M. A. 1982. Is equilibration important? A view from Artificial Intelligence. *British Journal of Psychology* 73: 165–173.

Bolger, F. 1988. Children's Notational Competence. Doctoral dissertation, MRC Cognitive Development Unit and University College, London.

Bolger, F., and Karmiloff-Smith, A. 1990. The development of communicative competence: Are notational systems like language? *Archvies de Psychologie* 58: 257–273.

Bonvillian, J. D., Orlansky, M. D., and Novack, L. L. 1983. Developmental milestones: Sign language and motor development. *Child Development* 54: 1435–1445.

Bornstein, B. 1963. Prosopagnosia. In Halpern (ed.), *Problems of Dynamic Neurology*. Hadassah Medical Organisation, Jerusalem.

Bornstein, M., Ferdinandsen, K., and Gross, C. G. 1981. Perception of symmetry in infancy. *Developmental Psychology* 17: 82–86.

Bovet, M. C., Dasen, P. R., Inhelder, B., and Othenin-Girard, C. 1972. Etapes de l'intélligence sensori-motrice chez l'enfant baoulé. *Archives de Psychologie* 41: 363–386.

Bowerman, M. 1973. *Early Syntactic Development: A Crosslinguistic Study with Special Reference to Finnish*. Cambridge University Press.

Bowerman, M. 1989. Learning a semantic system: What role do cognitive predispositions play? In M. L. Rice and R. L. Schiefelbusch (eds.), *The Teachability of Language*. Paul H. Brookes.

Boysen, S. T., and Berntson, G. B. 1989. The emergence of numerical competence in the chimpanzee (*Pan troglodytes*). In S. T. Parker and K. R. Gibson (eds.), *Language and Intelligence in Animals: Developmental Perspectives*. Cambridge University Press.

Braine, M. D. S. 1987. What is learned in acquiring word classes? A step towards an acquisition theory. In B. MacWhinney (ed.), *Mechanisms of Language Acquisition*. Erlbaum.

Braine, M. D. S. 1991. What sort of innate structure is needed to "bootstrap" into syntax? Manuscript, New York University.

Bresnan, J. (ed.) 1982. *The Mental Representation of Grammatical Relations*. MIT Press.

Broughton, J. 1978. Development of concepts of self, mind, reality, and knowledge. In W. Damon (ed.), *New Directions for Child Development*. Jossey-Bass.

Brown, A. L. 1990. Domain-specific principles affect learning and transfer in children. *Cognitive Science* 14: 107–133.

Brown, R. W. 1973. *A First Language: The Early Stages*. Harvard University Press.

Bruner, J. S. 1970. The growth and structure of skill. In K. Connolly (ed.), *Mechanisms of Motor Development*. Academic.

Bruner, J. S. 1974–75. From communication to language: A psychological perspective. *Cognition* 3: 255–287.

Bruner, J. S. 1978. On prelinguistic prerequisites of speech. In R. N. Campbell and P. T. Smith (eds.), *Recent Advances in the Psychology of Language: Language Development and Mother-Child Interaction*. Plenum.

Bryant, P. 1974. *Perception and Understanding in Young Children*. Methuen.

Butterworth, G. (ed.) 1981. *Infancy and Epistemology: An Evaluation of Piaget's theory*. Harvester.

Butterworth, G. 1991. The ontogeny and phylogeny of joint visual attention. In A. Whiten (ed.), *Natural Theories of Mind: Evolution, Development and Simulation of Everyday Mindreading*. Blackwell.

Campbell, J. A. 1990. Challenges for knowledge representation. Paper presented at International Symposium on Computational Intelligence, Milan.

Capaldi, E. J., and Miller, D. J. 1988. Counting in rats: Its functional significance and the independent cognitive processes that constitute it. *Journal of Experimental Psychology: Animal Behavior Processes* 14: 3–17.

Caplan, D. 1985. A neo-cartesian alternative. *Behavioral and Brain Sciences* 8: 6–7.

Carey, S. 1982. Semantic development: The state of the art. In E. Wanner and L. Gleitman (eds.), *Language Acquisition: The State of the Art*. Cambridge University Press.

Carey, S. 1985. *Conceptual Change in Childhood*. MIT Press.

Carey, S. 1988. Conceptual differences between children and adults. *Mind and Language* 3: 167–181.

Carey, S. 1990. Procedures toddlers use to constrain word meanings: Speculations and a little data. In E. Dromi (ed.), *Cognition and Language: Early Childhood Years*. Ablex.

Carraher, T. N., Carraher, D. W., and Schliemann, A. D. 1985. Mathematics in the streets and schools. *British Journal of Developmental Psychology* 3: 21–29.

Case, R. 1978. Intellectual development from birth to adulthood: A neo-Piagetian interpretation. In R. S. Siegler (ed.), *Children's Thinking: What Develops?*. Erlbaum.

Case, R. 1989. A neo-Piagetian analysis of the child's understanding of other people, and the internal conditions which motivate their behavior. Paper presented at Biennial Meeting of Society for Research in Child Development, Kansas City.

Chandler, M. J., and Boyes, M. 1982. Social-cognitive development. In B. B. Wolman (ed.), *Handbook of Developmental Psychology*. Prentice-Hall.

Changeux, J. P. 1985. *Neuronal Man: The Biology of Mind*. Pantheon.

Chi, M. T. H., and Klahr, D. 1975. Span and rate of apprehension in children and adults. *Journal of Experimental Child Psychology* 19: 434–439.

Chiat, S. 1986. Personal pronouns. In P. Fletcher and M. Garman (eds.), *Language Acquisition*. Cambridge University Press.

Choi, S., and Bowerman, M. 1991. Learning to express motion event in English and Korean: The influence of language-specific lexicalization patterns. *Cognition* 41: 83–121.

Chomsky, N. 1965. *Aspects of the Theory of Syntax*. MIT Press.

Chomsky, N. 1975. *Reflections on Language*. Pantheon.

Chomsky, N. 1981. *Lectures on Government and Binding*. Foris.

Chomsky, N. 1986. *Knowledge of Language: Its Nature, Origin and Use*. Praeger.

Chomsky, N. 1988. *Language and Problems of Knowledge*. MIT Press.

Cipolotti, L., Butterworth, B., and Denes, G. 1991. A specific deficit for numbers in a case of dense acalculia. *Brain* 114: 2619–2637.

Clark, A. 1987. The kludge in the machine. *Mind and Language* 2: 277–300.

Clark, A. 1989. *Microcognition: Philosophy, Cognitive Science, and Parallel Distributed Processing*. MIT Press.

Clark, A., and Karmiloff-Smith, A. 1993. The Cognizer's innards: a psychological and philosophical perspective on the development of thought. *Mind and Language* 8: 487–515.

Clark, E. V. 1973. What's in a word? On the child's acquisition of semantics in his first language. In T. E. Moore (ed.), *Cognitive Development and the Acquisition of Language*. Academic.

Clark, E. V. 1978. Awareness of language: Some evidence from what children say and do. In A. Sinclair, R. J. Jarvella, and W. Levelt (eds.), *The Child's Conception of Language*. Springer-Verlag.

Clark, E. V. 1987. The principle of contrast: A constraint on language acquisition. In B. MacWhinney (ed.), *The 20th Annual Carnegie Symposium on Cognition*. Erlbaum.

Cohen, S. R. 1985. The development of constraints on symbol-meaning structure in notation: Evidence from production, interpretation and forced-choice judgements. *Child Development* 56: 177–195.

Cole, M. 1989. Cultural psychology: A once and future discipline? In J. J. Berman ed., *Cross-Cultural Perspectives: Nebraska Symposium on Motivation*, vol. 37 University of Nebraska Press.

Cole, M., and Scribner, S. 1974. *Culture and Thought: A Psychological Introduction*. Wiley.

Cooper, R. G., Jr. 1984. Early number development: Discovering number space with addition and subtraction. In C. Sophian (ed.), *Origins of Cognitive Skills*. Erlbaum.

Cossu, G., and Marshall, J. C. 1990. Are cognitive skills a prerequisite for learning to read and write? *Cognitive Neuropsychology* 7: 21–40.

Cossu, G., and Marshall, J. C. 1986. Theoretical implications of the hyperlexia syndrome: Two new Italian cases. *Cortex* 22: 579–589.

Cowan, R. 1987. Assessing children's idea of one-to-one correspondence. *British Journal of Developmental Psychology* 5: 149–154.

Cox, M. V. 1985. One object behind another. Young children's use of array-specific or view-specific representations. In N. H. Freeman and M. V. Cox (eds.), *Visual Order: The Nature and Development of Pictorial Representation*. Cambridge University Press.

Crain, S., and Fodor, J. D. In press. Competence and performance in child language. In E. Dromi (ed.), *Language and Cognition: A Developmental Perspective*. Ablex.

Cromer, R. F. 1983. Hierarchical planning disability in the drawings and constructions of a special group of severely aphasic children. *Brain and Cognition* 2: 144–164.

Cromer, R. F. 1994. A case study of dissociation between language and cognition. In H. Tager-Flusberg (ed.), *Constraints on Language Acquisition: Studies of Atypical Children*. Erlbaum.

Curtiss, S. 1977. *Genie: A Psycholinguistic Study of a Modern Day "Wild Child."* Academic.

Dasen, P., Inhelder, B., Lavallee, M., and Retschitzki, J. 1978. *Naissance de l'Intélligence chez l'Enfant Baoulé de Côte d'Ivoire*. Huber.

Dasser, V., Ulbaeck, L., and Premack, D. 1989. The perception of intention. *Science* 243: 365–367.

Davis, A. M. 1985. The canonical bias: Young children's drawing of familiar objects. In Freeman, N. H., and Cox, M. V. (eds.), *Visual Order: The Nature and Development of Pictorial Representation*. Cambridge University Press.

Davis, H, and Perusse, R. 1988. Numerical competence in animals. *Behavioral and Brain Sciences* 11: 561–615.

Dawson, G., Hill, D., Spencer, A., Galpert, L., and Watson, L. 1990. Affective exchanges between young autistic children and their mothers. *Journal of Abnormal Child Psychology* 18: 335–345.

Dean, A. L., Scherzer, E., and Chabaud, S. 1986. Sequential ordering in children's representations of rotation movements. *Journal of Experimental Child Psychology* 42: 99–114.

DeMany, L., McKenzie, B., and Vurpillot, E. 1977. Rhythm perception in early infancy. *Nature* 266: 718–719.

Dennett, D. C. 1971. Intentional systems. *Journal of Philosophy* 68: 87–106.

Dennett, D. C. 1978. *Brainstorms: Philosophical Essays on Mind and Psychology*. Bradford.

Diamond, A. 1985. Development of the ability to use recall to guide action, as indicated by infants' performance on A-not-B. *Child Development* 56: 868–883.

diSessa, A. 1982. Unlearning Aristotelian physics: A study of knowledge-based learning. *Cognitive Science* 6: 37–75.

Dockrell, J., and Campbell, R. 1986. Lexical acquisition strategies in the preschool child. In S. Kuczaj and M. Barrett (eds.), *The Development of Word Meaning*. Springer-Verlag.

Donaldson, M. 1978. *Children's Minds*. Fontana.

Dromi, E. 1987. *Early Lexical Development*. Cambridge University Press.

Eilers, R. E., Bull, D. H., Oller, K., and Lewis, D. C. 1984. The discrimination of vowel duration by infants. *Journal of the Acoustical Society of America* 75: 1213–1218.

Eimas, P. H., Siqueland, E. R., Jusczyk, P., and Vigorito, J. 1971. Speech perception in infants. *Science* 171: 303–306.

Elman, J. L. 1990. Finding structure in time. *Cognitive Science* 14: 179–211.

Elman, J. L. 1991. Distributed representations, simple recurrent networks, and grammatical structure. *Machine Learning* 7: 195–225.

Estes, D., Wellman, H. M., and Woolley, J. D. 1990. Children's understanding of mental phenomena. In H. Reese (ed.), *Advances in Child Development and Behavior*. Academic.

Farah, M. J. 1990. *Visual Agnosia: Disorders of Object Recognition and What They Tell Us about Normal Vision*. MIT Press.

Feldman, H., and Gelman, R. 1987. Otitis media and cognitive development. In J. F. Kavanagh (ed.), *Otitis Media and Child Development*. York.

Feldman, H., Goldin-Meadow, S., and Gleitman, L. 1978. Beyond Herodotus: The creation of language by linguistically deprived deaf children. In A. Locke (ed.), *Action, Symbol, and Gesture: The Emergence of Language*. Academic.

Fernald, A., and Kuhl, P. 1981. Fundamental frequency as an acoustic determinant of infant preference for motherese. Paper presented at meeting of the Society for Research in Child Development, Boston.

Fernandes, D. M., and Church, R. M. 1982. Discrimination of the number of sequential events by rats. *Animal Learning and Behavior* 10: 171–176.

Ferreiro, E. 1982. The relationship between oral and written language: The children's viewpoints. In Y. Goodman, M. Hausler, and D. Strickland (eds.), *Oral and Written language: Developmental Research*: The Impact on the Schools. National Council of Teachers.

Ferreiro, E., and Sinclair, H. 1971. Temporal relations in language. *International Journal of Psychology* 6: 39–47.

Ferreiro, E., and Teberosky, A. 1979. *Los sistemas de escritura en el desarolla del niño*. Siglo Veintiuno Editores.

Filmore, C. J. 1968. The case for case. In E. Bach and R. T. Harms (eds.), *Universals in Linguistic Theory*. Holt, Rinehart and Winston.

Fischer, K. W. 1980. A theory of cognitive development: The control and construction of hierarchies of skills. *Psychological Review* 87: 477–531.

Flavell, J. H. 1988. The development of children's knowledge about the mind: From cognitive connections to mental representations. In J. Astington, P. L. Harris, and D. R. Olson (eds.), *Developing Theories of Mind*. Cambridge University Press.

Flavell, J. H., Everett, B. A., Croft, K., and Flavell, E. R. 1981. Young children's knowledge about visual perception: Further evidence for the Level 1/Level 2 distinction. *Developmental Psychology* 17: 99–103.

Fodor, J. A. 1976. *The Language of Thought*. Harvester.

Fodor, J. A. 1978. Propositional attitudes. *Monist* 68: 501–523.

Fodor, J. A. 1983. *The Modularity of Mind*. MIT Press.

Fodor, J. A. 1985. Précis of *The Modularity of Mind*. *Behavioral and Brain Sciences* 8: 1–42.

Fodor, J. A. 1987. *Psychosemantics: The Problem of Meaning in the Philosophy of Mind*. MIT Press.

Forguson, L., and Gopnik, A. 1988. The ontogeny of common sense. In J. Astington, P. L. Harris, and D. R. Olson (eds.), *Developing Theories of Mind*. Cambridge University Press.

Fowler, C. A., Smith, M. R., and Tassinary, L. G. 1986. Perception of syllable timing by prebabbling infants. *Journal of the Acoustical Society of America* 79: 814–825.

Freeman, N. H. 1980. *Strategies of Representation in Young Children: Analysis of Spatial Skills and Drawing Processes*. Academic.

Freeman, N. H. 1987. Current problems in the development of representational picture production. *Archives de Psychologie* 55: 127–152.

Freeman, N. H. 1990. Unpublished manuscript, Bristol University.

Frith, U. 1989. *Autism: Explaining the Enigma*. Blackwell.

Frye, D. Rawling, P., Moore, C., and Myers, I. 1983. Object-person discrimination and communication at 3 and 10 months. *Developmental Psychology* 19: 303–309.

Frydman, O., and Bryant, P. 1988. Sharing and the understanding of number equivalence by young children. *Cognitive Development* 3: 323–339.

Fuson, K. C. 1988. Children's counting and concepts of number. In C. J. Brainerd (ed.), *Springer Series in Cognitive Development*. Springer-Verlag.

Fuson, K., Richards, J., and Brians, D. 1982. The acquisition and elaboration of the number word sequence. In C. J. Brainerd (ed.), *Children's Logical and Mathematical Cognition*. Springer-Verlag.

Gallistel, C. R. 1990. *The Organization of Learning*. MIT Press.

Gallistel, C. R., and Gelman, R. 1991. The what and how of counting. In W. F. Kesser, A. Ortony, and F. Craik (eds.), *Essays in Honor of George Mandler*. Erlbaum.

Gardner, H. 1985. *Frames of Mind: The Theory of Multiple Intelligences*. Basic Books.

Gardner, R. A., and Gardner, B. T. 1969. Teaching sign language to a chimpanzee. *Science* 165: 664–672.

Garnham, A. 1991. Did two farmers leave or three? Comment on Starkey, Spelke & Gelman: Numerical abstraction by human infants. *Cognition* 39: 167–170.

Gazdar, G. 1982. Phrase structure grammar. In P. Jacobson and G. Pullum (eds.), *The Nature of Syntactic Representation*. Reidel.

Gelman, R. 1982. Accessing onetoone correspondence: Still another paper about conservation. *British Journal of Psychology* 73: 209–220.

Gelman, R. 1990a. Structural constraints on cognitive development. *Cognitive Science* 14: 39.

Gelman, R. 1990b. First principles organize attention to and learning about relevant data: Number and animate-inanimate distinction as examples. *Cognitive Science* 14: 79–106.

Gelman, R., and Cohen, M. 1988. Qualitative differences in the way Down's Syndrome and normal children solve a novel counting problem. In L. Nadel (ed.), *The Psychobiology of Down's Syndrome*. MIT Press.

Gelman, R., Cohen, M., and Hartnett, P. 1989. To know mathematics is to go beyond thinking that "Fractions aren't numbers." In *Proceedings of the Eleventh Annual Meeting of the North American Chapter*. International Group for Psychology of Mathematics of Education.

Gelman, R., and Gallistel, C. R. 1978. *The Child's Understanding of Number*. Harvard University Press.

Gelman, R., and Greeno, J. G. 1989. On the nature of competence: Principles for understanding in a domain. In L. B. Resnick (ed.), *Knowing and Learning: Issues for a Cognitive Science of Instruction*. Erlbaum.

Gelman, R., Massey, C. M., and McManus, M. 1991. Characterizing supporting environments for cognitive development: Lessons from children in a museum. In J. M. Levine and L. B. Resnick (eds.), *Perspectives on Socially Shared Cognition*. American Psychological Association.

Gelman, R., and Meck, E. 1986. The notion of principle: The case of counting. In J. Hiebert (ed.), *The Relationship Between Procedural and Conceptual Competence*. Erlbaum.

Gelman, S. A., and Coley, J. D. 1991. Language and categorization: The acquisition of natural kind terms. In S. A. Gelman and J. P. Brynes (eds.), *Perspectives on Language and Thought: Interrelations in Development*. Cambridge University Press.

Gelman, S. A., and Markman, E. 1986. Categories and induction in young children. *Cognition* 23: 183–209.

Gerhardt, J. 1988. From discourse to semantics: The development of verb morphology and forms of self-reference in the speech of a 2-year-old. *Journal of Child Language* 15: 337–393.

Gerken, L. 1987. Telegraphic speech does not imply telegraphic listening. *Papers and Reports on Child Language Development* 26: 48–55.

Gerken, L., Landau, B., and Remez, R. E. 1990. Function morphemes in young children's speech perception and production. *Developmental Psychology* 26: 204–216.

Gibson, E. J. 1970. The development of perception as an adaptive process. *American Scientist* 58: 98–107.

Gibson, E. J., and Spelke, E. 1983. The development of perception. In J. H. Flavell and E. Markman (eds.), *Cognitive Development* (volume 3 of P. H. Mussen's *Handbook of Cognitive Psychology*,) Wiley.

Gilliéron, C. 1976. Décalages et sériation. *Archives de Psychologie* 44, Monographie 3.

Gilliéron, C. 1982. Conservation: Forty-five years later. *Journal of Structured Learning* 7: 167–174.

Gleitman, L. 1990. The structural sources of verb meanings. *Language Acquisition* 1: 3–55.

Gleitman, L. R., Gleitman, H., and Shipley, E. F. 1972. The emergence of the child as grammarian. *Cognition* 1: 137–164.

Gleitman, L. R., Gleitman, H., Landau, B., and Wanner, E. 1988. Where learning begins: Initial representations for language learning. In F. Newmeyer, (ed.), *The Cambridge Linguistic Survey, Volume III: Language: Psychological and Biological Aspects*. Cambridge University Press.

Gleitman, L. R., and Wanner, E. 1982. Language acquisition: The state of the state of the art. In E. Wanner and L. R. Gleitman (eds.), *Language Acquisition: State of the Art*. Cambridge University Press.

Gold, R. S. 1978. On the meaning of non-conservation. In A. M. Lesgold, J. W. Pellegrino, S. D. Fokkema, and R. Glaser (eds.), *Cognitive Psychology and Instruction*. Plenum.

Gold, R. S. 1985. The "failure to communicate a change of mind" explanation of young children's non-conservation responses. *Journal of Genetic Psychology* 146: 171–180.

Gold, R. S. 1987. *The Description of Cognitive Development: Three Piagetian themes*. Oxford University Press.

Goldin-Meadow, S., and Feldman, H. 1979. The development of language-like communication without a language model. *Science* 197: 401–403.

Golinkoff, R. M. 1983. The preverbal negotiation of failed messages: Insights into the transition period. In R. M. Golinkoff (ed.), *The Transition from Prelinguistic to Linguistic Communication*. Erlbaum.

Golinkoff, R. M., Harding, C. G., Carlson-Luden, V., and Sexton, M. 1984. The infant's perception of causal events: The distinction between animate and inanimate objects. In L. P. Lipsitt (ed.), *Advances in Infancy Research*, Ablex.

Golinkoff, R. M., and Hirsh-Pasek, K. 1990. Let the mute speak: What infants can tell us about language acquisition. *Merrill-Palmer Quarterly* 36: 67–92.

Gomez, J. C. 1991. Visual behaviour as a window for reading the mind of others in primates. In A. Whiten (ed.), *Natural Theories of Mind: Evolution, Development and Simulation of Everyday Mindreading*. Blackwell.

Gonzales, R. C., and Wintz, P. 1977. *Digital Image Processing*. Addison-Wesley.

Goodnow, J. J., and Levine, R. A. 1973. The grammar of action: Sequence and syntax in children's copying. *Cognitive Psychology* 4: 82–98.

Goodson, B. D., and Greenfield, P. M. 1975. The search for structural principles in children's manipulative play: A parallel with linguistic development. *Child Development* 46: 734–746.

Gopnik, A., and Astington, J. 1988. Children's understanding of representational change and its relation to the understanding of false-belief and the appearance-reality distinction. *Child Development* 59: 26–37.

Gopnik, A., and Astington, J. 1991. Theoretical explanations of children's understanding of the mind. *British Journal of Developmental Psychology* 9, no. 1: 7–13.

Gopnik, A., and Graf, P. 1988. Knowing how you know: Young children's ability to identify and remember the sources of their beliefs. *Child Development* 59: 26–37.

Gordon, P. 1991. The Piraha tribe of Amazonia. Colloquium, University of Pittsburgh.

Greenfield, P. M., Nelson, K., and Saltzman, E. 1972. The development of rulebound strategies for manipulating seriated cups: A parallel between action and grammar. *Cognitive Psychology* 3: 291–310.

Greenfield, P. M., and Schneider, L. 1977. Building a tree structure: The development of hierarchical complexity and interrupted strategies in children's construction activity. *Developmental Psychology* 13: 299–313.

Greenfield, P. M., and Smith, J. H. 1976. *The Structure of Communication in Early Language Development*. Academic.

Greenough, W. T., Black, J. E., and Wallace, C. S. 1987. Experience and brain development. *Child Development* 58: 539–559.

Groen, G., and Resnick, L. B. 1977. Can preschool children invent addition algorithms? *Journal of Educational Psychology* 69: 645–652.

Gruber, H. E., and Voneche, J. 1977. *The Essential Piaget*. Routledge & Kegan Paul.

Hadenius, A. M., Hagberg, B., Hyttnas-Bensch, K., and Sjogren I. 1962. The natural prognosis of infantile hydrocephalus. *Acta Paediatrica* 51: 117–118.

Halford, G. S. 1982. *The Development of Thought*. Erlbaum.

Hall, D. G. 1991. Acquiring word meanings: How children constrain the possibilities. Paper presented at annual conference of British Psychological Society Developmental Section, Cambridge.

Harris, P. L. 1989. Object permanence in infants. In A. Slater and J. G. Bremner (eds.), *Infant Development*. Erlbaum.

Hawkins, J. 1983. *Word Order Universals*. Academic.

Hermelin, B., and O'Connor, N. 1983. Flawed genius or Clever Hans? *Psychological Medicine* 13: 479–481.

Hermelin, B., and O'Connor, N. 1986. Idiot savant calendrical calculators: Rules and regularities. *Psychological Medicine* 16: 885–893.

Hermelin, B., and O'Connor, N. 1989. Intelligence and musical improvisation. *Psychological Medicine* 19: 447–457.

Hirsch-Pasek, K., Gleitman, H., Gleitman, L. R., Golinkoff, R., and Naigles, L. 1988. Syntactic bootstrapping: Evidence from comprehension. Paper presented at Boston Language Conference.

Hirsch-Pasek, K., Golinkoff, R., Fletcher, A., DeGaspe Beaubien, F., and Cauley, K. 1985. In the beginning: One-word speakers comprehend word order. Paper presented at Boston Language Conference.

Hirsh-Pasek, K., Kemler-Nelson, D. G., Jusczyk, P. W., Wright Cassidy, K., Druss, B., and Kennedy, L. 1987. Clauses are perceptual units for young infants. *Cognition* 26: 269–286.

Horn, G., and Johnson, M. H. 1989. Memory systems in the chick: Dissociations and neuronal analysis. *Neuropsychologia* 27: 122.

Horton, M. S., and Markman, E. M. 1980. Developmental differences in the acquisition of basic and superordinate categories. *Child Development* 51: 708–719.

Hoyles, C. 1985. Culture and Computers in the Mathematics Classroom. Inaugural lecture, University of London Institute of Education Publications.

Hughes, M. 1986. *Children and Number: Difficulties in Learning Mathematics*. Blackwell.

Huttenlocher, J., and Smiley, P. 1987. Early word meanings: The case for object names. *Cognitive Psychology* 19: 63–89.

Hyams, N. 1986. *The Acquisition of Parameterized Grammars*, Reidel.

Inhelder, B., and Piaget, J. 1958. *The Growth of Logical Thinking from Childhood to Adolescence*. Basic Books.

Johnson, M. H. 1988. Memories of mother. *New Scientist* 18 (February): 60–62.

Johnson, M. H. 1990a. Cortical maturation and the development of visual attention in early infancy. *Journal of Cognitive Neuroscience* 2: 81–95.

Johnson, M. H. 1990b. Cortical maturation and perceptual development. In H. Bloch and B. I. Bertenthal (eds.), *Sensory Motor Organisations and Development in Infancy and Early Childhood*. Kluwer.

Johnson, M. H. 1993. Constraints on cortical plasticity. In M. H. Johnson (ed.), *Brain Development and Cognition: A Reader*. Blackwell.

Johnson, M. H., and Bolhuis, J. J. 1991. Imprinting, predispositions and filial preference in the chick. In R. J. Andrew (ed.), *Neural and Behavioural Plasticity*. Oxford University Press.

Johnson, M. H., Bolhuis, J. J., and Horn, G. 1985. Interaction between acquired preferences and developing predispositions during imprinting. *Animal Behaviour* 33: 1000–1006.

Johnson, M. H., Dziurawiec, S., Ellis, H., and Morton, J. 1991. Newborns' preferential tracking of facelike stimuli and its subsequent decline. *Cognition* 40: 1–19.

Johnson, M. H., and Horn, G. 1988. The development of filial preferences in the dark-reared chick. *Animal Behavior* 36: 675–683.

Johnson, M. H., and Karmiloff-Smith, A. 1989. The right tools for the job? (peer commentary on "Spontaneous tool use and sensorimotor intelligence in *Cebus* compared with other monkeys and men"). *Behavioral and Brain Sciences* 12: 600.

Johnson, M. H., and Karmiloff-Smith, A. 1992. Can neural selectionism be applied to cognitive development and its disorders? *New Ideas in Psychology* 10: 35–46.

Johnson, M. H., and Morton, J. 1991. *Biology and Cognitive Development: The Case of Face Recognition*. Blackwell.

Johnson, J. S., and Newport, E. L. 1989. Critical period effects in second language learning: the influence of maturational state on the acquisition of English as a second language. *Cognitive Psychology* 21: 60–99.

Johnson-Laird, P. N. 1982. Thinking as a skill. *Quarterly Journal of Experimental Psychology* 34A. 1–29.

Jusczyk, P. W. 1990. How to get Dis-connected: A user's manual. *Contemporary Psychology* 35: 645–646.

Jusczyk, P. W., and Bertoncini, J. 1988. Viewing the development of speech perception as an innately guided learning process. *Language and Speech* 31: 217–238.

Jusczyk, P., Hirsh-Pasek, K., Kemler-Nelson, D., Kennedy, L., Woodward, A., and Piwoz, J. 1988. Perception of acoustic correlates of major phrasal units by young infants. Unpublished manuscript, University of Oregon.

Just, M. A., and Carpenter, P. A. 1992. A capacity theory of comprehension: Individual differences in working memory. *Psychological Review* 1: 122–149.

Kacelnik, A., and Houston, A. I. 1984. Some effects of energy costs on foraging strategies. *Animal Behaviour* 32: 609–614.

Karmiloff-Smith, A. 1971a. The Development Of Children's Thinking. UNRWA/UNESCO publication P/EP/6, 147.

Karmiloff-Smith, A. 1971b. Selected Aspects of Piaget's Theory: Implications for a Theoretical Basis to the Education Programme of UNRWA/UNESCO. UNWRA/UNESCO publication P/EP/7, 128.

Karmiloff-Smith, A. 1975. Les Métaphores dans l'action chez les enfants de 5 et de 12 ans. Paper given at symposium of International Center for Genetic Epistemology, Geneva.

Karmiloff-Smith, A. 1979a. *A Functional Approach to Child Language*. Cambridge University Press.

Karmiloff-Smith, A. 1979b. Micro- and macro-developmental changes in language acquisition and other representational systems. *Cognitive Science* 3: 81–118.

Karmiloff-Smith, A. 1979c. Problem-solving procedures in children's construction and representation of closed railway circuits. *Archives de Psychologie* 1807: 37–59.

Karmiloff-Smith, A. 1980. Psychological processes underlying pronominalization and non-pronominalization in children's connected discourse. In J. Kreiman and E. Ojedo (eds.), *Papers from the Parasession on Pronouns and Anaphora*. Chicago Linguistics Society.

Karmiloff-Smith, A. 1981. Getting developmental differences or studying child development? *Cognition* 10: 151–158.

Karmiloff-Smith, A. 1983. A new abstract code or the new possibility of multiple codes? *Behavioral and Brain Sciences*, 6 (1): 149–150.

Karmiloff-Smith, A. (1984). Children's problem solving. In M. E. Lamb, A. L. Brown, and B. Rogoff (eds.), *Advances in Developmental Psychology*, volume III. Erlbaum.

Karmiloff-Smith, A. 1985. A constructivist approach to modelling linguistic and cognitive development. *Archives de Psychologie* 53: 113–126.

Karmiloff-Smith, A. 1986. From metaprocesses to conscious access: Evidence from children's metalinguistic and repair data. *Cognition* 23: 95–147.

Karmiloff-Smith, A. 1987. A developmental perspective on human consciousness. Invited Address, British Psychological Society Annual Conference, Sussex.

Karmiloff-Smith, A. 1988. The child is a scientist, not an inductivist. *Mind and Language* 3 (3): 183–195.

Karmiloff-Smith, A. 1990a. Constraints on representational change: Evidence from children's drawing. *Cognition* 34: 57–83.

Karmiloff-Smith, A. 1990b. The human printout facility: Extending biological constraints by cultural tools, or "Electronic mail is ruining evolution!" Talk given at Conference on Domain Specificity and Cultural Knowledge, University of Michigan.

Karmiloff-Smith, A. 1990c. Piaget and Chomsky on language acquisition: Divorce or Marriage? *First Language* 10: 255–270.

Karmiloff-Smith, A. 1991. Beyond modularity: Innate constraints and developmental change. In S. Carey and R. Gelman (eds.), *Epigenesis of Mind: Essays in Biology and Knowledge*. Erlbaum.

Karmiloff-Smith, A., and Inhelder, B. 1974/75. If you want to get ahead, get a theory. *Cognition* 3: 195–212.

Karmiloff-Smith, A., Bellugi, U., Klima, E., and Grant, J. 1991. Talk prepared for British Psychological Society's Developmental Annual Conference, Cambridge.

Karmiloff-Smith, A., Grant, J., Jones, M.-C., and Cuckle, P. 1991. Rethinking metalinguistic awareness: Representing and accessing knowledge about what counts as a word. Unpublished.

Karmiloff-Smith, A., Johnson, H., Grant, J., Jones, Karmiloff, Y.-N., Bartrip, J., and Cuckle C. 1993. From sentential to discourse functions: Detection and explanation of speech repairs in children and adults. *Discourse Processes* 16: 565–584.

Katz, N., Baker, E., and Macnamara, J. 1974. What's in a name? A study of how children learn common and proper names. *Child Development* 45: 469–473.

Kazak, S., Collis, G., and Lewis, V. 1991. Autistic children's ability to attribute "knowing" and "guessing" to themselves and others. Paper presented at annual conference of British Psychological Society, Developmental Section, Cambridge.

Keil, F. C. 1979. *Semantic and Conceptual Development: An Ontological Perspective*. Harvard University Press.

Keil, F. C. 1986. On the structure-dependent nature of stages of cognitive development. In I. Levin (ed.), *Stage and Structure: Reopening the Debate*. Ablex.

Keil, F. C. 1989. *Concepts, Kinds and Cognitive Development*. MIT Press.

Keil, F. C. 1990. Constraints on constraints: Surveying the epigenetic landscape. *Cognitive Science* 14: 135–168.

Keil, F. C. 1991. Godzilla vs. Mothra and the Sydney Opera House: Boundary conditions on functional architecture in infant visual perception and beyond. *Mind & Language* 6 (3): 239–251.

Kellman, P. J., and Spelke, E. S. 1983. Perception of partly occluded objects in infancy. *Cognitive Psychology* 15: 483–524.

Kitcher, P. 1982. Genes. *British Journal for the Philosophy of Science* 33: 337–359.

Kitcher, P. 1988. The child as parent of the scientist. *Mind and Language* 3: 217–228.

Klahr, D. 1992. Information-processing approaches to cognitive development. In Bornstein, M. H., and Lamb, M. E. (eds.), *Developmental Psychology: An advanced textbook*, third edition. Erlbaum.

Klahr, D., and Dunbar, K. 1988. Dual search space during scientific reasoning. *Cognitive Science* 12: 1–48.

Klahr, D., Langley, P., and Neches, R. (eds.), 1987. *Production System Models of Learning and Development*. MIT Press.

Klahr, D., and Robinson, M. 1981. Formal assessment of problem-solving and planning processes in preschool children. *Cognitive Psychology* 13: 113–148.

Klima, E., and Bellugi, U. 1979. *The Signs of Language*. Harvard University Press.

Klin, A. 1988. The Emergence of Self, Symbolic Functions and Early Infantile Autism. Doctoral dissertation, London School of Economics and Political Science.

Klin, A. 1991. Young autistic children's listening preferences in regard to speech: A possible characterization of the symptom of social withdrawal. *Journal of Autism and Developmental Disorders* 21: 29–42.

Kosslyn, S. M., Cave, C. B., Provost, D. A., and von Gierke, S. M. 1988. Sequential processes in image generation. *Cognitive Psychology* 20: 319–343.

Kosslyn, S. M., Heldmeyer, K. H., and Locklear, E. P. 1977. Children's drawings as data about internal representations. *Journal of Experimental Child Psychology* 23: 191–211.

Kuhl, P. K. 1983. The perception of auditory equivalence classes for speech in early infancy. *Infant Behaviour and Development* 6: 263–285.

Kuhn, T. 1962. *The Structure of Scientific Revolutions*. University of Chicago Press.

Kuhn, D., Amsel, E., and O'Loughlin, M. 1988. *The Development of Scientific Thinking Skills*. Academic Press.

Kuhn, D., and Phelps, E. 1982. The developmental of problem-solving strategies. In H. Reese (ed.), *Advances in Child Development and Behavior*, volume 17. Academic.

Lachter, J., and Bever, T. G. 1988. The relation between linguistic structure and associative theories of language learning: A constructive critique of some connectionist learning models. *Cognition* 28: 195–247.

Landau, B., and Gleitman, L. 1985. *Language and Experience: Evidence from the Blind Child*. Harvard University Press.

Langley, P., Simon, H. A., Bradshaw, G. L., and Zytkow, J. M. 1987. *Scientific Discovery: Computational Explorations of the Creative Processes*. MIT Press.

Lashley, K. S. 1951. The problem of serial order in behavior. In L. A. Jeffress (ed.), *Cerebral Mechanisms in Behaviors: The Hixon Symposium*. Wiley.

Laszlo, J. I., and Broderick, P. A. 1985. The perceptual-motor skill of drawing. In N. H. Freeman and M. V. Cox (eds.), *Visual Order: The Nature and Development of Pictorial Representation*. Cambridge University Press.

Lawson, G., Baron, J., and Siegel, L. 1974. The role of number and length cues in children's quantitative judgements. *Child Development* 45: 731–736.

Lenneberg, E. 1967. *Biological Foundations of Language*. Wiley.

Leslie, A. M. 1984. Infant perception of a manual pickup event. *British Journal of Developmental Psychology* 2: 19–32.

Leslie, A. M. 1987. Pretense and representation: The origins of "theory of mind." *Psychological Review* 94: 412–426.

Leslie, A. M. 1988. The necessity of illusion: Perception and thought in infancy. In L. Weiskrantz (ed.), *Thought Without Language*. Oxford University Press.

Leslie, A. M. 1990. Pretence, autism and the basis of "theory of mind." *The Psychologist* 3: 120–123.

Leslie, A. M., and Frith, U. 1987. Metarepresentation and autism: How not to lose one's marbles. *Cognition* 27: 291–294.

Leslie, A. M., and Frith, U. 1990. Prospects for a cognitive neuropsychology of autism: Hobson's choice. *Psychological Review* 97: 122–131.

Leslie, A. M., and Happe, F. 1989. Autism and ostensive communication: The relevance of metarepresentation. *Development and Psychopathology* 1: 205–212.

Lewis, D. 1969. *Convention: A Philosophical Study*. Harvard University Press.

Li, K., and Karmiloff-Smith, A. 1991a. Cognitive Constraints on Notations: Encoding States versus Transformations. Unpublished manuscript.

Li, K., and Karmiloff-Smith, A. 1991b. Adapting notations to the Communicative Needs of Children of Different Ages. Manuscript in preparation.

Liben, L. S., and Downs, R. M. 1989. Understanding maps as symbols: The development of map concepts in children. In H. W. Reese (ed.), *Advances in Child Development*, volume 22. Academic.

Logan, G. D. 1988. Toward an instance theory of automatization. *Psychological Review* 95 (4): 492–527.

Luria, A. R., and Tzvetkova, L. S. 1978. Disturbance of intellectual function in patients with front lobe lesions. In M. Cole (ed.), *The Selected Writings of A. R. Luria*. Sharp.

MacNamara, J. 1982. *Names for Things: A Study of Human Learning.* MIT Press.

MacWhinney, B. 1978. The acquisition of morphophonology. *Monographs of the Society for Research in Child Development* 43: 1.

MacWhinney, B. 1987. The competition model. In B. MacWhinney (ed.), *Mechanisms of Language Acquisition.* Erlbaum.

Madore, B. F., and Freedman, W. L. 1987. Self-organizing structures. *American Scientist* 75: 252–259.

Mandler, G., and Shebo, B. J. 1982. Subitizing: An analysis of its component processes. *Journal of Experimental Psychology: General* 111: 1–22.

Mandler, J. M. 1983. Representation. In J. Flavell and E. Markman (eds.), *Handbook of Child Psychology*, vol. 3. Wiley.

Mandler, J. M. 1988. How to build a baby: On the development of an accessible representational system. *Cognitive Development* 3: 113–136.

Mandler, J. M. 1992. How to build a baby II: Conceptual primitives. *Psychological Review* 99: 587–604.

Mandler, J. M., and Bauer, P. J. 1988. The cradle of categorization: Is the basic level basic? *Cognitive Development* 3: 247–264.

Maratsos, M. P. 1976. *The Use of Definite and Indefinite Reference in Young Children.* Cambridge University Press.

Maratsos, M., and Chalkley, M. A. 1980. The internal language of children's syntax. The ontogenesis and representation of syntactic categories. In K. Nelson (ed.), *Children's Language*, vol. II. Erlbaum.

Markman, E. 1979. Classes, collections, and principles of psychological organization. Paper presented at biennial meeting of Society for Research in Child Development, San Francisco.

Markman, E. M. 1987. How children constrain the possible meanings of words. In U. Neisser (ed.), *Concepts and Conceptual Development: Ecological and Intellectual Factors in Categorization.* Cambridge University Press.

Markman, E. M. 1989. *Categorization and Naming in Children: Problems of Induction.* MIT Press.

Markman, E. M. 1990. Constraints children place on word meanings. *Cognitive Science* 14: 57–77.

Markman, E. M., and Wachtel, G. F. 1988. Children's use of mutual exclusivity to constrain the means of words. *Cognitive Psychology* 20: 121–157.

Marler, P. 1991. The instinct to learn. In S. Carey and R. Gelman (eds.), *Epigenesis of the Mind: Essays in Biology and Knowledge.* Erlbaum.

Marr, D. 1976. Artificial intelligence: A personal view. *Artificial Intelligence* 9: 37–48.

Marr, D. 1982. *Vision: A Computational Investigation into the Human Representation and Processing of Visual Information.* Freeman.

Marshall, J. C. 1980. The new organology. *Behavioral and Brain Sciences* 2: 472–473.

Marshall, J. C. 1984. Multiple perspectives on modularity. *Cognition* 17: 209–242.

Marshall, J. C., and Morton, J. 1978. On the mechanics of EMMA. In A. Sinclair, R. J. Javella, and W. Levelt (eds.), *The Child's Conception of Language.* Springer-Verlag.

Marslen-Wilson, W. D., Levy, E., and Tyler, L. K. 1982. Producing interpretable discourse. In R. J. Jarvella and W. Klein (eds.), *Speech, Place and Action.* Wiley.

Marslen-Wilson, W. D., and Tyler, L. K. 1987. Against modularity. In J. L. Garfield (ed.), *Modularity in Knowledge Representations and Natural-Language Understanding.* MIT Press.

Massey, C., and Gelman, R. 1988. Preschoolers' ability to decide whether pictured or unfamiliar objects can move themselves. *Developmental Psychology* 24: 307–317.

Maurer, D. 1976. Infant visual perception: Methods of study. In L. B. Cohen and P. Salapatek (eds.), *Infant Perception: From Sensation to Cognition*, Vol. 1. Academic.

McClelland, J. L. 1989. Parallel distributed processing: Implications for cognition and development. In R. G. M. Morris (ed.), *Parallel Distributed Processing: Implications for Psychology and Neurobiology*. Oxford University Press.

McClelland, J. L. 1990. Toward a theory of information processing in graded, random, interactive networks. *Attention and Performance* 14.

McClelland, J. L. 1991. Paper given at meeting of Society for Research in Child Development, Seattle.

McClelland, J. L., and Jenkins, E. 1990. Nature, nurture and connectionism: Implications for connectionist models for cognitive development. In K. van Lehn (ed.), *Architectures for Intelligence*. Erlbaum.

McClelland, J. L., Rumelhart, D. E., and the PDP Research Group. 1986. *Parallel Distributed Processing: Explorations in the Microstructure of Cognition*, vol. 2. MIT Press.

McGarrigle, J., and Donaldson, M. 1975. Conservation accidents. *Cognition* 3: 341–350.

McManus, C., and Bryden, M. P. 1993. The neurobiology of handedness, language and cerebral dominance: A model for the molecular genetics of behaviour. In M. H. Johnson (ed.), *Brain Development and Cognition: A Reader*. Blackwell.

McManus, I. C. 1991. Evolution of a genetic basis for reading and writing within the historical time-period. Unpublished manuscript, University College London.

McShane, J. 1979. The development of naming. *Linguistics* 17: 879–905.

McShane, J. 1991. *Cognitive Development*. Blackwell.

McTear, M. 1987. *The Articulate Computer*. Blackwell.

Mehler, J., and Bertoncini, J. 1988. Development: A question of properties, not change? *Cognition* 115: 121–133.

Mehler, J., and Fox, R. (eds.), 1985. *Neonate Cognition: Beyond the Blooming Buzzing Confusion*. Erlbaum.

Mehler, J., Lambertz, G., Jusczyk, P., and Amiel-Tison, C. 1986. Discrimination de la langue maternelle par le nouveau-né. *Comptes Rendes Academie des Sciences* 303, Serie III: 637–640.

Meier, R. P., and Newport, E. L. 1990. Out of the hands of babes: On a possible sign advantage in language acquisition. *Language* 66: 1–23.

Meltzoff, A. N. 1988. Infant imitation and memory: Nine-month-olds in immediate and deferred tests. *Child Development* 59: 217–225.

Meltzoff, A. N. 1990. Towards a developmental cognitive science: The implications of cross-modal matching and imitation for the development of memory in infancy. *Annals of the New York Academy of Sciences* 608: 1–37.

Meltzoff, A. N., and Moore, M. K. 1977. Imitation of facial and manual gestures by human neonates. *Science* 198: 75–78.

Merriman, W. E., and Bowman, L. L. 1989. The mutual exclusivity bias in children's word learning. *Monographs of the Society for Research in Child Development* 220.

Moore, D., Benenson, J., Reznick, S., Peterson, M., and Kagan, J. 1987. Effect of auditory numerical information on infants' looking behavior: Contradictory evidence. *Developmental Psychology* 23: 665–670.

Morton, J. 1986. Developmental contingency modelling. In P. van Geehrt (ed.), *Theory Building in Developmental Psychology*. Elsevier.

Morton, J., and Johnson, M. H. 1991. CONSPEC and CONLERN: A two-process theory of infant face recognition. *Psychological Review* 98: 164–181.

Moshman, D. 1979. To really get ahead, get a metatheory. In D. Kuhn (ed.), *Intellectual Development Beyond Childhood: New Directions for Child Development*, Vol. 5. Jossey-Bass.

Mounoud, P. 1986. Similarities between developmental sequences at different age periods. In I. Levin (ed.), *Stage and Structure: Reopening the Debate*. Ablex.

Movellan, J. R., and McClelland, J. L. 1991. Learning continuous probability distributions with the contrastive Hebbian algorithm. TR.PDP.CNS.91.2.

Mundy, P., and Sigman, M., 1989. The theoretical implications of joint-attention deficits in autism. *Development and Psychopathology* 1: 173–183.

Nelson, K. 1973. Structure and strategy in learning to talk. *Monographs of the Society for Research in Child Development*, no. 149.

Nelson, K. 1986. *Event Knowledge, Structure and Function in Development*. Erlbaum.

Nelson, K. 1988. Constraints on word learning? *Cognitive Development* 3: 221–246.

Neville, H. J. 1991. Neurobiology of cognitive and language processing: Effects of early experience. In K. R. Gibson and A. C. Petersen (eds.), *Brain Maturation and Cognitive Development: Comparative and Cross-Cultural Perspectives*. Aldine deGruyter.

Newell, A. 1990. *Unified Theories of Cognition*. Harvard University Press.

Newport, E. L. 1981. Constraints on structure: Evidence from American Sign Language and language learning. In W. A. Collins (ed.), *Aspects of the Development of Competence: Minnesota Symposia on Child Psychology*, vol. 14. Erlbaum.

Newport, E. L. 1990. Maturational constraints on language learning. *Cognitive Science* 14: 11–28.

Newport, E. L., and Supalla, T. In press. A critical period effect in the acquisition of a primary language. *Science*.

Nicolle, J. 1965. *La Symétrie*. Presses Universitaires de France.

Nicolich, L. M. 1977. Beyond sensorimotor intelligence: Assessment of symbolic maturity through analysis of pretend play. *Merill-Palmer Quarterly* 23: 89–99.

Nooteboom, S. 1980. Speaking and unspeaking: Detection and correction of phonological and lexical errors in spontaneous speech. In V. A. Fromkin (ed.), *Errors in Linguistic Performance*. Academic.

Norris, R., and Millan, S. 1991. Theory of mind: New directions. Social Psychology seminar, University of Oxford.

O'Connor, N., and Hermelin, B. 1984. Idiot savant calendrical calculators: Maths or memory? *Psychological Medicine* 14: 801–806.

Olson, D. R. 1988. On the origins of beliefs and other intentional states in children. In J. Astington, P. L. Harris, and D. R. Olson (eds.), *Developing Theories of Mind*. Cambridge University Press.

Olson, D. R., Astington, J. W., and Harris, P. L. 1988. Introduction. In J. Astington, P. L. Harris, and D. R. Olson (eds.), *Developing Theories of Mind*. Cambridge University Press.

Olson, D. R., and Bialystok, E. 1983. *Spatial Cognition*. Erlbaum.

Oyama, S. 1985. *The Ontogeny of Information: Developmental Systems and Evolution*. Cambridge University Press.

Parisi, D. 1990. Connectionism and Piaget's sensory-motor intelligence. Paper presented at conference on "Evolution and Cognition: The Heritage of Jean Piaget's epistemology," Bergamo, Italy.

Pascual-Leone, J. 1976. On learning and development, Piagetian-style: II. A critical historical analysis of Geneva's research programme. *Canadian Psychological Review* 17: 270–280.

Pascual-Leone, J. 1987. Organismic processes for neo-Piagetian theories: A dialectical causal account of cognitive development. *International Journal of Psychology* 22: 531–570.

Pemberton, E. F., and Nelson, K. E. 1987. Using interactive graphic challenges to foster young children's drawing ability. *Visual Arts Research* 13: 29–41.

Perner, J. 1988. Developing semantics for theories of mind: From propositional attitudes to mental representation. In J. W. Astington, P. L. Harris, and D. R. Olson (eds.), *Developing Theories of Mind*. Cambridge University Press.

Perner, J. 1991. *Understanding the Representational Mind*. MIT Press.

Perner, J., Leekam, S., and Wimmer, H. 1987. Threeyearolds' difficulty with false belief: The case for a conceptual deficit. *British Journal of Developmental Psychology* 5: 125–137.

Perner, J., and Wimmer, H. 1985. "John thinks that Mary thinks that . . .": Attribution of second-order false beliefs by 5- to 10-year-old children. *Journal of Experimental Child Psychology* 39: 437–471.

Peters, A. M. 1983. *The Units of Language Acquisition*. Cambridge University Press.

Peterson, S. E., Fox, P. T., Posner, M. I., Mintun, M., and Raichle, M. E. 1989. Positron emission tomography studies of the processing of single words. *Journal of Cognitive Neuroscience* 1: 153–170.

Petitto, A. L. 1978. Mathematical Thinking in Tailors and Merchants in Ivory Coast. Doctoral dissertation, Cornell University.

Petitto, L. A. 1987. On the autonomy of language and gesture: Evidence from the acquisition of personal pronouns in American Sign Language. *Cognition* 27: 1–52.

Philips, W. A., Inall, M., and Lauder, E. 1985. On the discovery, storage and use of graphic descriptions. In N. H. Freeman and M. V. Cox (eds.), *Visual Order: The Nature and Development of Pictorial Representation*. Cambridge University Press.

Piaget, J. 1929. *The Child's Conception of the World*. Routledge and Kegan Paul.

Piaget, J. 1932. *The Moral Judgement of the Child*. Kegan Paul, Trench Trubner.

Piaget, J. 1951. *Play, Dreams and Imitation in Childhood*. Routledge & Kegan Paul.

Piaget, J. 1952a. *The Child's Conception of Number*. Humanities Press.

Piaget, J. 1952b. *The Origins of Intelligence in Children*. International University Press.

Piaget, J. 1955a. *The Child's Construction of Reality*. Routledge and Kegan Paul.

Piaget, J. 1955b. *The Language and Thought of the Child*. Meridian Books.

Piaget, J. 1967. *Biologie et Connaissance*. Gallimard.

Piaget, J. 1968. Quantification, conservation, and nativism. *Science* 162: 976–979.

Piaget, J., and Inhelder, B. 1948. *La Représentation de l'Espace chez l'Enfant*. Presses Universitaires de France.

Piaget, J., and Karmiloff-Smith, A. 1990. Un cas particulier de symétrie inférentielle. In J. Piaget (ed.), *Recherches sur les Catégories*. Presses Universitaires de France.

Piaget, J., Karmiloff-Smith, A., and Bronckart, J. P. 1978. Généralisations relative à la pression et à la réaction. In J. Piaget (ed.), *Recherches sur la Généralisation*. Presses Universitaires de France.

Piatelli-Palmarini, M. 1989. Evolution, selection, and cognition: From "learning" to parameter setting in biology and the study of language. *Cognition* 31: 1–44.

Pinker, S. 1984. *Language Learnability and Language Development*. Harvard University Press.

Pinker, S. 1987. The bootstrapping problem in language acquisition. In B. MacWhinney (ed.), *Mechanisms of Language Acquisition*. Erlbaum.

Pinker, S. 1989a. *Learnability and Cognition: The Acquisition of Argument Structure*. MIT Press.

Pinker, S. 1989b. Rules of language. *Science* 253: 530–534.

Pinker, S., and Mehler, J. (eds.) 1988. Connectionism and symbol systems: Special edition. *Cognition* 28.

Pinker, S., and Prince, A. 1988. On language and connectionism: Analysis of a Parallel Distributed Processing model of language acquisition. *Cognition* 28: 73–193.

Plunkett, K., and Marchman, V. 1991. Ushaped learning and frequency effects in a multilayered perceptron: Implications for child language acquisition. *Cognition* 38: 43–102.

Poizner, H., Klima, E. S., and Bellugi, U. 1987. *What the Hands Reveal about the Brain.* MIT Press.

Posner, M. I., and Snyder, C. R. R. 1975. Facilitation and inhibition in the processing of signals. In P. M. A. Rabbitt and S. Dornic (eds.), *Attention and Performance.* Academic.

Posner, M. I., Peterson, S. E., Fox, P. T., and Raichle, M. E. 1988. Localization of cognitive functions in the human brain. *Science* 240: 1627–1631.

Premack, D. 1975. Putting a face together. *Science* 188: 228–236.

Premack, D. 1986. *Gavagai! Or the Future History of the Animal Language Controversy.* MIT Press.

Premack, D. 1988. "Does the chimpanzee have a theory of mind?" revisited. In R. Byrne and A. Whitten (eds.), *Machiavellian Intelligence.* Clarendon.

Premack, D. 1990. Words: What are they, and do animals have them? *Cognition* 37: 197–212.

Premack, D. 1991. "Does the chimpanzee have a theory of mind?" revisited. In R. Byrne and A. Whiten (eds.), *Machiavellian Intelligence.* Oxford Science Publications.

Premack, D., and Premack, A. J. 1983. *The Mind of an Ape.* Norton.

Premack, D., and Woodruff, G. 1978. Does the chimpanzee have a theory of mind? *Behavioral and Brain Sciences* 1: 515–526.

Pylyshyn, Z. W. 1980. Computation and cognition: Issues in the foundations of cognitive science. *Behavioral and Brain Sciences* 3: 111–132.

Pylyshyn, Z. W. 1987. What's in a mind? *Synthese* 70: 97–122.

Quine, W. V. O. 1960. *Word and Object.* MIT Press.

Reddy, V. 1991. Playing with others' expectations: Teasing and mucking about in the first year. In A. Whitten (ed.), *Natural Theories of Mind: Evolution, Development and Simulation of Everyday Mindreading.* Blackwell.

Reichmann, R. 1978. Conversational coherency. *Cognitive Science* 2: 283–327.

Resnick, L. B. 1986. The development of mathematical intuition. In M. Perlmutter (ed.), *Perspectives on Intellectual Development: Minnesota Symposia on Child Psychology,* vol. 19. Erlbaum.

Resnick, L. B., and Greeno, J. G. 1990. Conceptual growth of number and quantity. Unpublished manuscript.

Restle, F. 1970. Theory of serial pattern learning: Structural trees. *Psychological Review* 77: 481–495.

Rilling, M. 1967. Number of responses as a stimulus in fixed interval and fixed ratio schedules. *Journal of Comparative and Physiological Psychology* 63: 60–65.

Rilling, M., and McDiarmid, C. 1965. Signal detection in fixed ratio schedules. *Science* 148: 526–527.

Ristau, C. A. 1988. Thinking, communicating and deceiving: Means to master the social environment. In G. Greenburg and E. Tobach (eds.), *Evolution of Social Behavior and Integrative Levels.* Erlbaum.

Roeper, T. 1987. The modularity of meaning in language acquisition. In S. Modgil and C. Modgil (eds.), *Noam Chomsky: Consensus and Controversy.* Falmer.

Rolls, E. T. 1991. Theoretical and neurophysiological analysis of the functions of the primate hippocampus in memory. *Cold Spring Harbor Symposia in Quantitative Biology* 55: 995–1006.

Rumelhart, D. E., McClelland, J. L., and the PDP Research Group. 1986. *Parallel Distributed Processing: Explorations in the Microstructure of Cognition,* vol. 1. MIT Press.

Rutkowska, J. C. 1987. Computational models and developmental psychology. In J. C. Rutkowska and C. Cook (eds.), *Computation and Development*. Wiley.

Rutkowska, J. C. 1991. Looking for 'constraints' in infants' perceptual-cognitive development. *Mind and Language* 6 (3): 215–238.

Rutter, M. 1983. Cognitive deficits in the pathogenesis of autism. *Journal of Child Psychology and Psychiatry* 24: 513–531.

Saxe, G. B. 1981. Body parts as numerals: A developmental analysis of numeration among remote Oksapmin village populations in Papua New Guinea. *Child Development* 52: 306–316.

Schaffer, H. R. (ed.). 1977. *Studies in Mother-Infant Interaction*. Academic.

Schank, R. C., and Abelson, R. P. 1977. *Plans, Goals and Understanding: An Inquiry into Human Knowledge Structures*. Erlbaum.

Schauble, L. 1990. Belief revision in children: The role of prior knowledge and strategies for generating evidence. *Journal of Experimental Child Psychology* 1: 31–57.

Schlesinger, I. M. 1971. The grammar of sign language and the problem of linguistic universals. In J. Morton (ed.), *Biological and Social Factors in Psycholinguistics*. Logos.

Schmandt-Besserat, D. 1977. An archaic recording system and the origins of writing. *Syro-Mesopotamian Studies* 1/2: 132.

Schmandt-Besserat, D. 1978. The earliest precursor of writing. *Scientific American* 238: 38–47.

Schmandt-Besserat, D. 1981. From tokens to tablets: A revaluation of the so called "numerical tablets." *Visible Language* 15: 321–344.

Schmidt, H. H., Spelke, E. S., and LaMorte, X. 1986. The development of Gestalt perception in infancy. Paper presented at International Conference on Infant Studies, Los Angeles.

Schneider, W. 1987. Connectionism: Is it a paradigm shift for psychology? *Behaviour Research Methods, Instruments and Computers* 19 (2): 73–83.

Schultz, T. R. 1991a. Simulating stages of human cognitive development with connectionist models. In L. Birnbaum and G. Collins (eds.), *Machine Learning: Proceedings of the Eighth International Workshop*. Morgan Kaufmann.

Schultz, T. R. 1991b. A cascade-correlation model of balance scale phenomena. Unpublished manuscript.

Seidenberg, M. S. 1985. Evidence from great apes concerning the biological bases of language. In A. Marras and W. Demopolous (eds.), *Language Learnability and Concept Acquisition*. Ablex.

Seidenberg, M. S. 1992. Connectionism without tears. In S. Davis (eds.), *Connectionism: Theory and Practice*. Oxford University Press.

Seidenberg, M. S., and Petitto, L. A. 1987. Communication, symbolic communication, and language. *Journal of Experimental Psychology, General* 116: 279–287.

Selfe, L. 1985. Anomalous drawing development: Some clinical studies. In N. H. Freeman and M. V. Cox (eds.), *Visual Order: The Nature and Development of Pictorial Representation*. Cambridge University Press.

Servan-Schreiber, D., Cleeremans, A., and McClelland, J. L. 1988. Encoding Sequential Structure in Simple Recurrent Networks. Technical report CMU-CS-88-183, Computer Science Department, Carnegie-Mellon University.

Shallice, T. 1988. *From Neuropsychology to Mental Structure*. Cambridge University Press.

Shatz, M. 1983. Communication. In P. H. Mussen (ed.), *Handbook of Child Psychology*, vol. 3: *Cognitive Development*. Wiley.

Shiffrin, R. M., and Schneider, W. 1977. Controlled and automatic human information processing. II: Perceptual learning, automatic attending, and a general theory. *Psychological Review* 84: 127–190.

Shipley, E. F., and Shepperson, B. 1990. Countable entities: Developmental changes. *Cognition* 34: 109–136.

Siegler, R. S. (ed.), 1978. *Children's Thinking: What Develops?* Erlbaum.

Siegler, R. S. 1981. Developmental sequences within and between concepts. *Monographs of the Society for Research in Child Development* 46 (189).

Siegler, R. S. 1989a. Mechanisms of cognitive development. *Annual Review of Psychology* 40: 453–479.

Siegler, R. S. 1989b. How domain-general and domain-specific knowledge interact to produce strategy choices. *Merrill-Palmer Quarterly* 35 (1): 1–26.

Siegler, R. S., and Crowley, K. 1991. The microgenetic method: A direct means for studying cognitive development. *American Psychologist* 46 (6): 606–620.

Siegler, R. S., and Jenkins, E. 1989. *How Children Discover New Strategies*. Erlbaum.

Siegler, R. S., and Robinson, M. 1982. The development of numerical understanding. In H. W. Reese and L. P. Lipsett (eds.), *Advances in Child Development and Behavior*, vol. 16. Academic.

Sigman, M., Mundy, P., Sherman, T., and Ungerer, J. 1986. Social interactions of autistic, mentally retarded, and normal children and their caregivers. *Journal of Child Psychology and Psychiatry* 27: 647–656.

Sinclair, H. 1971. Sensorimotor action patterns as the condition for the acquisition of syntax. In R. Huxley and E. Ingrams (eds.), *Language Acquisition: Models and Methods*. Academic.

Sinclair, H. 1987. Language: A gift of nature or a homemade tool? In S. Modgil and C. Modgil (eds.), *Noam Chomsky: Consensus and Controversy*. Falmer.

Sinclair, A., Siegrist, F., and Sinclair, H. 1983. Young children's ideas about the written number systems. In D. Rogers and J. Sloboda (eds.), *The Acquisition of Symbolic Skills*. Plenum.

Skinner, B. F. 1953. *Science and Human Behaviour*. Macmillan.

Slater, A. 1988. Habituation and visual fixation in infants: Information processing, reinforcement, and what else? *Cahiers de Psychologie Cognitive* 8: 517–523.

Slater, A. 1990. Size constancy and complex visual processing at birth. Poster presented at Fourth European Conference on Developmental Psychology, University of Stirling.

Slater, A., and Bremner, J. G. (eds.). 1989. *Infant Development*. Erlbaum.

Slater, A., Earle, D. C., Morison, V., and Rose, D. 1985. Pattern preferences at birth and their interaction with habituation-induced novelty preferences. *Journal of Experimental Child Psychology* 39: 37–54.

Slater, A., and Morison, V. 1991. Visual attention and memory at birth. In M. J. Weiss and P. Zelazo (eds.), *Newborn Attention*. Ablex.

Slater, A., Morison, V., and Rose, D. 1983. Perception of shape by the newborn baby. *British Journal of Developmental Psychology* 1: 135–142.

Slater, A., Morison, V., Somers, M., Mattock, A., Brown, E., and Taylor, D. 1990. Newborn and older infants' perception of partly occluded objects. *Infant Behaviour and Development* 13: 33–49.

Slobin, D. I. 1973. Cognitive prerequisites for the development of grammar. In C. A. Ferguson and D. I. Slobin (eds.), *Studies of Child Language Development*. Holt, Rinehart and Winston.

Slobin, D. I. 1985. Crosslinguistic evidence for the language-making capacity. In Slobin, D. I. (ed.), *Crosslinguistic study of child language*. Erlbaum.

Smith, L. 1989. In defense of perceptual similarity. Paper presented at biennial meeting of Society for Research in Child Development, Kansas City.

Soja, N., Carey, S., and Spelke, E. 1985. Constraints on word learning. Paper presented at biennial meeting of Society for Research in Child Development, Toronto.

Sokol, S. M., Goodman-Schulman, R., and McCloskey, M. 1989. In defense of a modular architecture for the number-processing system. *Journal of Experimental Psychology* 118, no. 1: 105–110.

Sophian, C., and Adams, N. 1987. Infants' understanding of numerical transformations. *British Journal of Developmental Psychology* 5: 257–264.

Spelke, E. S. 1985. Preferential-looking methods as tools for the study of cognition in infancy. In G. Gottlieb and N. A. Krasnegor (eds.), *Measurement of Audition and Vision in the First Year of Postnatal Life: A Methodological Overview.* Ablex.

Spelke, E. S. 1988. Where perceiving ends and thinking begins: The apprehension of objects in infancy. In A. Yonas (ed.), *Perceptual Development in Infancy.* Erlbaum.

Spelke, E. S. 1990. Principles of object perception. *Cognitive Science* 14: 29–56.

Spelke, E. S. 1991. Physical knowledge in infancy: Reflections on Piaget's theory. In S. Carey and R. Gelman (eds.), *Epigenesis of the Mind: Essays in Biology and Knowledge.* Erlbaum.

Spelke, E. S., Breinlinger, K., Macomber, J., and Jacobson, K. 1992. *Psychological Review* 99: 605–632.

Sperber, D. 1985. Anthropology and psychology: Towards an epidemiology of representations. *Man* 20: 74–89.

Sperber, D., and Wilson, D. 1986. *Relevance: Communication and Cognition.* Blackwell.

Spring, D. R., and Dale, P. S. 1977. Discrimination of linguistic stress in early infancy. *Journal of Speech and Hearing Research* 20: 224–232.

Starkey, P., and Cooper, R. G. 1980. Perception of number by human infants. *Science* 200: 1033–1035.

Starkey, P., Gelman, R., and Spelke, E. 1983. Detection of 1-to-1 correspondences by human infants. *Science* 210: 1033–1035.

Starkey, P., Gelman, R., and Spelke, E. S. 1985. Response to Davis, Albert & Baron's Detection of number or numerousness by human infants. *Science* 228: 1222–1223.

Starkey, P., Spelke, E. S., and Gelman, R. 1983. Detection of intermodal correspondences by human infants. *Science* 222: 179–181.

Starkey, P., Spelke, E. S., and Gelman, R. 1990. Numerical abstraction by human infants. *Cognition* 36: 97–127.

Stich, S. 1983. *From Folk Psychology to Cognitive Science.* MIT Press.

Stiles-Davies, J. 1987. Paper presented at MacArthur Workshop on the Production of Drawing, San Diego.

Strauss, M. S., and Curtis, L. E. 1981. Infants' perception of numerosity. *Child Development* 52: 1146–1152.

Strauss, M. S., and Curtis, L. E. 1984. Development of numerical concepts in infancy. In C. Sophian (ed.), *Origins of Cognitive Skills.* Erlbaum.

Streri, A., and Spelke, E. S. 1988. Haptic perception of objects in infancy. *Cognitive Psychology* 20: 1–23.

Sullivan, J. W., and Horowitz, F. D. 1983. The effects of intonation on infant attention: The role of the rising intonation contour. *Journal of Child Language* 10: 521–534.

Swischer, L. P., and Pinsker, E. J. 1971. The language characteristics of hyperverbal, hydrocephalic children. *Developmental Medicine and Child Neurology* 13: 746–755.

Tager-Flusberg, H. 1989. An analysis of discourse ability and internal state lexicons in a longitudinal study of autistic children. Paper presented at Biennial Meeting of Society for Research in Child Development, Kansas City.

Tager-Flusberg, H., Calkins, S., Nolin, T., Baumberger, T., Anderson, M., and Chadwick-Dias, A. 1990. A longitudinal study of language acquisition in autistic and Down Syndrome children. *Journal of Autism and Developmental Disorders* 20: 1–20.

Tanz, C. 1980. *Studies in the Acquisition of Deictic Terms*. Cambridge University Press.

Taylor, M., and Gelman, S. A. 1988. Adjectives and nouns: Children's strategies for learning new words. *Child Development* 59: 411–419.

Tew, B. 1979. The "cocktail party syndrome" in children with hydrocephalus and spina bifida. *British Journal of Disorders of Communication* 14: 89–101.

Thelen, E. 1989. Self-organization in developmental processes: Can systems approaches work? In M. Gunnar and E. Thelen (eds.), *Systems and Development. Minnesota Symposium in Child Psychology*, vol. 22. Erlbaum.

Thibadeau, R., Just, M. A., and Carpenter, P. A. 1982. A model of the time course and content of reading. *Cognitive Science* 6: 157–203.

Tolchinsky-Landsmann, L. 1986. Literacy development and pedagogical implications: Evidences from the Hebrew written system. Paper presented to World Congress of International Reading Association, London.

Tolchinsky-Landsmann, L. 1990. Early writing development: Evidence from different orthographic systems. In M. Spoolders (ed.), *Literacy Acquisition*.

Tolchinsky-Landsmann, L., and Karmiloff-Smith. A. 1992. Children's understanding of notations as domains of knowledge versus referential-communicative tools. *Cognitive Development* 7, no. 3.

Tolchinsky-Landsmann, L., and Levin, I. 1985. Writing in preschoolers: An agerelated analysis. *Applied Psycholinguistics* 6: 319–339.

Tolchinsky-Landsmann, L., and Levin, I. 1987. Writing in four to six years old: Representation of semantic and phonetic similarities and differences. *Journal of Child Language* 14: 127–144.

Tollefsrud-Anderson, L., Campbell, R. L., Starkey, P., and Cooper, R. G. 1992. Number conservation: Distinguishing quantifier from operator solutions. In C. Meljac and J. Bideaud (eds.), *Pathways to Number*. Erlbaum.

Trevarthen, C. 1987. Sharing makes sense: Intersubjectivity and the making of an infant's meaning. In K. Steele and T. Threadgold (eds.), *Language Topics: Essays in Honour of Michael Halliday*. Benjamins.

Tunmer, W. E., Bowey, J. A., and Grieve, R. 1983. The development of young children's awareness of the word as a unit of spoken language. *Journal of Psycholinguistic Research* 12: 567–594.

Turkewitz, G., and Kenny, P. A. 1982. Limitations on input as a basis for neural organization and perceptual development: A preliminary theoretical statement. *Developmental Psychobiology* 15: 357–368.

Tyler, L. K. 1981. Syntactic and interpretative factors in the development of language comprehension. In W. Deutsch (ed.), *The Child's Construction of Language*. Academic.

Tyler, L. K. 1983. The development of discourse mapping processes: The online interpretation on anaphoric expressions. *Cognition* 13: 309–341.

Tyler, L. K. 1988. Spoken language comprehension in a fluent aphasic patient. *Cognitive Neuropsychology* 5: 375–400.

Tyler, L. K. 1992. *Spoken Language Comprehension: An Experimental Approach to Disordered and Normal processing*. MIT Press.

Tyler, L. K., and Marslen-Wilson, W. D. 1978. Some developmental aspects of sentence processing and memory. *Journal of Child Language* 5: 113–129.

Tyler, L. K., and Marslen-Wilson, W. D. 1981. Children's processing of spoken language. *Journal of Verbal Learning and Verbal Behaviour* 20: 400–416.

Udwin, O., Yule, W., and Martin, N. 1987. Cognitive abilities and behavioural characteristics of children with ideopathic infantile hypercalcaemia. *Journal of Child Psychology and Psychiatry* 28: 297–309.

Udwin, O., and Yule, W. 1991. A cognitive and behavioural phenotype in Williams Syndrome. *Journal of Clinical and Experimental Neuropsychology* 2: 232–244.

Valian, V. 1986. Syntactic categories in the speech of young children. *Developmental Psychology* 22: 562–579.

Valian, V. 1990. Null subjects: A problem for parameter-setting models of language acquisition. *Cognition* 35: 105–122.

Van Geehrt, P. 1991. A dynamic systems model of cognitive and language growth. *Psychological Review* 98: 3–53.

Van Sommers, P. 1984. *Drawing and Cognition: Descriptive and Experimental Studies of Graphic Production Processes*. Cambridge University Press.

Vinter, A. 1984. *L'Imitation chez le Nouveau-né*. Delalchaux & Niestlé.

Vinter, A. 1986. The role of movement in eliciting early imitation. *Child Development* 57: 66–71.

von Glaserfeld, H. 1982. Subitizing: The role of figural patterns in the development of numerical concepts. *Archives de Psychologie* 50: 191–218.

Vygotsky, L. 1962. *Thought and Language*. MIT Press.

Warden, D. A. 1976. The influence of context on children's use of identifying expressions and references. *British Journal of Psychology* 67: 101–112.

Waxman, S. R. 1985. *Hierarchies in Classification and Language: Evidence from Preschool Children*. Doctoral dissertation, University of Pennsylvania.

Wellman, H. M. 1983. Metamemory revisited. In M. T. H. Chi (ed.), *Trends in Memory Development*. Karger.

Wellman, H. M. 1988. First steps in the child's theorizing about the mind. In J. W. Astington, P. L. Harris, and D. R. Olson (eds.), *Developing Theories of Mind*. Cambridge University Press.

Wellman, H. M. 1990. *The Child's Theory of Mind*. MIT Press.

Wellman, H. M., and Miller, K. G. 1986. Thinking about nothing: Development of concepts of zero. *British Journal of Developmental Psychology* 4: 31–42.

Wilks, Y. 1982. Machines and Consciousness. Report CSCM-8, Cognitive Studies Centre, University of Essex.

Willats, J. 1977. How children learn to draw realistic pictures. *Quarterly Journal of Experimental Psychology* 29: 367–382.

Willats, P. 1989. Development of problem-solving. In A. Slater and J. G. Bremner (eds.), *Infant Development*. Erlbaum.

Wimmer, H., Hogrefe, J., and Sodian, B. 1988. A second stage in the child's conception of mental life: Understanding informational access as a source of knowledge. In J. Astington, P. Harris, and D. Olson (eds.), *Developing Theories of Mind*. Cambridge University Press.

Wimmer, H., and Perner, J. 1983. Beliefs about beliefs. Representation and constraining function of wrong beliefs in young children's understanding of deception. *Cognition* 13: 103–128.

Winner, E., and Gardner, H. 1977. The comprehension of metaphor in brain damaged patients. *Brain* 100: 717–729.

Wynn, K. 1990. Children's understanding of counting. *Cognition* 36: 155–193.

Zaitchik, D. 1990. When representations conflict with reality: The preschooler's problem with false beliefs and "false" photographs. *Cognition* 35: 41–68.

Zaitchik, D. 1991. Is only seeing really believing? Sources of true belief in the false belief task. *Cognitive Development* 6 (1): 91–103.

Zaslavsky, C. 1973. *Africa Counts*. Prindle, Weber & Schmidt.

Index